PRAISE FO

At a time of severe partisanship that has infected many accounts of our nation's past, this brilliant new history, *Land of Hope*, written in lucid and often lyrical prose, is much needed. It is accurate, honest, and free of the unhistorical condescension so often paid to the people of America's past. This generous but not uncritical story of our nation's history ought to be read by every American. It explains and justifies the right kind of patriotism.

GORDON S. WOOD

author of *Friends Divided: John Adams and Thomas Jefferson*

Those who are acquainted with Wilfred McClay's writing will not be surprised that *Land of Hope*, his latest book, is a lucid and engaging account of the "great American story." McClay is a charming storyteller – and a first-rate scholar and appreciator of America's political and cultural development.

MICHAEL BARONE

resident fellow at the American Enterprise Institute,
senior political analyst at the Washington Examiner,
and coauthor of *The Almanac of American Politics*

We've long needed a readable text that truly tells the American story, neither hiding the serious injustices in our history nor soft-pedaling our nation's extraordinary achievements. Such a text cannot be a mere compilation of facts, and it certainly could not be written by someone lacking a deep understanding and appreciation of America's constitutional ideals and institutions. Bringing his impressive skills as a political theorist, historian, and writer to bear, Wilfred McClay has supplied the need.

ROBERT P. GEORGE

McCormick Professor of Jurisprudence,
Princeton University

In a time when America seems pulled in opposite directions, Wilfred McClay has written a necessary book – the most balanced, nuanced history of the United States I have read in the past fifty years.

DANIEL HENNINGER

deputy editor, editorial page, *The Wall Street Journal*

Wilfred McClay has written more than a textbook. His affirmative, even-handed review of American history, institutions, and character is refreshing, and comes none too soon, when so many accounts are merely trying to settle scores. Beautifully written and fair minded, *Land of Hope* ranks among the finest surveys of the nation's past.

GILBERT T. SEWALL
Director, American Textbook Council

No one has told the story of America with greater balance or better prose than Wilfred McClay. *Land of Hope* is a history book that you will not be able to put down. From the moment that "natives" first crossed here over the Bering Strait, to the founding of America's great experiment in republican government, to the horror and triumph of the Civil War, and to the stirring election of Barack Obama, McClay's account will capture your attention while offering an unforgettable education.

JAMES W. CEASER
Professor of Politics, University of Virginia

I wish *Land of Hope* had been there when I was teaching U.S. history. It is history as literature – broad, detailed, compassionate – and it can help anyone who wants to know where we came from and how we got here. Professor McClay has made a welcome gift to the history of our country.

WILL FITZHUGH
Founder, *The Concord Review*

This is the most cheerful and inspiring history of America written so far this century. Where most historians emphasize fragmentation and oppression, McClay makes the case for a unified national story characterized by optimism and achievement. Without downplaying dismaying episodes, past and present, he shows how they have been offset by the American pursuit of reform, revival, and improvement. Old heroes like George Washington are restored to their rightful place. America is far from perfect, McClay admits, but it is genuinely dedicated to the ideals of equality and democracy, and there is much to be proud of. I can imagine schools and colleges assigning this book with a sense of gratitude and confidence.

PATRICK ALLITT
Cahoon Family Professor of American History,
Emory University

In *Land of Hope*, Bill McClay succeeds at multitasking. He has written not only a learned and readable history of the United States, from Columbus to Trump, with balance and integrity but has provided an insightful primer on the meaning of citizenship itself. McClay reminds us that although history holds no easy lessons, its honest practice proves indispensable in preventing the future from proceeding in darkness. Those entrusted with teaching young minds about the discipline of history as well as history will find in this volume much to fortify them.

ROBERT PAQUETTE
Professor of History and President,
The Alexander Hamilton Institute

Land of Hope is in every way a remarkable piece of work, clearly written and as balanced and fair-minded as any American history you will ever read. *Land of Hope* operates on the assumption that the past remains a necessary part of us, something we must both understand and learn from. It refuses the all-too-common view that we today are simply superior to our own history, a history that amounts to little more than a grab bag of chicanery, venality, and self-interest. Instead, it is an attempt to lay out the political history of our nation, the dilemmas we faced, the choices we made, and the ideas that shaped and reshaped our American creed.

JOHN AGRESTO
Professor of Political Science, former President of St. John's College,
and author of *Rediscovering America*

Land of Hope seems written for such a time as this, when ideology, combined with a profound historical ignorance, has left several generations belonging to no internalized story larger than their own experiences. Here we encounter a habitable story that comes complete with the principles, obligations, and privileges of citizenship.

TED MCALLISTER
Law & Liberty

To hear many historians today tell it, the American past offers a choice: you can love your country or you can learn its history – but not both. McClay rejects this dichotomy. *Land of Hope* proves that patriotism is not only compatible with a clear view of America's past – it should proceed from it as well.

TIM RICE
City Journal

The antidote to the damage caused by Howard Zinn's wretched *A People's History of the United States*. Give it to every millennial on your Christmas list.

GEORGE WEIGEL
First Things

Written most immediately for high school students taking Advanced Placement courses, the book looks and feels the part of a history textbook. But unlike most of those dreary tomes, it reads like a bestselling thriller. In finely wrought yet readable prose, history comes alive in McClay's expansive and thoughtful appraisal of the American story.

MIKE SABO
Intercollegiate Studies Institute

Professors and teachers across America should cancel their fall book orders and replace their current textbooks with Wilfred McClay's *Land of Hope*. McClay, the G.T. and Libby Blankenship Chair in the History of Liberty at the University of Oklahoma, satisfies the promise made in the title of his latest work. In it, he invites everyone to learn how ideals drove America's creation and success.

STEPHEN TOOTLE
National Review

Wilfred McClay's new book *Land of Hope* is a gift for Americans aiming to revive a more unifying approach to national history and civics. McClay is clear from the start: He aspires to tell America's story in a way that is both accurate and inspiring. This book is not an academic screed, but a compelling narrative spun across centuries. Key moments are smoothly tied together so students can see history's progression from the Boston Tea Party to the Louisiana Purchase to the closing of the frontier, and so on.

ANDY SMARICK
Philanthropy Magazine

McClay's book does not whitewash our history, but presents an honest and fair accounting that recognizes the astonishing success of the American experiment. If any U.S. history survey in recent memory has a chance to unseat Zinn in the classroom, it just might be McClay's delightfully written tome.

THE EDITORS
Real Clear Books

Student Workbook for

LAND OF HOPE

AN INVITATION TO
THE GREAT AMERICAN STORY

Wilfred M. McClay
and John D. McBride

Student Workbook for

LAND OF HOPE

An Invitation to the Great American Story

Encounter
BOOKS
New York · London

First American edition published in 2021 by Encounter Books,
an activity of Encounter for Culture and Education, Inc.,
a nonprofit, tax-exempt corporation.
Encounter Books website address: www.encounterbooks.com

Manufactured in the United States and printed on
acid-free paper. The paper used in this publication meets
the minimum requirements of ANSI/NISO Z39.48 − 1992
(R 1997) (*Permanence of Paper*).

FIRST AMERICAN EDITION

To our fellow students of the American past

CONTENTS

USING THE *WORKBOOK*

ELCOME TO OUR *Student Workbook,* which has been designed to accompany Wilfred M. McClay's book *Land of Hope: An Invitation to the Great American Story* and help students get the most out of reading it.

To begin, each of the book's chapters is provided with its own study questions, objective questions, one or two primary-source documents related to the chapter's chief themes, and study questions to accompany each of the documents.

Study Questions. The study questions generally follow the contents of the book closely. In a few cases, a question may require you to draw on additional insights or information *not* taken from the book. Such questions will let you know that you will need to consult outside sources before answering.

Some questions may feature a statement, sometimes (but not always) a direct quotation from the book, with key words or phrases omitted. Following is an example from chapter 2:

> 6. Sea power trumps land power. The defeat of the _____ in 1588 changed the course of world history and especially of what became the United States. How? (pp. 21–22)

The purpose of such fill-in-the-blank exercises is to call attention to key words and ideas. You should be able, after class discussion, to restate these ideas in your own words. Whenever blanks are to be filled in, the corresponding page numbers in *Land of Hope* are provided, to make it easier for you to locate the original sources of direct quotations taken from the text.

Occasionally, one of the chapter questions will ask you for a judgment or an opinion – but needless to say, it must be an informed one! Here's an example from chapter 11:

24. Assess the degree of success and failure of Reconstruction.

Objective Questions. Following each of the chapter questions, we have provided objective questions. These are mostly put-in-order exercises, with some matching exercises as well. The items to be put in proper time sequence are either quite far apart in time or have an important cause-and-effect relationship, for example,

Put in order:

_____ Alien and Sedition Acts
_____ Virginia and Kentucky Resolutions
_____ XYZ Affair

The XYZ Affair led directly to the Alien and Sedition Acts, which in turn led to the Virginia and Kentucky Resolutions.

Documents and Questions. Each chapter includes, immediately after the objective questions, one or two primary-source documents. The readings have in many instances been pared back a bit from the originals, to save space in the printed text. We have also provided study questions with these readings, designed mainly to help you get the most out of reading these original texts.

Map Exercises. The *Workbook* provides a map section, a set of twelve map exercises starting on page 265, each of which features a list of places and directions, as well as an outline map to accompany it, on which you will be able to write and draw directly, in response to the directions.

Supplemental Resources. In addition to the chapter-by-chapter materials, we have included supplemental resources to be used as you or your teacher sees fit. We have provided a "Quick and Easy Guide to the English and British Monarchy," which outlines the dynasties and persons occupying the throne from the age of exploration up to the time of the American Revolution. We also have included the text of the Declaration of Independence and the U.S. Constitution, a "Table of Presidential Elections," and a list of "Suggested Topics for Additional Research," which is meant to give you topic ideas for research papers and other such projects.

A workbook brings both opportunity and danger. The questions are given in the order found in the text, and point to the main ideas, in effect providing an outline of each chapter. That's the opportunity. But you must not merely skim the text to find the answers. If you do that, you'll get only isolated fragments of information that lack context and are hard to remember. That's the danger.

Instead, read the chapter slowly and carefully, highlighter in hand, looking for the main ideas. Then check the questions and see if your highlighted sentences answer them. If so, you are highlighting correctly – and that's a skill you will need to develop. Then copying the answers into the space provided in the workbook (or onto your own sheet of paper, if you need the extra space) will help get the main ideas into your long-term memory. Write the answers neatly so that you can read them a month later. Develop your own set of shorthand abbreviations. The ability to read for the main idea and then record it in a compressed and concise form is a skill that will have value for you far beyond your history course.

If you read the text carefully once and answer the questions correctly, your workbook – in effect, your notes – will be the ideal tool for studying for tests or final exams and for organizing more extensive papers on topics such as those listed at the end of the book. Take the time to do it right the first time, and you will not have to find the time to do it over again.

ONE LONG STORY

Summary

THE EPIGRAPH AND INTRODUCTION to *Land of Hope* are reflections on the meaning and value of history, including some initial thoughts about what it means to be a "land of hope."

For that reason, we are encouraging teachers and students alike to give close attention to them, especially the epigraph, a quotation from the novelist John Dos Passos. In many books, such quotations are merely decorative in character, but in *Land of Hope*, the epigraph is a key to the meaning of all that follows. It appears in the book immediately after the dedication page and before the table of contents, but here it is in its entirety, for your convenience:

Document

DOS PASSOS, "THE USE OF THE PAST," *FROM THE GROUND WE STAND ON: SOME EXAMPLES FROM THE HISTORY OF A POLITICAL CREED*

Every generation rewrites the past. In easy times history is more or less of an ornamental art, but in times of danger we are driven to the written record by a pressing need to find answers to the riddles of today. We need to know what kind of firm ground other men, belonging to generations before us, have found to stand on. In spite of changing conditions of life they were not very different from ourselves, their thoughts were the grandfathers of our thoughts, they managed to meet situations as difficult as those we have to face, to meet them sometimes lightheartedly, and in some measure to make their hopes prevail. We need to know how they did it.

In times of change and danger when there is a quicksand of fear under men's reasoning, a sense of continuity with generations gone before can stretch like a lifeline across the scary present and get us past that idiot delusion of the exceptional Now that blocks good thinking. That is why, in times like ours, when old institutions are caving in and being replaced by new institutions not necessarily in accord with most men's preconceived hopes, political thought has to look backwards as well as forwards.

Epigraph Questions

Some answers may require more space than provided.

1. When do we need history? Why?

2. What do you think Dos Passos means by "the idiot delusion of the exceptional Now"?

3. Do the conditions Dos Passos is describing apply today? That is, are old institutions caving in and being replaced by new institutions? Give some examples.

4. Dos Passos wrote this in 1941. Are our problems today greater or more frightening than then? Do we suffer from the same "idiot delusion" as did previous times and peoples?

Introduction Questions

1. What does this book seek to accomplish? What are its guiding intentions? (p. xi)

2. What does the author mean by "citizenship"? (p. xi)

3. "We are, at our core, _____ and _____ creatures, and _____ are one of the chief ways we find meaning in the flow of events." (pp. xi–xii)

4. "_____ is to civilized society what _____ is to individual identity." (p. xii)

5. "A culture without _____ will necessarily be barbarous and easily tyrannized, even if it is technologically advanced." (p. xii)

6. Where do we most reliably find our lives' meaning?

7. What aspect of American history does the author emphasize, treating it as "the skeleton of the story"?

8. "History is the study of _____ through _____,... but it must be _____ if it is to be intelligible." (p. xiii)

9. History means "_____" again and again. "The past does not speak for itself, and it cannot speak to us directly. We must first ask." (pp. xiii–xiv)

10. "Hope has both _____ and _____ meanings, _____ ones as well as _____ ones." (p. xiv)

11. What is the danger of having high ideals?

12. "All human beings are _____, as are all human enterprises. To believe otherwise is to be _____, and much of what passes for cynicism in our time is little more than naiveté in deep disguise." (p. xiv)

13. "The history of the United States, and of the West more generally, includes the activity of _____ self-_____ as part of its foundational makeup." (p. xiv)

14. "One of the worst sins of the present ... is its tendency to _____ toward the past." (p. xiv)

CHAPTER ONE

BEGINNINGS

Settlement and Unsettlement

Questions

Some answers may require more space than provided.

1. You should assume that the author chose the title and subtitle of the chapter as indicative of its major themes. Look at and read through the portraits and pictures following p. 224 and select the three you believe best embody or exemplify these themes. Consider all the images from the beginning to the present day: which individuals and which pictures most suggest "beginnings" and "settlement" and "unsettlement"?

2. There are fewer than twenty named individuals in this chapter, of whom two are worldwide religious figures (Christ and Mohammed) and two are modern writers (Mumford and Frost). Excluding those four, which THREE of the remainder seem to you most significant in the story of what will become the United States of America?

3. In what sense can it be said that America was an idea before it became a reality?

4. "History always begins in _____." (p. 3)

5. "What we call history is a _____, organized wisely and _____." (p. 4)

6. "The goal [of the book], in short, is to 'be full members of a _____ of which we are already a part.'" (p. 4)

7. Who "can truly be called 'native' to America"? (p. 4) Why?

8. "The lost civilizations of _____, and the explorations of the _____ and _____ do not play an important role in this book, simply because _____." (pp. 5–6)

9. Name groups that stand outside of the history of the United States but nevertheless "point to the presence of America in the world's imagination as a land of hope and refuge."

10. "We will start our history of America in the _____ of Europe's history." (p. 7)

11. America would be "an unusual kind of offshoot": un_____, un_____, un_____. (p. 7)

12. "The settlement of America had its origins in the unsettlement of Europe." What did Mumford mean by this?

13. "A great upsurge in fresh energies and disruptions, converging from many different directions at once, was unsettling a great deal of what had become familiar in the older world." What were these fresh energies and disruptions, which were economic, social, religious, technological, and cultural?

14. How did the Crusades indirectly create economic wants among Europeans? What were the barriers to satisfying these wants?

15. What technological innovations aided in overcoming the barriers mentioned above?

16. Trade and exploration empowered but were also enabled by the rise of two new socioeconomic and political groups: a merchant class, who might become merchant-princes, and national monarchies, of which the first four to emerge were _____. (pp. 9–10)

17. _____ took the lead under the guidance of _____. What was the goal of this national effort? How, when, and by whom was it achieved? (p. 10)

18. Why did the success of the Portuguese make them *less* interested in Columbus's project but the Spanish *more* interested?

19. Examine the Martellus map carefully (p. 2). Is the world depicted as mostly land or mostly water? What was Columbus right about? What was Columbus wrong about?

20. Why is Columbus an example of what Frost means, that America is hard to see? (p. 13)

21. "What we _____ is not always what we were _____, and what we _____ is not always what we _____." (p. 13)

Objective Questions

Put in order:

_____ Balboa discovers the Pacific Ocean
_____ Columbus discovers America
_____ Dias discovers the Cape of Good Hope

Match the individual with his nation: (*answers may be used more than once or not at all*)

_____ Bartolomeu Dias   A. England
_____ Columbus   B. France
_____ Prince Henry the Navigator   C. Portugal
_____ Vasco da Gama   D. Spain

COLUMBUS'S LOG OF HIS FIRST VOYAGE, 1492

NOTE: *Columbus was interested in everything. In the interest of brevity, what follows has been edited to remove most of the geographic and botanical information. The entire log is much longer.*

Thursday, 11 October. At two o'clock in the morning the land was discovered, at two leagues' distance; they took in sail and remained under the square-sail lying to till day, which was Friday, when they found themselves near a small island, called in the Indian language Guanahani. Presently they descried people, naked, and the Admiral landed in the boat, which was armed, along with Martin Alonzo Pinzon, and Vincent Yanez his brother, captain of the Nina. The Admiral bore the royal standard; this contained the initials of the names of the King and Queen each side of the cross, and a crown over each letter Arrived on shore, they saw trees very green many streams of water, and diverse sorts of fruits. The Admiral called upon the two Captains to bear witness that he took possession of that island for the King and Queen his sovereigns, making the requisite declarations.

Numbers of the people of the island straightway collected together. Here follow the precise words of the Admiral: "As I saw that they were very friendly to us, and perceived that they could be much more easily converted to our holy faith by gentle means than by force, I presented them with some red caps, and strings of beads to wear upon the neck, and many other trifles of small value, wherewith they were much delighted, and became wonderfully attached to us. Afterwards they came swimming to the boats, bringing parrots, balls of cotton thread, javelins, and many other things which they exchanged for articles we gave them, such as glass beads, and hawk's bells; which trade was carried on with the utmost good will.

But they seemed on the whole to me, to be a very poor people. They all go completely naked, even the women, though I saw but one girl. All whom I saw were young, not above thirty years of age, well made, with fine shapes and faces; their hair short, and coarse like that of a horse's tail, combed toward the forehead, except a small portion which they suffer to hang down behind, and never cut. Some paint the face, and some the whole body; others only the eyes, and others the nose. Weapons they have none, nor are acquainted with them, for I showed them swords which they grasped by the blades, and cut themselves through ignorance. They have no iron, their javelins being without it, and nothing more than sticks, though some have fish-bones or other things at the ends. They are all of a good size and stature, and handsomely formed.

I saw some with scars of wounds upon their bodies, and demanded by signs the origin of them; they answered me in the same way, that there came people from the other islands in the neighborhood who endeavored to make prisoners of them, and they defended themselves. I thought then, and still believe, that these were from the continent.

It appears to me, that the people are ingenious, and would be good servants and I am of opinion that they would very readily become Christians, as they appear to have no religion. They very quickly learn such words as are spoken to them. If it please our Lord, I intend at my return to carry home six of them to your Highnesses, that they may learn our language. I saw no beasts in the island, nor any sort of animals except parrots." These are the words of the Admiral.

Saturday, 13 October. At daybreak great multitudes of men came to the shore, all young and of fine shapes, very handsome; their hair not curled but straight and coarse like horse-hair, and all with foreheads and heads much broader than any people I had hitherto seen; their eyes were large and very beautiful; they were not black, but the color of the inhabitants of the Canaries, which is a very natural circumstance, they being in the same latitude with the island of Ferro in the Canaries. They were straight-limbed without exception, and not with prominent bellies but handsomely shaped. They came to the ship in canoes, made of a single trunk of a tree, wrought in a wonderful manner considering the country; some of them large enough to contain forty or forty-five men, others of different sizes down to those fitted to hold but a single person. They rowed with an oar like a baker's peel, and wonderfully swift. If they happen to upset, they all jump into the sea, and swim till they have righted their canoe and emptied it with the calabashes they carry with them. They came loaded with balls of cotton, parrots, javelins, and other things too numerous to mention; these they exchanged for whatever we chose to give them.

I was very attentive to them, and strove to learn if they had any gold. Seeing some of them with little bits of this metal hanging at their noses, I gathered from them by signs that by going southward or steering round the island in that direction, there would be found a king who possessed large vessels of gold, and in great quantities. I endeavored to procure them to lead the way thither, but found they were unacquainted with the route. I determined to stay here till the evening of the next day, and then sail for the southwest; for according to what I could learn from them, there was land at the south as well as at the southwest and northwest and those from the northwest came many times and fought with them and proceeded on to the southwest in search of gold and precious stones.

The natives are an inoffensive people, and so desirous to possess any thing they saw with us, that they kept swimming off to the ships with whatever they could find, and readily bartered for any article we saw fit to give them in return, even such as broken platters and fragments of glass. I saw in this manner sixteen balls of cotton thread which weighed above twenty-five pounds, given for three Portuguese ceutis. This traffic I forbade, and suffered no one to take their cotton from them, unless I should order it to be procured for your Highnesses, if proper quantities could be met with. It grows in this island, but from my short stay here I could not satisfy myself fully concerning it; the gold, also, which they wear in their noses, is found here, but not to lose time, I am determined to proceed onward and ascertain whether I can reach Cipango. At night they all went on shore with their canoes.

Sunday, 14 October. In the morning, I ordered the boats to be got ready, and coasted along the island toward the north- northeast to examine that part of it, we having landed first at the eastern part. Presently we discovered two or three villages, and the people all came down to the shore, calling out to us, and giving thanks to God. Some brought us water, and others victuals: others seeing that I was not disposed to land, plunged into the sea and swam out to us, and we perceived that they interrogated us if we had come from heaven. An old man came on board my boat; the others, both men and women cried with loud voices – "Come and see the men who have come from heavens. Bring them victuals and drink." There came many of both sexes, every one bringing something, giving thanks to God, prostrating themselves on the earth, and lifting up their hands to heaven.

It was to view these parts that I set out in the morning, for I wished to give a complete relation to your Highnesses, as also to find where a fort might be built. I discovered a tongue of land which appeared like an island though it was not, but might be cut through and made so in two days; it contained six houses. I do not, however, see the necessity of fortifying the place, as the people here are simple in war-like matters, as your Highnesses will see by those seven which I have ordered to be taken and carried to Spain in order to learn our language and return, unless your Highnesses should choose to have them all transported to Castile, or held captive in the island. I could conquer the whole of them with fifty men, and govern them as I pleased. I returned to the ship, and setting sail, discovered such a number of islands that I knew not which first to visit; the natives whom I had taken on board informed me by signs that there were so many of them that they could not be numbered; they repeated the names of more than a hundred. I determined to steer for the largest, which is about five leagues from San Salvador; the others were some at a greater, and some at a less distance from that island. They are all very level, without mountains, exceedingly fertile and populous, the inhabitants living at war with one another, although a simple race, and with delicate bodies.

Monday, 15 October. About sunset we anchored near the cape which terminates the island towards the west to enquire for gold, for the natives we had taken from San Salvador told me that the people here wore golden bracelets upon their arms and legs. I believed pretty confidently that they had invented this story in order to find means to escape from us, still I determined to pass none of these islands without taking possession, because being once taken, it would answer for all times. We anchored and remained till Tuesday, when at daybreak I went ashore with the boats armed. The people we found naked like those of San Salvador, and of the same disposition. They suffered us to traverse the island, and gave us what we asked of them.

The natives we found like those already described, as to personal appearance and manners, and naked like the rest. Whatever they possessed, they bartered for what we chose to give them. I saw a boy of the crew purchasing javelins of them with bits of platters and broken glass. Those who went for water informed me that they had entered their houses and found them very clean and neat, with beds and coverings of cotton nets. Their houses are all built in the shape of tents, with very high chimneys. None of the villages which I saw contained more than twelve or fifteen of them. Here it was remarked that the married women wore cotton breeches, but the younger females were without them, except a few who were as old as eighteen years. Dogs were seen of a large and small size, and one of the men had hanging at his nose a piece of gold half as big as a castellailo, with letters upon it. I endeavored to purchase it of them in order to ascertain what sort of money it was but they refused to part with it.

Source: http://www.christopher-columbus.eu/logs.htm

Document Questions

Some answers may require more space than provided.

1. What was Columbus's first priority? Why?

2. Assuming that different goals and motives are mentioned in the log more or less in order of importance — is this a reasonable assumption? — what was Columbus's second priority after claiming the territory for Spain?

3. What two topics does Columbus consider next?

4. Were the natives ignorant of war?

5. Some historians have interpreted the following to mean that Columbus immediately envisioned the natives as slaves: "It appears to me, that the people are ingenious, and would be good servants and I am of opinion that they would very readily become Christians, as they appear to have no religion. They very quickly learn such words as are spoken to them." What are some possible interpretations of this passage? Try to think of at least two.

CHAPTER TWO

THE SHAPING OF BRITISH NORTH AMERICA

Questions

Some answers may require more space than provided.

1. Name the three great dynasties that ruled over England between 1485 and 1776. (For the names and sequence of individual kings and queens, you may wish to consult the "Quick and Easy Guide to the English and British Monarchy" on page 296 of this *Workbook*.)

2. The Reformation was a huge event in world history, bringing to an end the dominant role of _____ in medieval religious life, reinforcing the rise of the modern nation-state (including national churches, such as the Church of England), and igniting a century and a half of religious wars, mainly in Europe but also worldwide. But the reformers (who came to be collectively termed _____) also divided among themselves. Name the two principal divisions. (pp. 14–18)

3. What did Calvinists believe? Why did English Calvinists come to be called Puritans? How did Queen Elizabeth settle the tension between Anglicans and Calvinists?

4. Why and how was Spain the dominant power in the western hemisphere (and indeed in the world) from 1500 to, say, 1588?

5. What was the single most important factor in the destruction of various indigenous peoples after contact with Europeans? What was the Columbian Exchange? Could the deadly diseases have been avoided?

6. Sea power trumps land power. The defeat of the _____ in 1588 changed the course of world history, and especially the history of what became the United States. How? (pp. 21–22)

7. How were Spanish (and later French) governance and institutions fundamentally different from those of England?

8. English colonization of the New World was not _____. (p. 23)

9. What is a joint-stock company? Why is this form of business organization best for financing risky endeavors? (pp. 23–24)

10. Why did Jamestown nearly perish? Why did it finally survive?

11. Who was Nathaniel Bacon?

12. What is the (only real) difference between the Pilgrims and the Puritans?

13. What is the "social contract"?

14. What was John Winthrop's vision for Puritan Massachusetts?

15. Be able to contrast the motives and experiences and principles of Virginia and New England. Which do you think has shaped America more? Be prepared to defend your answer in class or in writing.

16. How did dissidence among the Massachusetts Puritans lead (in two opposite directions) to two new colonies?

17. How did Pennsylvania come to be?

18. Which was the last colony to be founded? When and why?

19. To what extent were colonies founded in pursuit of high ideals, and to what extent by practical desires like wealth? (p. 30)

20. "Being a land of hope also means, at times, being a land of _____." (p. 30)

21. "Colonial life was _____, and even when _____ fail, something important is learned from them." (p. 30)

Objective Questions

Put in order:

_____ Elizabeth I
_____ Henry VIII
_____ Mary I

Match the individual with the colony: (*some answers may not be used*)

____ John Winthrop	A. Georgia
____ James Oglethorpe	B. Massachusetts
____ Roger Williams	C. Pennsylvania
____ John Smith	D. Rhode Island
____ William Penn	E. South Carolina
	F. Virginia

Document 1

THE MAYFLOWER COMPACT (AGREEMENT BETWEEN THE SETTLERS AT NEW PLYMOUTH), 1620

IN THE NAME OF GOD, AMEN. We, whose names are underwritten, the Loyal Subjects of our dread Sovereign Lord King James, by the Grace of God, of Great Britain, France, and Ireland, King, Defender of the Faith, &c. Having undertaken for the Glory of God, and Advancement of the Christian Faith, and the Honour of our King and Country, a Voyage to plant the first Colony in the northern Parts of Virginia; Do by these Presents, solemnly and mutually, in the Presence of God and one another, covenant and combine ourselves together into a civil Body Politick, for our better Ordering and Preservation, and Furtherance of the Ends aforesaid: And by Virtue hereof do enact, constitute, and frame, such just and equal Laws, Ordinances, Acts, Constitutions, and Officers, from time to time, as shall be thought most meet and convenient for the general Good of the Colony; unto which we promise all due Submission and Obedience. IN WITNESS whereof we have hereunto subscribed our names at Cape-Cod the eleventh of November, in the Reign of our Sovereign Lord King James, of England, France, and Ireland, the eighteenth, and of Scotland the fifty-fourth, Anno Domini; 1620.

Source: https://avalon.law.yale.edu/17th_century/mayflower.asp

Document 1 Questions

Some answers may require more space than provided.

1. What, in this context, is meant by a covenant or compact?

2. What is the purpose of the establishment of the Plymouth Colony?

3. The Pilgrims secured a land patent from the Virginia Company, permitting them to establish an English colony where they could practice their faith freely. Yet they made landfall in 1620 at what is today Cape Cod, which created a problem for the group. What was the problem?

4. What did the Mayflower Compact do?

5. What did they believe to be the function of government?

6. The men who signed the Compact obviously were bound by it. Who *else* was bound by it?

JOHN WINTHROP, "A MODELL OF CHRISTIAN CHARITY," 1630 (EXCERPTS)

The end [of our actions] is to improve our lives to do more service to the Lord; the comfort and increase of the body of Christ, whereof we are members; that ourselves and posterity may be the better preserved from the common corruptions of this evil world, to serve the Lord and work out our Salvation under the power and purity of his holy ordinances.

For the means whereby this must be effected: they are twofold, a conformity with the work and end we aim at. These we see are extraordinary, therefore we must not content ourselves with usual ordinary means. Whatsoever we did, or ought to have, done, when we lived in England, the same must we do, and more also, where we go. That which the most in their churches maintain as truth in profession only, we must bring into familiar and constant practice; as in this duty of love, we must love brotherly without dissimulation, we must love one another with a pure heart fervently. We must bear one another's burdens. We must not look only on our own things, but also on the things of our brethren. Neither must we think that the Lord will bear with such failings at our hands as he do the from those among whom we have lived....

Thus stands the cause between God and us. We are entered into covenant with Him for this work. We have taken out a commission. The Lord hath given us leave to draw our own articles. We have professed to enterprise these and those accounts, upon these and those ends. We have hereupon besought Him of favor and blessing. Now if the Lord shall please to hear us, and bring us in peace to the place we desire, then hath he ratified this covenant and sealed our Commission, and will expect a strict performance of the articles contained in it; but if we shall neglect the observation of these articles which are the ends we have propounded, and, dissembling with our God, shall fall to embrace this present world and prosecute our carnal intentions, seeking great things for ourselves and our posterity, the Lord will surely break out in wrath against us; be revenged of such a [sinful] people and make us know the price of the breaches of such a covenant.

Now the only way to avoid this shipwreck, and to provide for our posterity, is to follow the counsel of Micah, to do justly, to love mercy, to walk humbly with our God. For this end, we must be knit together, in this work, as one man. We must entertain each other in brotherly affection. We must be willing to abridge ourselves of our superfluities, for the supply of other's necessities. We must uphold a familiar commerce together in all meekness, gentleness, patience and liberality. We must delight in each other; make other's conditions our own; rejoice together, mourn together, labor and suffer together, always having before our eyes our commission and community in the work, as members of the same body. So shall we keep the unity of the spirit in the bond of peace. The Lord will be our God, and delight to dwell among us, as his own people, and will command a blessing upon us in all our ways. So that we shall see much more of his wisdom, power, goodness and truth, than formerly we have been acquainted with. We shall find that the God of Israel is among us, when ten of us shall be able to resist a thousand of our enemies; when he shall make us a praise and glory that men shall say of succeeding plantations, "the Lord make it like that of New England." For we must consider that we shall be as a city upon a hill. The eyes of all people are upon us. So that if we shall deal falsely with our God in this work we have undertaken, and so cause him to withdraw his present help from us, we shall be made a story and a by-word through the world. We shall open the mouths of enemies to speak evil of the ways of God, and all professors for God's sake. We shall shame the faces of many of God's worthy servants, and cause their prayers to be turned into curses upon us till wee be consumed out of the good land whither we are a going.

I shall shut up this discourse with that exhortation of Moses, that faithful servant of the Lord, in his last farewell to Israel, Deut. 30: Beloved there is now set before us life and good, Death and evil, in that we are commanded this day to love the Lord our God, and to love one another, to walk in his ways and to keep his Commandments and his Ordinance and his laws, and the articles of our Covenant with him, that we may live and be multiplied, and that the Lord our God may blesse us in the land whither we go to possess it. But if our hearts shall turn away, so that we will not obey, but shall be seduced, and worship and serve other Gods, our pleasure and profits, and serve them; it is propounded unto us this day, we shall surely perish out of the good land whither we pass over this vast sea to possess it;

Therefore let us choose life – that we, and our seed may live, by obeying His voice and cleaving to Him, for He is our life and our prosperity.

Source: From John Winthrop, "A Model of Christian Charity," Collections of the Massachusetts Historical Society (Boston, 1838), 3rd series 7:31–48. https://teachingamericanhistory.org/library/document/a-model-of-christian-charity/

Some answers may require more space than provided.

1. Winthrop lists four "ends" (purposes) of actions. Which comes first, and which comes last? What might that order tell us about the character of the colony Winthrop was founding?

2. What is the difference between the churches in England and those in Massachusetts?

3. What will happen if Massachusetts fails to live up to its "commission" or covenant with God?

4. What are the obligations of one to another within the community or body?

5. What powerful scriptural image (later picked up by Ronald Reagan) does Winthrop employ?

6. How will Massachusetts know whether it is doing God's will?

CHAPTER THREE

THE REVOLUTION OF SELF-RULE

Questions

Some answers may require more space than provided.

1. Why were the colonies mostly left to their own devices? Why was this a good thing?

2. What difference did it make that the British Empire came to dominate North America as opposed to the Spanish and French Empires?

3. Who could participate in government?

4. "The French and Indian War was enormously consequential." Why?

5. Fighting the French and Indians had given the colonists some sense of themselves as members of a larger American culture; the first occasion for Franklin's famous *Unite or Die* cartoon (in the gallery following p. 224) was the 1754 Albany conference to develop a joint strategy against the French threat. Were there other important sources of national consciousness?

6. What was the Enlightenment? How did it affect America? How did it coexist with the Great Awakening?

7. How did Britain first attempt to raise revenue in America? What resulted?

8. The second attempt to tax the colonies was the Townshend Acts (1767, repealed 1770), taxing imports of tea, glass, lead, paint, and paper. How did the colonies respond? What resulted?

9. The third attempt to tax the colonies was the Tea Act, and the issue by now had shifted from revenue to authority. Parliament provided a subsidy to the East India Tea Company (which was the largest corporation in the world) so that the company could sell taxed tea at an irresistibly lower price to the colonists – establishing the principle that the colonies would pay a tax, and also perhaps giving the company a monopoly on tea in America – which prospect terrified American merchants. How did the colonists respond?

10. How did the Continental Congress respond to the Coercive Acts?

11. Was war inevitable? Was independence?

12. The argument in Jefferson's Declaration of Independence is derived from what source?

13. Why are governments instituted?

14. What does it mean to say that "all men are created equal"?

Objective Questions

Put in order:

_____ Declaratory Act
_____ Stamp Act
_____ Townsend Acts

Put in order:

_____ Boston Massacre
_____ Intolerable Acts
_____ Tea Party

Matching:

_____ Ben Franklin   A. Enlightenment
_____ George Whitefield   B. Great Awakening
_____ Isaac Newton   C. Middle Ages
_____ Jonathan Edwards

THOMAS PAINE, *COMMON SENSE* (EXCERPTS), 1775–76

Volumes have been written on the subject of the struggle between England and America. Men of all ranks have embarked in the controversy, from different motives, and with various designs; but all have been ineffectual, and the period of debate is closed. Arms, as the last resource, decide this contest; the appeal was the choice of the king, and the continent hath accepted the challenge....

The sun never shined on a cause of greater worth. 'Tis not the affair of a city, a county, a province, or a kingdom, but of a continent – of at least one eighth part of the habitable globe. 'Tis not the concern of a day, a year, or an age; posterity are virtually involved in the contest, and will be more or less affected, even to the end of time, by the proceedings now. Now is the seed-time of continental union, faith and honour. The least fracture now will be like a name engraved with the point of a pin on the tender rind of a young oak; the wound will enlarge with the tree, and posterity read it in full grown characters.

By referring the matter from argument to arms, a new era for politics is struck; a new method of thinking hath arisen. All plans, proposals, &c. prior to the nineteenth of April, i.e. to the commencement of hostilities, are like the almanacs of the last year; which, though proper then are superseded and use-less now. Whatever was advanced by the advocates on either side of the ques-tion then, terminated in one and the same point. viz. a union with Great-Britain: the only difference between the parties was the method of effecting it; the one proposing force, the other friendship; but it hath so far happened that the first hath failed, and the second hath withdrawn her influence.

As much hath been said of the advantages of reconciliation which, like an agreeable dream, hath passed away and left us as we were, it is but right, that we should examine the contrary side of the argument, and inquire into some of the many material injuries which these colonies sustain, and always will sustain, by being connected with, and dependent on Great Britain: To examine that con-nection and dependence, on the principles of nature and common sense, to see what we have to trust to, if separated, and what we are to expect, if dependant.

I have heard it asserted by some, that as America hath flourished under her former connection with Great Britain that the same connection is necessary towards her future happiness, and will always have the same effect. Nothing can be more fallacious than this kind of argument. We may as well assert that because a child has thrived upon milk that it is never to have meat, or that the first twenty years of our lives is to become a precedent for the next twenty. But even this is admitting more than is true, for I answer roundly, that America would have flourished as much, and probably much more, had no European power had any thing to do with her. The commerce, by which she hath enriched herself, are the necessaries of life, and will always have a market while eating is the custom of Europe.

But she has protected us, say some. That she has engrossed us is true, and defended the continent at our expense as well as her own is admitted, and she would have defended Turkey from the same motive, viz. the sake of trade and dominion.

Alas, we have been long led away by ancient prejudices, and made large sacrifices to superstition. We have boasted the protection of Great Britain, without considering, that her motive was INTEREST not ATTACHMENT; that she did not protect us from OUR ENEMIES on OUR ACCOUNT, but from HER ENEMIES on HER OWN ACCOUNT, from those who had no quarrel with us on any OTHER ACCOUNT, and who will always be our enemies on the SAME ACCOUNT. Let Britain wave her pretensions to the continent, or the continent throw off the dependence, and we should be at peace with France and Spain were they at war with Britain. The miseries of Hanover's last war ought to warn us against connections.

It has lately been asserted in parliament, that the colonies have no relation to each other but through the parent country, i. e. that Pennsylvania and the Jerseys, and so on for the rest, are sister colonies by the way of England; this is certainly a very round-about way of proving relationship, but it is the nearest and only true way of proving enemyship, if I may so call it. France and Spain never were, nor perhaps ever will be our enemies as AMERICANS, but as our being the subjects of GREAT BRITAIN.

But Britain is the parent country, say some. Then the more shame upon her conduct. Even brutes do not devour their young, nor savages make war upon their families; wherefore the assertion, if true, turns to her reproach; but it happens not to be true, or only partly so and the phrase PARENT or MOTHER COUNTRY hath been jesuitically adopted by the king and his parasites, with a low papistical design of gaining an unfair bias on the credulous weakness of our minds. Europe, and not England, is the parent country of America. This new world hath been the asylum for the persecuted lovers of civil and religious liberty from EVERY PART of Europe. Hither have they fled, not from the tender embraces of the mother, but from the cruelty of the monster; and it is so far true of England, that the same tyranny which drove the first emigrants from home, pursues their descendants still.

In this extensive quarter of the globe, we forget the narrow limits of three hundred and sixty miles (the extent of England) and carry our friendship on a larger scale; we claim brotherhood with every European Christian, and triumph in the generosity of the sentiment.

It is pleasant to observe by what regular gradations we surmount the force of local prejudice, as we enlarge our acquaintance with the world. A man born in any town in England divided into parishes, will naturally associate most with his fellow-parishioners (because their interests in many cases will be common) and distinguish him by the name of NEIGHBOUR; if he meet him but a few miles from home, he drops the narrow idea of a street, and salutes him by the name of TOWNSMAN; if he travel out of the county, and meet him in any other, he forgets the minor divisions of street and town, and calls him COUNTRYMAN, i. e. COUNTRYMAN; but if in their foreign excursions they should associate in France or any other part of EUROPE, their local remembrance would be enlarged into that of ENGLISHMEN. And by a just parity of reasoning, all Europeans meeting in America, or any other quarter of the globe, are COUNTRYMEN; for England, Holland, Germany, or Sweden, when compared with the whole, stand in the same places on the larger scale, which the divisions of street, town, and county do on the smaller ones; distinctions too limited for continental minds. Not one third of the inhabitants, even of this province, are of English descent. Wherefore I reprobate the phrase of parent or mother country applied to England only, as being false, selfish, narrow and ungenerous.

But admitting, that we were all of English descent, what does it amount to? Nothing. Britain, being now an open enemy, extinguishes every other name and title: And to say that reconciliation is our duty, is truly farcical. The first king of England, of the present line (William the Conqueror) was a Frenchman, and half the Peers of England are descendants from the same country; therefore, by the same method of reasoning, England ought to be governed by France.

Much hath been said of the united strength of Britain and the colonies, that in conjunction they might bid defiance to the world. But this is mere presumption; the fate of war is uncertain, neither do the expressions mean any thing; for this continent would never suffer itself to be drained of inhabitants, to support the British arms in either Asia, Africa, or Europe.

Besides what have we to do with setting the world at defiance? Our plan is commerce, and that, well attended to, will secure us the peace and friendship of all Europe; because, it is the interest of all Europe to have America a FREE PORT. Her trade will always be a protection, and her barrenness of gold and silver secure her from invaders.

I challenge the warmest advocate for reconciliation, to shew, a single advantage that this continent can reap, by being connected with Great Britain.

I repeat the challenge, not a single advantage is derived. Our corn will fetch its price in any market in Europe, and our imported goods must be paid for, buy them where we will.

But the injuries and disadvantages we sustain by that connection, are without number; and our duty to mankind at large, as well as to ourselves, instruct us to renounce the alliance: Because, any submission to, or dependence on Great Britain, tends directly to involve this continent in European wars and quarrels; and sets us at variance with nations, who would otherwise seek our friendship, and against whom, we have neither anger nor complaint. As Europe is our market for trade, we ought to form no partial connection with any part of it. It is the true interest of America to steer clear of European contentions, which she never can do, while by her dependence on Britain, she is made the make-weight in the scale of British politics.

Europe is too thickly planted with kingdoms to be long at peace, and whenever a war breaks out between England and any foreign power, the trade of America goes to ruin, BECAUSE OF HER CONNECTION WITH ENGLAND....

No man was a warmer wisher for reconciliation than myself, before the [clashes at Lexington and Concord on the] fatal nineteenth of April 1775, but the moment the event of that day was made known, I rejected the hardened, sullen tempered Pharaoh of England for ever; and disdain the wretch, that with the pretended title of FATHER OF HIS PEOPLE can unfeelingly hear of their slaughter, and composedly sleep with their blood upon his soul....

But where, says some, is the King of America? I'll tell you. Friend, he reigns above, and doth not make havoc of mankind like the Royal Brute of Britain. Yet that we may not appear to be defective even in earthly honors, let a day be solemnly set apart for proclaiming the charter; let it be brought forth placed on the divine law, the word of God; let a crown be placed thereon, by which the world may know, that so far as we approve of monarchy, that in America THE LAW IS KING. For as in absolute governments the King is law, so in free countries the law OUGHT to be King; and there ought to be no other. But lest any ill use should afterwards arise, let the crown at the conclusion of the ceremony, be demolished, and scattered among the people whose right it is.

A government of our own is our natural right: And when a man seriously reflects on the precariousness of human affairs, he will become convinced, that it is infinitely wiser and safer, to form a constitution of our own in a cool deliberate manner, while we have it in our power, than to trust such an interesting event to time and chance. If we omit it now, some Massanello may hereafter arise, who laying hold of popular disquietudes, may collect together the desperate and the discontented, and by assuming to themselves the powers of government, may sweep away the liberties of the continent like a deluge. Should the government of America return again into the hands of Britain, the tottering situation of things will be a temptation for some desperate adventurer to try his fortune; and in such a case, what relief can Britain give? Ere she could hear the news, the fatal business might be done; and ourselves suffering like the wretched Britons under the oppression of the Conqueror. Ye that oppose independence now, ye know not what ye do; ye are opening a door to eternal tyranny, by keeping vacant the seat of government. There are thousands, and tens of thousands, who would think it glorious to expel from the continent that barbarous and hellish power, which hath stirred up the Indians and Negroes to destroy us; the cruelty hath a double guilt, it is dealing brutally by us, and treacherously by them.

To talk of friendship with those in whom our reason forbids us to have faith, and our affections wounded through a thousand pores instruct us to detest, is madness and folly. Every day wears out the little remains of kindred between us and them, and can there be any reason to hope, that as the relationship expires, the affection will increase, or that we shall agree better, when we have ten times more and greater concerns to quarrel over than ever?

Ye that tell us of harmony and reconciliation, can ye restore to us the time that is past? Can ye give to prostitution its former innocence? Neither can ye reconcile Britain and America. The last cord now is broken, the people of England are presenting addresses against us. There are injuries which nature cannot forgive; she would cease to be nature if she did. As well can the lover forgive the ravisher of his mistress, as the continent forgive the murders of Britain. The Almighty hath implanted in us these unextinguishable feelings for good and wise purposes. They are the guardians of his image in our hearts. They distinguish us from the herd of common animals. The social compact would dissolve, and justice be extirpated from the earth, or have only a casual existence were we callous to the touches of affection. The robber, and the murderer, would often escape unpunished, did not the injuries which our tempers sustain, provoke us into justice.

O ye that love mankind! Ye that dare oppose, not only the tyranny, but the tyrant, stand forth! Every spot of the old world is overrun with oppression. Freedom hath been hunted round the globe. Asia, and Africa, have long expelled her – Europe regards her like a stranger, and England hath given her warning to depart. O! receive the fugitive, and prepare in time an asylum for mankind....

Source: https://teachingamericanhistory.org/library/document/common-sense/

Document Questions and Answers

Some answers may require more space than provided.

1. How, in Paine's view, has the debate changed?

2. If reconciliation is now impossible, what is Paine's argument for a war to achieve independence?

3. How does Paine refute "England is our mother country"?

4. Does England protect the colonies in wartime?

5. Who (or what) should be king in America?

6. Is Paine familiar with Locke's theory of government?

7. How does Paine criticize the British for attempting to use slaves and Indians against the rebellious colonies? What does he mean when he says "the cruelty hath a double guilt"?

8. Can peace and reconciliation restore the old relationship?

UNDERSTANDING THE DECLARATION OF INDEPENDENCE

To understand the first part of the Declaration, it is necessary to understand the meanings of key words and phrases and also their implications. Provide a precise explanation of each of these crucially important sentences or phrases drawn from the Declaration. Feel free to draw upon the complete text of the Declaration, which is provided immediately after this list, and also in the Supplemental Materials on page 292.

… the Laws of Nature and of Nature's God

We hold these truths to be self-evident …

… that all men are created equal,

… that they are endowed by their Creator

… with certain unalienable Rights

… that among these are Life, Liberty and the pursuit of Happiness

That to secure these rights, Governments are instituted among Men

… deriving their just powers

… from the consent of the governed….

THE DECLARATION OF INDEPENDENCE

In Congress, July 4, 1776.

The unanimous Declaration of the thirteen united States of America.

When in the Course of human events, it becomes necessary for one people to dissolve the political bands which have connected them with another, and to assume among the powers of the earth, the separate and equal station to which the Laws of Nature and of Nature's God entitle them, a decent respect to the opinions of mankind requires that they should declare the causes which impel them to the separation.

We hold these truths to be self-evident, that all men are created equal, that they are endowed by their Creator with certain unalienable Rights, that among these are Life, Liberty and the pursuit of Happiness. – That to secure these rights, Governments are instituted among Men, deriving their just powers from the consent of the governed, – That whenever any Form of Government becomes destructive of these ends, it is the Right of the People to alter or to abolish it, and to institute new Government, laying its foundation on such principles and organizing its powers in such form, as to them shall seem most likely to effect their Safety and Happiness. Prudence, indeed, will dictate that Governments long established should not be changed for light and transient causes; and accordingly all experience hath shewn, that mankind are more disposed to suffer, while evils are sufferable, than to right themselves by abolishing the forms to which they are accustomed. But when a long train of abuses and usurpations, pursuing invariably the same Object evinces a design to reduce them under absolute Despotism, it is their right, it is their duty, to throw off such Government, and to provide new Guards for their future security. – Such has been the patient sufferance of these Colonies; and such is now the necessity which constrains them to alter their former Systems of Government. The history of the present King of Great Britain is a history of repeated injuries and usurpations, all having in direct object the establishment of an absolute Tyranny over these States. To prove this, let Facts be submitted to a candid world.

He has refused his Assent to Laws, the most wholesome and necessary for the public good.

He has forbidden his Governors to pass Laws of immediate and pressing importance, unless suspended in their operation till his Assent should be obtained; and when so suspended, he has utterly neglected to attend to them.

He has refused to pass other Laws for the accommodation of large districts of people, unless those people would relinquish the right of Representation in the Legislature, a right inestimable to them and formidable to tyrants only.

He has called together legislative bodies at places unusual, uncomfortable, and distant from the depository of their public Records, for the sole purpose of fatiguing them into compliance with his measures.

He has dissolved Representative Houses repeatedly, for opposing with manly firmness his invasions on the rights of the people.

He has refused for a long time, after such dissolutions, to cause others to be elected; whereby the Legislative powers, incapable of Annihilation, have returned to the People at large for their exercise; the State remaining in the mean time exposed to all the dangers of invasion from without, and convulsions within.

He has endeavoured to prevent the population of these States; for that purpose obstructing the Laws for Naturalization of Foreigners; refusing to pass others to encourage their migrations hither, and raising the conditions of new Appropriations of Lands.

He has obstructed the Administration of Justice, by refusing his Assent to Laws for establishing Judiciary powers.

He has made Judges dependent on his Will alone, for the tenure of their offices, and the amount and payment of their salaries.

He has erected a multitude of New Offices, and sent hither swarms of Officers to harass our people, and eat out their substance.

He has kept among us, in times of peace, Standing Armies without the Consent of our legislatures.

He has affected to render the Military independent of and superior to the Civil power.

He has combined with others to subject us to a jurisdiction foreign to our constitution, and unacknowledged by our laws; giving his Assent to their Acts of pretended Legislation:

For Quartering large bodies of armed troops among us:

For protecting them, by a mock Trial, from punishment for any Murders which they should commit on the Inhabitants of these States:

For cutting off our Trade with all parts of the world:

For imposing Taxes on us without our Consent:

For depriving us in many cases, of the benefits of Trial by Jury:

For transporting us beyond Seas to be tried for pretended offences

For abolishing the free System of English Laws in a neighbouring Province, establishing therein an Arbitrary government, and enlarging its Boundaries so as to render it at once an example and fit instrument for introducing the same absolute rule into these Colonies:

For taking away our Charters, abolishing our most valuable Laws, and altering fundamentally the Forms of our Governments:

For suspending our own Legislatures, and declaring themselves invested with power to legislate for us in all cases whatsoever.

He has abdicated Government here, by declaring us out of his Protection and waging War against us.

He has plundered our seas, ravaged our Coasts, burnt our towns, and destroyed the lives of our people.

He is at this time transporting large Armies of foreign Mercenaries to compleat the works of death, desolation and tyranny, already begun with circumstances of Cruelty & perfidy scarcely paralleled in the most barbarous ages, and totally unworthy the Head of a civilized nation.

He has constrained our fellow Citizens taken Captive on the high Seas to bear Arms against their Country, to become the executioners of their friends and Brethren, or to fall themselves by their Hands.

He has excited domestic insurrections amongst us, and has endeavoured to bring on the inhabitants of our frontiers, the merciless Indian Savages, whose known rule of warfare, is an undistinguished destruction of all ages, sexes and conditions.

In every stage of these Oppressions We have Petitioned for Redress in the most humble terms: Our repeated Petitions have been answered only by repeated injury. A Prince whose character is thus marked by every act which may define a Tyrant, is unfit to be the ruler of a free people.

Nor have We been wanting in attentions to our Brittish brethren. We have warned them from time to time of attempts by their legislature to extend an unwarrantable jurisdiction over us. We have reminded them of the circumstances of our emigration and settlement here. We have appealed to their native justice and magnanimity, and we have conjured them by the ties of our common kindred to disavow these usurpations, which, would inevitably interrupt our connections and correspondence. They too have been deaf to the voice of justice and of consanguinity. We must, therefore, acquiesce in the necessity, which denounces our Separation, and hold them, as we hold the rest of mankind, Enemies in War, in Peace Friends.

We, therefore, the Representatives of the united States of America, in General Congress, Assembled, appealing to the Supreme Judge of the world for the rectitude of our intentions, do, in the Name, and by Authority of the good People of these Colonies, solemnly publish and declare, That these United Colonies are, and of Right ought to be Free and Independent States; that they are Absolved from all Allegiance to the British Crown, and that all political connection between them and the State of Great Britain, is and ought to be totally dissolved; and that as Free and Independent States, they have full Power to levy War, conclude Peace, contract Alliances, establish Commerce, and to do all other Acts and Things which Independent States may of right do. And for the support of this Declaration, with a firm reliance on the protection of divine Providence, we mutually pledge to each other our Lives, our Fortunes and our sacred Honor.

UNDERSTANDING THE CONSTITUTION

Provide a detailed answer to each of the following three questions, with special attention to explaining the meaning of the boldfaced terms.

1. The United States is a **federal system** with several levels of government, including a national government and the state (and local) governments. What is the relationship between We the People and our various levels of government?

2. The U.S. government is **"mixed and balanced."** What does that mean?

3. What view of **human nature** does the Constitution rest upon?

CHAPTER FOUR

A WAR, A NATION, AND A WOUND

Questions

Some answers may require more space than provided.

1. What were the main problems facing the newly independent United States in winning the war?

2. What advantages did the Americans have?

3. Washington's defense of New York City was probably doomed from the start, and he was fortunate to extract his army from Long Island in the face of British naval superiority. Driven out of New York and across New Jersey in a series of defeats, his army dwindled from twenty-eight thousand in August 1776 to three thousand in December. This was the crisis. What happened to turn things around?

4. The British called 1777 "the year of the hangman" when the rebellion would be crushed. What was their plan? What part of it worked, and what part failed?

5. What happened at Valley Forge over the winter of 1777–78?

6. Who was George Rogers Clark? (p. 57)

7. What happened when the British under Lord Cornwallis moved into the South?

8. Was the war a fight for independence or a truly revolutionary struggle? Was it about "home rule" or "who should rule at home"?

9. What sort of national government did the Articles of Confederation provide for the United States? Why did it not matter that they were not finally ratified until 1781?

10. What was the "singularly impressive and enduring accomplishment" of Congress under the Articles?

11. What problems did the United States face after the war? How effective was the Confederation Congress in dealing with them?

12. How serious a threat was Shays' Rebellion in Massachusetts?

13. Who was the intellectual leader among the many very talented men at the Philadelphia convention?

14. What did the Philadelphia convention agree on from the start?

15. What was the fundamental problem?

16. Why was there reluctance to create a strong executive? Why did they do so anyway?

17. What was the great issue regarding representation? How was it resolved?

18. What are the three functions of government? How was the system of checks and balances achieved?

19. "We are forever about the business of making a workable _____ out of our unworkable _____, and our Constitution accepted the inevitability of our _____ in such things, and the inevitability of _____ arising out of our differences." (p. 69)

20. What would counteract the ambitions of powerful men?

21. "Unlike the Declaration of Independence, the Constitution's spirit is _____, _____; it would be revealed not through words but through _____, through _____, and through _____ that would express the unfolding demands of history." (p. 69)

22. What was the main labor system during the seventeenth century?

23. Why did black chattel slavery supplant the indenture system?

24. How do we understand the irony and contradictions of the Founders' acceptance of slavery in an otherwise free society?

25. How is slavery recognized, and how not, in the Constitution?

26. How did slavery in the southern states compare with the situation in Latin America?

27. "We live today on the other side of a great transformation in moral sensibility … that was not yet completed, in the very years that the United States was being formed. Hence it would be profoundly wrong to contend, as some do, that the United States was '_____' slavery. No, it was *founded* on other principles entirely, on principles of _____ and _____, that … would win out in the end, though not without much struggle and striving, and eventual bloodshed." (p. 73)

Objective Questions

Put in order:

    ____ Articles of Confederation
    ____ Philadelphia Convention
    ____ Shays' Rebellion

Matching:

____ Charles Cornwallis   A. American
____ Comte de Grasse   B. British
____ Friedrich von Steuben   C. French
____ George Washington   D. Prussian
____ George Rogers Clark
____ John Burgoyne
____ Marquis de Lafayette

Document

THE NORTHWEST ORDINANCE, JULY 13, 1787

An Ordinance for the government of the Territory of the United States northwest of the River Ohio.

Sec. 1. Be it ordained by the United States in Congress assembled, that the said territory, for the purposes of temporary government, be one district, subject, however, to be divided into two districts, as future circumstances may, in the opinion of Congress, make it expedient.

Sec. 2. Be it ordained by the authority aforesaid, that the estates, both of resident and nonresident proprietors in the said territory, dying intestate, shall descend to, and be distributed among their children, and the descendants of a deceased child, in equal parts; the descendants of a deceased child or grandchild to take the share of their deceased parent in equal parts among them: And where there shall be no children or descendants, then in equal parts to the next of kin in equal degree; and among collaterals, the children of a deceased brother or sister of the intestate shall have, in equal parts among them, their deceased parents' share; and there shall in no case be a distinction between kindred of the whole and half blood; saving, in all cases, to the widow of the intestate her third part of the real estate for life, and one third part of the personal estate; and this law relative to descents and dower, shall remain in full force until altered by the legislature of the district. And until the Governor and judges shall adopt laws as hereinafter mentioned, estates in the said territory may be devised or bequeathed by wills in writing, signed and sealed by him or her in whom the estate may be (being of full age), and attested by three witnesses; and real estates may be conveyed by lease and release, or bargain and sale, signed, sealed and delivered by the person being of full age, in whom the estate may be, and attested by two witnesses, provided such wills be duly proved, and such conveyances be acknowledged, or the execution thereof duly proved, and be recorded within one year after proper magistrates, courts, and registers shall be appointed for that purpose; and personal property may be transferred by delivery; saving, however to the French and Canadian inhabitants, and other settlers of the Kaskaskies, St. Vincents and the neighboring villages who have heretofore professed themselves citizens of Virginia, their laws and customs now in force among them, relative to the descent and conveyance, of property.

Sec. 3. Be it ordained by the authority aforesaid, that there shall be appointed from time to time by Congress, a Governor, whose commission shall continue in force for the term of three years, unless sooner revoked by Congress; he shall reside in the district, and have a freehold estate therein in 1,000 acres of land, while in the exercise of his office.

Sec. 4. There shall be appointed from time to time by Congress, a secretary, whose commission shall continue in force for four years unless sooner revoked; he shall reside in the district, and have a freehold estate therein in 500 acres of land, while in the exercise of his office. It shall be his duty to keep and preserve the acts and laws passed by the legislature, and the public records of the district, and the proceedings of the Governor in his executive department, and transmit authentic copies of such acts and proceedings, every six months, to the secretary of Congress: There shall also be appointed a court to consist of three judges, any two of whom to form a court, who shall have a common law jurisdiction, and reside in the district, and have each therein a freehold estate in 500 acres of land while in the exercise of their offices; and their commissions shall continue in force during good behavior.

Sec. 5. The Governor and judges, or a majority of them, shall adopt and publish in the district such laws of the original states, criminal and civil, as may be necessary and best suited to the circumstances of the district, and report them to Congress from time to time: which laws shall be in force in the district until the organization of the General Assembly therein, unless disapproved of by Congress; but afterwards the Legislature shall have authority to alter them as they shall think fit.

Sec. 6. The Governor, for the time being, shall be commander in chief of the militia, appoint and commission all officers in the same below the rank of general officers; all general officers shall be appointed and commissioned by Congress.

Sec. 7. Previous to the organization of the General Assembly, the Governor shall appoint such magistrates and other civil officers in each county or township, as he shall find necessary for the preservation of the peace and good order in the same: After the General Assembly shall be organized, the powers and duties of the magistrates and other civil officers shall be regulated and defined by the said assembly; but all magistrates and other civil officers not herein otherwise directed, shall during the continuance of this temporary government, be appointed by the Governor.

Sec. 8. For the prevention of crimes and injuries, the laws to be adopted or made shall have force in all parts of the district, and for the execution of process, criminal and civil, the Governor shall make proper divisions thereof; and he shall proceed from time to time as circumstances may require, to lay out the parts of the district in which the Indian titles shall have been extinguished, into counties and townships, subject, however, to such alterations as may thereafter be made by the legislature.

Sec. 9. So soon as there shall be five thousand free male inhabitants of full age in the district, upon giving proof thereof to the Governor, they shall receive authority, with time and place, to elect a representative from their counties or townships to represent them in the General Assembly: Provided, that, for every five hundred free male inhabitants, there shall be one representative, and so on progressively with the number of free male inhabitants shall the right of representation increase, until the number of representatives shall amount to twenty-five; after which, the number and proportion of representatives shall be regulated by the legislature: Provided, that no person be eligible or qualified to act as a representative unless he shall have been a citizen of one of the United States three years, and be a resident in the district, or unless he shall have resided in the district three years; and, in either case, shall likewise hold in his own right, in fee simple, two hundred acres of land within the same; Provided, also, that a freehold in fifty acres of land in the district, having been a citizen of one of the states, and being resident in the district, or the like freehold and two years residence in the district, shall be necessary to qualify a man as an elector of a representative.

Sec. 10. The representatives thus elected, shall serve for the term of two years; and, in case of the death of a representative, or removal from office, the Governor shall issue a writ to the county or township for which he was a member, to elect another in his stead, to serve for the residue of the term.

Sec. 11. The General Assembly or legislature shall consist of the Governor, Legislative Council, and a House of Representatives. The Legislative Council shall consist of five members, to continue in office five years, unless sooner removed by Congress; any three of whom to be a quorum: and the members of the council shall be nominated and appointed in the following manner, to wit: As soon as representatives shall be elected, the Governor shall appoint a time and place for them to meet together; and, when met, they shall nominate ten persons, residents in the district, and each possessed of a freehold in five hundred acres of land, and return their names to Congress; five of whom Congress shall appoint and commission to serve as aforesaid; and, whenever a vacancy shall happen in the council, by death or removal from office, the house of representatives shall nominate two persons, qualified as aforesaid, for each vacancy, and return their names to Congress; one of whom congress shall appoint and commission for the residue of the term. And every five years, four months at least before the expiration of the time of service of the members of council, the said house shall nominate ten persons, qualified as aforesaid, and return their names to Congress; five of whom Congress shall appoint and commission to serve as members of the council five years, unless sooner removed. And the Governor, legislative council, and house of representatives, shall have authority to make laws in all cases, for the good government of the district, not repugnant to the principles and articles in this ordinance established and declared. And all bills, having passed by a majority in the house, and by a majority in the council, shall be referred to the Governor for his assent; but no bill, or legislative act whatever, shall be of any force without his assent. The Governor shall have power to convene, prorogue, and dissolve the General Assembly, when, in his opinion, it shall be expedient.

Sec. 12. The Governor, judges, legislative council, secretary, and such other officers as Congress shall appoint in the district, shall take an oath or affirmation of fidelity and of office; the Governor before the president of congress, and all other officers before the Governor. As soon as a legislature shall be formed in the district, the council and house assembled in one room, shall have authority, by joint ballot, to elect a delegate to Congress, who shall have a seat in Congress, with a right of debating but not voting during this temporary government.

Sec. 13. And, for extending the fundamental principles of civil and religious liberty, which form the basis whereon these republics, their laws and constitutions are erected; to fix and establish those principles as the basis of all laws, constitutions, and governments, which forever hereafter shall be formed in the said territory: to provide also for the establishment of states, and permanent government therein, and for their admission to a share in the federal councils on an equal footing with the original States, at as early periods as may be consistent with the general interest:

Sec. 14. It is hereby ordained and declared by the authority aforesaid, That the following articles shall be considered as articles of compact between the original States and the people and States in the said territory and forever remain unalterable, unless by common consent, to wit:

Art. 1. No person, demeaning himself in a peaceable and orderly manner, shall ever be molested on account of his mode of worship or religious sentiments, in the said territory.

Art. 2. The inhabitants of the said territory shall always be entitled to the benefits of the writ of habeas corpus, and of the trial by jury; of a proportionate representation of the people in the legislature; and of judicial proceedings according to the course of the common law. All persons shall be bailable, unless for capital offenses, where the proof shall be evident or the presumption great. All fines shall be moderate; and no cruel or unusual punishments shall be inflicted. No man shall be deprived of his liberty or property, but by the judgment of his peers or the law of the land; and, should the public exigencies make it necessary, for the common preservation, to take any person's property, or to demand his particular services, full compensation shall be made for the same. And, in the just preservation of rights and property, it is understood and declared, that no law ought ever to be made, or have force in the said territory, that shall, in any manner whatever, interfere with or affect private contracts or engagements, bona fide, and without fraud, previously formed.

Art. 3. Religion, morality, and knowledge, being necessary to good government and the happiness of mankind, schools and the means of education shall forever be encouraged. The utmost good faith shall always be observed towards the Indians; their lands and property shall never be taken from them without their consent; and, in their property, rights, and liberty, they shall never be invaded or disturbed, unless in just and lawful wars authorized by Congress; but laws founded in justice and humanity, shall from time to time be made for preventing wrongs being done to them, and for preserving peace and friendship with them.

Art. 4. The said territory, and the states which may be formed therein, shall forever remain a part of this Confederacy of the United States of America, subject to the Articles of Confederation, and to such alterations therein as shall be constitutionally made; and to all the acts and ordinances of the United States in Congress assembled, conformable thereto. The inhabitants and settlers in the said territory shall be subject to pay a part of the federal debts contracted or to be contracted, and a proportional part of the expenses of government, to be apportioned on them by Congress according to the same common rule and measure by which apportionments thereof shall be made on the other states; and the taxes for paying their proportion shall be laid and levied by the authority and direction of the legislatures of the district or districts, or new states, as in the original states, within the time agreed upon by the United States in Congress assembled. The legislatures of those districts or new states, shall never interfere with the primary disposal of the soil by the United States in Congress assembled, nor with any regulations Congress may find necessary for securing the title in such soil to the bona fide purchasers. No tax shall be imposed on lands the property of the United States; and, in no case, shall nonresident proprietors be taxed higher than residents. The navigable waters leading into the Mississippi and St. Lawrence, and the carrying places between the same, shall be common highways and forever free, as well to the inhabitants of the said territory as to the citizens of the United States, and those of any other states that may be admitted into the confederacy, without any tax, impost, or duty therefor.

Art. 5. There shall be formed in the said territory, not less than three nor more than five states; and the boundaries of the states, as soon as Virginia shall alter her act of cession, and consent to the same, shall become fixed and established as follows.... And, whenever any of the said states shall have sixty thousand free inhabitants therein, such state shall be admitted, by its delegates, into the Congress of the United States, on an equal footing with the original states in all respects whatever, and shall be at liberty to form a permanent constitution and State government: Provided, the constitution and government so to be formed, shall be republican, and in conformity to the principles contained in these articles; and, so far as it can be consistent with the general interest of the confederacy, such admission shall be allowed at an earlier period, and when there may be a less number of free inhabitants in the state than sixty thousand.

Art. 6. There shall be neither slavery nor involuntary servitude in the said territory, otherwise than in the punishment of crimes whereof the party shall have been duly convicted: Provided, always, that any person escaping into the same, from whom labor or service is lawfully claimed in any one of the original states, such fugitive may be lawfully reclaimed and conveyed to the person claiming his or her labor or service as aforesaid.

Be it ordained by the authority aforesaid, that the resolutions of the 23rd of April, 1784, relative to the subject of this ordinance, be, and the same are hereby repealed and declared null and void.

Done by the United States, in Congress assembled, the 13th day of July, in the year of our Lord 1787, and of their sovereignty and independence the twelfth.

Document Questions

Some answers may require more space than provided.

1. What is remarkable about Section 2 of the Ordinance?

2. Where do you see Daniel Boorstin's "add a state plan" idea in this document?

3. What does the Ordinance have to say about slavery?

4. What about education?

5. What about the treatment of the native population?

6. And religious liberty?

Special Unit

UNDERSTANDING THE BILL OF RIGHTS

Consult the text of the Bill of Rights, provided on pages 313–23 in the book, and supply the missing keywords in each of the first ten Amendments.

First Amendment: Congress shall make no law respecting an establishment of _____ or prohibiting the free exercise thereof; or abridging the freedom of _____, or of the _____; or the right of the people peaceably to _____, and to petition the Government for a redress of grievances.

Second Amendment: A well regulated Militia, being necessary to the security of a free State, the right of the people to keep and bear _____, shall not be infringed.

Third Amendment: No Soldier shall, in time of peace be _____ in any house, without the consent of the Owner, nor in time of war, but in a manner to be prescribed by law.

Fourth Amendment: The right of the people to be secure in their persons, houses, papers, and effects, against unreasonable _____, shall not be violated, and no Warrants shall issue, but upon probable cause, supported by Oath or affirmation, and particularly describing the place to be searched, and the persons or things to be seized.

Fifth Amendment: No person shall be held to answer for a capital, or otherwise infamous crime, unless on a presentment or indictment of a _____, except in cases arising in the land or naval forces, or in the Militia, when in actual service in time of War or public danger; nor shall any person be subject for the same offence to be twice put in_____ of life or limb; nor shall be compelled in any criminal case to be a witness against himself, nor be deprived of life, liberty, or property, without _____; nor shall private property be taken _____, without just compensation.

Sixth Amendment: In all criminal prosecutions, the accused shall enjoy the right to a speedy and public _____, by an impartial jury of the State and district wherein the crime shall have been committed, which district shall have been previously ascertained by law, and to be informed of the nature and cause of the accusation; to be confronted with the witnesses against him; to have compulsory process for obtaining witnesses in his favor, and to have the Assistance of Counsel for his defense.

Seventh Amendment: In Suits at common law, where the value in controversy shall exceed twenty dollars, the right of trial by jury shall be preserved, and no fact tried by a jury, shall be otherwise re-examined in any Court of the United States, than according to the rules of _____.

Eighth Amendment: Excessive bail shall not be required, nor excessive fines imposed, nor _____ and _____ punishments inflicted.

Ninth Amendment: The enumeration in the Constitution, of certain rights, shall not be construed to deny or disparage others retained by _____.

Tenth Amendment: The powers not delegated to the United States by the Constitution, nor prohibited by it to the States, are reserved to the _____ respectively, or to the _____.

CHAPTER FIVE

THE EXPERIMENT BEGINS

Questions

Some answers may require more space than provided.

1. Of the fourteen individuals named in this chapter, seven are pictured or alluded to in the book's inserted picture gallery: Washington, Jefferson, Madison, Hamilton, the Adamses, and L'Enfant's plan for the capital city; go back and study (look at and read) the material there about each of them. Try to capture each individual's life in a sentence.

2. Of the remaining eight, one (Flexner) is a modern biographer, and one (Tally-rand) was a foreign diplomat. Which two of the remaining five (Jay, Henry, Knox, Randolph, and Burr) were most important in their impact on the new nation?

3. Consult a reference source about Aaron Burr and write a paragraph describing his relationships with Thomas Jefferson and with Alexander Hamilton.

4. By what process was the U.S. Constitution ratified? Why was this important?

5. The Federalists of 1787–88 were really nationalists favoring a strong central government, an unpopular idea. So they called themselves Federalists, which *was* a popular idea, and labeled their opponents *Anti*-Federalists, even though the Articles of Confederation had also created a federal union. What then was the "persistent tension" that divided the Federalists and Anti-Federalists and that persists to this day?

6. Who wrote *The Federalist* (or *The Federalist Papers*)? Why are they classics? Where were they first published, and what does this suggest about the state of public debate today?

7. According to *Federalist* 10, what is the cure for the problem of factions?

8. According to *Federalist* 51, what protects the rights of the people?

9. What view of human nature does the Constitution rest on?

10. Why is the writing and ratification of the U.S. Constitution an important event in world history?

11. What did the Anti-Federalists contribute to the outcome of this struggle?

12. Why is the irony of the opponents of the Constitution contributing so greatly to its success "not as ironic as it might seem"?

13. What remained to be done when Washington was sworn in as the first president? Why did Flexner call him "the indispensable man"? Why did Washington agonize over every decision?

14. What was Washington's attitude toward political parties? Who was in his first cabinet?

15. What were the three main elements of Hamilton's financial plan? How well did each succeed?

16. What was the debate over the creation of the national bank?

17. Describe the rival views of Hamilton and Jefferson, including their visions for what sort of republic the United States should be, what examples it should follow, how it should be governed, and what its position should be in the conduct of its foreign policy.

18. How did the wars of the French Revolution and Napoleon (1791–1815, almost without interruption), which meant a worldwide war between the two superpowers, the British and French Empires, affect the development of the fledgling United States?

19. What was Washington's policy regarding the wars in Europe? Why was this both necessary and unpopular, as exemplified in the Jay Treaty?

20. How bitter and intense did party conflict become during the 1790s? Why?

21. Why is Washington's Farewell Address an American classic? What rule did it lay down for the United States' relationships with other countries?

22. Why was John Adams's presidency so contentious? Who was Adams's vice president? Why was the path of Adams's presidency powerful evidence that the Framers of the Constitution who met in the Philadelphia convention neither wanted nor anticipated political parties?

23. What was the XYZ Affair? How did it lead to the Alien and Sedition Acts? How did those lead to the Virginia and Kentucky Resolutions?

24. What was the state of the public press (newspapers) in the 1790s?

25. How did each party portray its opponent during the election of 1800?

26. How did it happen that Hamilton was responsible for the election of his arch-rival Jefferson? Why was the Twelfth Amendment necessary after 1796 and 1800?

27. What was "revolutionary" about the "Revolution of 1800"?

28. How did Jefferson address the nation in his First Inaugural? What did Jefferson change, and what did he leave, of Hamilton's plan after he gained power in 1800?

29. How did L'Enfant's layout of Washington, D.C., shape its development as a city?

Objective Questions

Put in order:

____ Hamilton and Jefferson debate the national bank
____ The Constitution is ratified
____ Washington is sworn in as first president

Put in order:

____ Alien and Sedition Acts
____ Virginia and Kentucky Resolutions
____ XYZ Affair

Matching: (author to document)

____ Declaration of Independence   A. Alexander Hamilton
____ *Federalist Papers*   B. James Madison
____ U.S. Constitution   C. John Adams
                                      D. Thomas Jefferson

Document 1

JAMES MADISON, *FEDERALIST* 10

Among the numerous advantages promised by a well-constructed union, none deserves to be more accurately developed, than its tendency to break and control the violence of faction. The friend of popular governments, never finds himself so much alarmed for their character and fate, as when he contemplates their propensity to this dangerous vice. He will not fail, therefore, to set a due value on any plan which, without violating the principles to which he is attached, provides a proper cure for it.... Complaints are everywhere heard from our most considerate and virtuous citizens, equally the friends of public and private faith, and of public and personal liberty, that our governments are too unstable; that the public good is disregarded in the conflicts of rival parties; and that measures are too often decided, not according to the rules of justice, and the rights of the minor party, but by the superior force of an interested and overbearing majority. However anxiously we may wish that these complaints had no foundation, the evidence of known facts will not permit us to deny that they are in some degree true....

By a faction, I understand a number of citizens, whether amounting to a majority or minority of the whole, who are united and actuated by some common impulse of passion, or of interest, adverse to the rights of other citizens, or to the permanent and aggregate interests of the community.

There are two methods of curing the mischiefs of faction: The one, by removing its causes; the other, by controlling its effects.

There are again two methods of removing the causes of faction: The one, by destroying the liberty which is essential to its existence; the other, by giving to every citizen the same opinions, the same passions, and the same interests.

It could never be more truly said, than of the first remedy, that it is worse than the disease. Liberty is to faction, what air is to fire, an element, without which it instantly expires. But it could not be a less folly to abolish liberty, which is essential to political life, because it nourishes faction, than it would be to wish the annihilation of air, which is essential to animal life, because it imparts to fire its destructive agency.

The second expedient is as impracticable, as the first would be unwise. As long as the reason of man continues fallible, and he is at liberty to exercise it, different opinions will be formed. As long as the connection subsists between his reason and his self-love, his opinions and his passions will have a reciprocal influence on each other; and the former will be objects to which the latter will attach themselves. The diversity in the faculties of men, from which the rights of property originate, is not less an insuperable obstacle to an uniformity of interests. The protection of these faculties, is the first object of government. From the protection of different and unequal faculties of acquiring property, the possession of different degrees and kinds of property immediately results; and from the influence of these on the sentiments and views of the respective proprietors, ensues a division of the society into different interests and parties.

The latent causes of faction are thus sown in the nature of man; and we see them everywhere brought into different degrees of activity, according to the different circumstances of civil society. A zeal for different opinions concerning religion, concerning government, and many other points, as well of speculation as of practice ... have, in turn, divided mankind into parties, inflamed them with mutual animosity, and rendered them much more disposed to vex and oppress each other, than to co-operate for their common good. So strong is this propensity of mankind, to fall into mutual animosities, that where no substantial occasion presents itself, the most frivolous and fanciful distinctions have been sufficient to kindle their unfriendly passions, and excite their most violent conflicts. But the most common and durable source of factions, has been the various and unequal distribution of property. Those who hold, and those who are without property, have ever formed distinct interests in society.... The regulation of these various and interfering interests, forms the principal task of modern legislation, and involves the spirit of party and faction in the necessary and ordinary operations of government....

It is in vain to say, that enlightened statesmen will be able to adjust these clashing interests, and render them all subservient to the public good. Enlightened statesmen will not always be at the helm: nor, in many cases, can such an adjustment be made at all, without taking into view indirect and remote considerations, which will rarely prevail over the immediate interest which one party may find in disregarding the rights of another, or the good of the whole.

The inference to which we are brought, is, that the causes of faction cannot be removed; and that relief is only to be sought in the means of controlling its effects.

If a faction consists of less than a majority, relief is supplied by the republican principle, which enables the majority to defeat its sinister views, by regular vote. It may clog the administration, it may convulse the society; but it will be unable to execute and mask its violence under the forms of the constitution. When a majority is included in a faction, the form of popular government, on the other hand, enables it to sacrifice to its ruling passion or interest, both the public good and the rights of other citizens. To secure the public good, and private rights, against the danger of such a faction, and at the same time to preserve the spirit and the form of popular government, is then the great object to which our inquiries are directed....

By what means is this object attainable? Evidently by one of two only. Either the existence of the same passion or interest in a majority, at the same time, must be prevented; or the majority, having such co-existent passion or interest, must be rendered, by their number and local situation, unable to concert and carry into effect schemes of oppression. If the impulse and the opportunity be suffered to coincide, we well know, that neither moral nor religious motives can be relied on as an adequate control. They are not found to be such on the injustice and violence of individuals, and lose their efficacy in proportion to the number combined together; that is, in proportion as their efficacy becomes needful....

A republic, by which I mean a government in which the scheme of representation takes place ... promises the cure for which we are seeking. Let us examine the points in which it varies from pure democracy, and we shall comprehend both the nature of the cure and the efficacy which it must derive from the union.

The two great points of difference, between a democracy and a republic, are, first, the delegation of the government, in the latter, to a small number of citizens elected by the rest; secondly, the greater number of citizens, and greater sphere of country, over which the latter may be extended.

The effect of the first difference is, on the one hand, to refine and enlarge the public views, by passing them through the medium of a chosen body of citizens, whose wisdom may best discern the true interest of their country, and whose patriotism and love of justice, will be least likely to sacrifice it to temporary or partial considerations. Under such a regulation, it may well happen, that the public voice, pronounced by the representatives of the people, will be more consonant to the public good, than if pronounced by the people themselves, convened for the purpose. On the other hand, the effect may be inverted. Men of factious tempers, of local prejudices, or of sinister designs, may by intrigue, by corruption, or by other means, first obtain the suffrages, and then betray the interests of the people. The question resulting is, whether small or extensive republics are most favorable to the election of proper guardians of the public weal; and it is clearly decided in favor of the latter by two obvious considerations.

In the first place, it is to be remarked, that however small the republic may be, the representatives must be raised to a certain number, in order to guard against the cabals of a few; and that, however large it may be, they must be limited to a certain number, in order to guard against the confusion of a multitude. Hence, the number of representatives in the two cases not being in proportion to that of the constituents, and being proportionally greatest in the small republic, it follows, that if the proportion of fit characters be not less in the large than in the small republic, the former will present a greater option, and consequently a greater probability of a fit choice.

In the next place, as each representative will be chosen by a greater number of citizens in the large than in the small republic, it will be more difficult for unworthy candidates to practice with success the vicious arts, by which elections are too often carried; and the suffrages of the people being more free, will be more likely to center in men who possess the most attractive merit, and the most diffusive and established characters.

It must be confessed, that in this, as in most other cases, there is a mean, on both sides of which inconveniences will be found to lie. By enlarging too much the number of electors, you render the representative too little acquainted with all their local circumstances and lesser interests; as by reducing it too much, you render him unduly attached to these, and too little fit to comprehend and pursue great and national objects. The federal constitution forms a happy combination in this respect; the great and aggregate interests, being referred to the national, the local and particular to the state legislatures.

The other point of difference is, the greater number of citizens, and extent of territory, which may be brought within the compass of republican, than of democratic government; and it is this circumstance principally which renders factious combinations less to be dreaded in the former, than in the latter. The smaller the society, the fewer probably will be the distinct parties and interests composing it; the fewer the distinct parties and interests, the more frequently will a majority be found of the same party; and the smaller the number of individuals composing a majority, and the smaller the compass within which they are placed, the more easily will they concert and execute their plans of oppression. Extend the sphere, and you take in a greater variety of parties and interests; you make it less probable that a majority of the whole will have a common motive to invade the rights of other citizens; or if such a common motive exists, it will be more difficult for all who feel it to discover their own strength, and to act in unison with each other. Besides other impediments, it may be remarked, that where there is a consciousness of unjust or dishonorable purposes, communication is always checked by distrust, in proportion to the number whose concurrence is necessary.

Hence it clearly appears, that the same advantage, which a republic has over a democracy, in controlling the effects of faction, is enjoyed by a large over a small republic, – is enjoyed by the union over the states composing it....

In the extent and proper structure of the union, therefore, we behold a republican remedy for the diseases most incident to republican government. And according to the degree of pleasure and pride we feel in being republicans, ought to be our zeal in cherishing the spirit, and supporting the character of federalists.

Source: https://teachingamericanhistory.org/library/document/federalist-no-10/

Document 1 Questions

Some answers may require more space than provided.

1. What does Madison mean by a "faction"?

2. What are the two methods of curing faction? Why are they undesirable or impossible?

3. What then is to be concluded about faction?

4. How does Madison distinguish between a republic and a democracy?

5. Why does "extending the sphere" offer relief from the problem of faction?

Document 2

ROBERT YATES, *BRUTUS* I

The first question that presents itself on the subject is, whether a confederated government be the best for the United States or not? Or in other words, whether the thirteen United States should be reduced to one great republic, governed by one legislature, and under the direction of one executive and judicial; or whether they should continue thirteen confederated republics, under the direction and control of a supreme federal head for certain defined national purposes only?

This enquiry is important, because, although the government reported by the convention does not go to a perfect and entire consolidation, yet it approaches so near to it, that it must, if executed, certainly and infallibly terminate in it.

This government is to possess absolute and uncontrollable power, legislative, executive and judicial, with respect to every object to which it extends, for by the last clause of section 8th, article Ist, it is declared "that the Congress shall have power to make all laws which shall be necessary and proper for carrying into execution the foregoing powers, and all other powers vested by this constitution, in the government of the United States; or in any department or office thereof." And by the 6th article, it is declared "that this constitution, and the laws of the United States, which shall be made in pursuance thereof, and the treaties made, or which shall be made, under the authority of the United States, shall be the supreme law of the land; and the judges in every state shall be bound thereby, any thing in the constitution, or law of any state to the contrary notwithstanding." It appears from these articles that there is no need of any intervention of the state governments, between the Congress and the people, to execute any one power vested in the general government, and that the constitution and laws of every state are nullified and declared void, so far as they are or shall be inconsistent with this constitution, or the laws made in pursuance of it, or with treaties made under the authority of the United States. The government then, so far as it extends, is a complete one, and not a confederation. It is as much one complete government as that of New-York or Massachusetts, has as absolute and perfect powers to make and execute all laws, to appoint officers, institute courts, declare offences, and annex penalties, with respect to every object to which it extends, as any other in the world. So far therefore as its powers reach, all ideas of confederation are given up and lost.

... It has authority to make laws which will affect the lives, the liberty, and property of every man in the United States; nor can the constitution or laws of any state, in any way prevent or impede the full and complete execution of every power given. The legislative power is competent to lay taxes, duties, imposts, and excises; there is no limitation to this power, unless it be said that the clause which directs the use to which those taxes, and duties shall be applied, may be said to be a limitation; but this is no restriction of the power at all, for by this clause they are to be applied to pay the debts and provide for the common defense and general welfare of the United States; but the legislature have authority to contract debts at their discretion; they are the sole judges of what is necessary to provide for the common defense, and they only are to determine what is for the general welfare: this power therefore is neither more nor less, than a power to lay and collect taxes, imposts, and excises, at their pleasure....

In the business therefore of laying and collecting taxes, the idea of confederation is totally lost, and that of one entire republic is embraced. It is proper here to remark, that the authority to lay and collect taxes is the most important of any power that can be granted; it connects with it almost all other powers, or at least will in process of time draw all other after it; it is the great mean of protection, security, and defense, in a good government, and the great engine of oppression and tyranny in a bad one....

The judicial power of the United States is to be vested in a supreme court, and in such inferior courts as Congress may from time to time ordain and establish. The powers of these courts are very extensive; their jurisdiction comprehends all civil causes, except such as arise between citizens of the same state; and it extends to all cases in law and equity arising under the constitution. One inferior court must be established, I presume, in each state at least, with the necessary executive officers appendant thereto. It is easy to see, that in the common course of things, these courts will eclipse the dignity, and take away from the respectability, of the state courts. These courts will be, in themselves, totally independent of the states, deriving their authority from the United States, and receiving from them fixed salaries; and in the course of human events it is to be expected, that they will swallow up all the powers of the courts in the respective states.

How far the clause in the 8th section of the Ist article may operate to do away all idea of confederated states, and to effect an entire consolidation of the whole into one general government, it is impossible to say. The powers given by this article are very general and comprehensive, and it may receive a construction to justify the passing almost any law. A power to make all laws, which shall be necessary and proper, for carrying into execution, all powers vested by the constitution in the government of the United States, or any department or officer thereof, is a power very comprehensive and definite, and may, for ought I know, be exercised in a such manner as entirely to abolish the state legislatures.

...The legislature of the United States are vested with the great and uncontrollable powers, of laying and collecting taxes, duties, imposts, and excises; of regulating trade, raising and supporting armies, organizing, arming, and disciplining the militia, instituting courts, and other general powers. And are by this clause invested with the power of making all laws, proper and necessary, for carrying all these into execution; and they may so exercise this power as entirely to annihilate all the state governments, and reduce this country to one single government. And if they may do it, it is pretty certain they will; for it will be found that the power retained by individual states, small as it is, will be a clog upon the wheels of the government of the United States; the latter therefore will be naturally inclined to remove it out of the way. Besides, it is a truth confirmed by the unerring experience of ages, that every man, and every body of men, invested with power, are ever disposed to increase it, and to acquire a superiority over everything that stands in their way....

Let us now proceed to enquire, as I at first proposed, whether it be best the thirteen United States should be reduced to one great republic, or not? It is here taken for granted, that all agree in this, that whatever government we adopt, it ought to be a free one; that it should be so framed as to secure the liberty of the citizens of America, and such a one as to admit of a full, fair, and equal representation of the people. The question then will be, whether a government thus constituted, and founded on such principles, is practicable, and can be exercised over the whole United States, reduced into one state?...

In every government, the will of the sovereign is the law. In despotic governments, the supreme authority being lodged in one, his will is law, and can be as easily expressed to a large extensive territory as to a small one. In a pure democracy the people are the sovereign, and their will is declared by themselves; for this purpose, they must all come together to deliberate, and decide. This kind of government cannot be exercised, therefore, over a country of any considerable extent; it must be confined to a single city, or at least limited to such bounds as that the people can conveniently assemble, be able to debate, understand the subject submitted to them, and declare their opinion concerning it.

In a free republic, although all laws are derived from the consent of the people, yet the people do not declare their consent by themselves in person, but by representatives, chosen by them, who are supposed to know the minds of their constituents, and to be possessed of integrity to declare this mind.

...If the people are to give their assent to the laws, by persons chosen and appointed by them, the manner of the choice and the number chosen, must be such, as to possess, be disposed, and consequently qualified to declare the sentiments of the people; for if they do not know, or are not disposed to speak the sentiments of the people, the people do not govern, but the sovereignty is in a few. Now, in a large extended country, it is impossible to have a representation, possessing the sentiments, and of integrity, to declare the minds of the people, without having it so numerous and unwieldly, as to be subject in great measure to the inconveniency of a democratic government.

The territory of the United States is of vast extent; it now contains near three millions of souls, and is capable of containing much more than ten times that number. Is it practicable for a country, so large and so numerous as they will soon become, to elect a representation, that will speak their sentiments, without their becoming so numerous as to be incapable of transacting public business? It certainly is not.

In a republic, the manners, sentiments, and interests of the people should be similar. If this be not the case, there will be a constant clashing of opinions;

and the representatives of one part will be continually striving against those of the other. This will retard the operations of government, and prevent such conclusions as will promote the public good. If we apply this remark to the condition of the United States, we shall be convinced that it forbids that we should be one government. The United States includes a variety of climates. The productions of the different parts of the union are very variant, and their interests, of consequence, diverse. Their manners and habits differ as much as their climates and productions; and their sentiments are by no means coincident. The laws and customs of the several states are, in many respects, very diverse, and in some opposite; each would be in favor of its own interests and customs, and, of consequence, a legislature, formed of representatives from the respective parts, would not only be too numerous to act with any care or decision, but would be composed of such heterogenous and discordant principles, as would constantly be contending with each other....

...The confidence which the people have in their rulers, in a free republic, arises from their knowing them, from their being responsible to them for their conduct, and from the power they have of displacing them when they misbehave: but in a republic of the extent of this continent, the people in general would be acquainted with very few of their rulers: the people at large would know little of their proceedings, and it would be extremely difficult to change them.... The different parts of so extensive a country could not possibly be made acquainted with the conduct of their representatives, nor be informed of the reasons upon which measures were founded. The consequence will be, they will have no confidence in their legislature, suspect them of ambitious views, be jealous of every measure they adopt, and will not support the laws they pass. Hence the government will be nerveless and inefficient, and no way will be left to render it otherwise, but by establishing an armed force to execute the laws at the point of the bayonet – a government of all others the most to be dreaded.

In a republic of such vast extent as the United-States, the legislature cannot attend to the various concerns and wants of its different parts. It cannot be sufficiently numerous to be acquainted with the local condition and wants of the different districts, and if it could, it is impossible it should have sufficient time to attend to and provide for all the variety of cases of this nature, that would be continually arising....

These are some of the reasons by which it appears, that a free republic cannot long subsist over a country of the great extent of these states. If then this new constitution is calculated to consolidate the thirteen states into one, as it evidently is, it ought not to be adopted.

Source: https://teachingamericanhistory.org/library/document/brutus-i-2/

Document 2 Questions

Some answers may require more space than provided.

1. What is the difference between a confederated government and "one great republic"?

2. What is Brutus's main objection to the U.S. government as defined in the new Constitution?

3. What power remains to the state governments?

4. Is there any limit on the power to tax?

5. What does Brutus think of the "necessary and proper" or "elastic clause"?

6. How likely does Brutus think it is that the central government will override the authority of the states?

7. What for Brutus is the difference between a democracy and a republic?

8. What is the problem with representation in large and diverse countries?

9. Does the growth of the country make things better or worse?

10. The last two parts of the Bill of Rights, the Ninth and Tenth Amendments, attempt to address some of Brutus's concerns. How effective have they been in doing that? Does this tend to confirm Brutus's point in Question 6?

11. This essay should be considered in direct comparison with Madison's *Federalist* 10. One historian commented that Madison's argument with regard to factions and the advantages of a large and diverse country was more clever; but Brutus's arguments may have proven more valid, particularly with the rise of political parties. What do you think?

CHAPTER SIX

FROM JEFFERSON TO JACKSON

The Rise of the Common Man

Questions

Some answers may require more space than provided.

1. How did Jefferson's presidential style differ from those of his predecessors? How effective was it?

2. Despite controlling the executive branch and the Congress, Jefferson's party was repeatedly stymied by the judiciary. How and why were the Supreme Court decisions of John Marshall, beginning with *Marbury v. Madison*, crucial in this resistance to the Jeffersonian party?

3. How did Jefferson respond to Marshall? How effective was each man in shaping the course and nature of the country? In particular, understand that even though Hamilton was dead and the Jeffersonians triumphant at the polls, Marshall ensured that Hamiltonian principles remained influential.

4. How did the Louisiana Purchase come to happen? How was it both a triumph for Jefferson and the nation and also a betrayal of his principles? What are the "layers of irony" in this situation?

5. Note that as the case of the Essex Junto (p. 99) shows, it was always the losing, out-of-power faction that appealed to secession or nullification. Perhaps it follows that every party likes a strong government when it is the one controlling the government?

6. What did the Lewis and Clark Expedition signal about America's future?

7. American foreign policy under Jefferson and Madison continued to focus on protecting America's _____ and its assertion of the principle of _____. (p. 100)

8. Both France and Britain interfered with American shipping, but the British also practiced _____ of American sailors into the British navy, a far greater and insulting grievance. (p. 101)

9. Why did Jefferson opt for the Embargo in 1807 instead of war? How successful was this?

10. Why did Jefferson not seek a third term?

11. Why did Jefferson consider the University of Virginia one of his most important achievements?

12. Madison (who was Jefferson's close friend and ally and had been his secretary of state) inherited all of Jefferson's problems. How effectively did he deal with them?

13. What is ironic about the U.S. declaration of war on Britain in 1812? What does this imply about the *real* reasons for the war? (Who were the War Hawks? Who was Tecumseh?)

14. Trace the destruction of the Federalist Party from the Hartford Convention through Jackson's victory at New Orleans to the election of 1816 and the Era of Good Feeling.

15. What was the "Virginia Dynasty"? What was the pattern of advancement in terms of who became the next president?

16. The story of how the United States acquired Florida was too complex to include in the text of *Land of Hope*, but the incident is very revealing about the complex relationship between Andrew Jackson, John Quincy Adams, and John C. Calhoun. Look it up in a reference source, and make a quick summary.

17. Be able to write several paragraphs about the Monroe Doctrine: how it came to be, what it said, and what its consequences and implications were. (pp. 105–6)

18. John Quincy Adams: The United States "goes not _____ in search of _____ to destroy." (p. 105)

19. How did Henry Clay's American Plan demonstrate the continuing influence of Hamiltonian ideas?

20. How were internal improvements mostly financed in the decades after the War of 1812?

21. What did the Erie Canal do?

22. How did population growth and economic development reshape America after the War of 1812?

23. What was the "fire bell in the night"? What did the Missouri Compromise settle? What did it *not* settle?

24. Jefferson: "We have the _____ by the _____, and we can neither _____ him, nor _____." (p. 110)

25. How did the election of 1824 destroy the Era of Good Feeling? Who ran? Who won? How? What was the "corrupt bargain"? Do you think it was really that corrupt?

26. How did politics change in the Jacksonian Era of the Common Man? What happened at Jackson's inauguration?

27. In what sense was Jackson the first populist?

28. How did Jackson deal with the Nullification Crisis?

29. Was Indian removal Jackson's idea?

30. Tocqueville saw many things in democracy to admire but also some to fear. Explain.

Objective Questions

Put in order:

____ Embargo Act
____ Lewis and Clark Expedition
____ Louisiana Purchase

Put in order:

____ Battle of New Orleans
____ Monroe Doctrine
____ Nullification Crisis

Put in order:

____ presidency of Andrew Jackson
____ presidency of James Monroe
____ presidency of John Quincy Adams

Document 1

ALEXIS DE TOCQUEVILLE, "WHY THE AMERICANS ARE SO RESTLESS IN THE MIDST OF THEIR PROSPERITY," FROM *DEMOCRACY IN AMERICA*, VOLUME 2, SECTION 2, CHAPTER 13

In certain remote corners of the Old World you may still sometimes stumble upon a small district that seems to have been forgotten amid the general tumult, and to have remained stationary while everything around it was in motion. The inhabitants, for the most part, are extremely ignorant and poor; they take no part in the business of the country and are frequently oppressed by the government, yet their countenances are generally placid and their spirits light.

In America I saw the freest and most enlightened men placed in the happiest circumstances that the world affords, it seemed to me as if a cloud habitually hung upon their brow, and I thought them serious and almost sad, even in their pleasures.

The chief reason for this contrast is that the former do not think of the ills they endure, while the latter are forever brooding over advantages they do not possess. It is strange to see with what feverish ardor the Americans pursue their own welfare, and to watch the vague dread that constantly torments them lest they should not have chosen the shortest path which may lead to it.

A native of the United States clings to this world's goods as if he were certain never to die; and he is so hasty in grasping at all within his reach that one would suppose he was constantly afraid of not living long enough to enjoy them. He clutches everything, he holds nothing fast, but soon loosens his grasp to pursue fresh gratifications.

In the United States a man builds a house in which to spend his old age, and he sells it before the roof is on; he plants a garden and lets it just as the trees are coming into bearing; he brings a field into tillage and leaves other men to gather the crops; he embraces a profession and gives it up; he settles in a place, which he soon afterwards leaves to carry his changeable longings elsewhere. If his private affairs leave him any leisure, he instantly plunges into the vortex of politics; and if at the end of a year of unremitting labor he finds he has a few days' vacation, his eager curiosity whirls him over the vast extent of the United States, and he will travel fifteen hundred miles in a few days to shake off his happiness. Death at length overtakes him, but it is before he is weary of his bootless chase of that complete felicity which forever escapes him.

At first sight there is something surprising in this strange unrest of so many happy men, restless in the midst of abundance. The spectacle itself, however, is as old as the world; the novelty is to see a whole people furnish an exemplification of it.

Their taste for physical gratifications must be regarded as the original source of that secret disquietude which the actions of the Americans betray and of that inconstancy of which they daily ford fresh examples. He who has set his heart exclusively upon the pursuit of worldly welfare is always in a hurry, for he has but a limited time at his disposal to reach, to grasp, and to enjoy it.

The recollection of the shortness of life is a constant spur to him. Besides the good things that he possesses, he every instant fancies a thousand others that death will prevent him from trying if he does not try them soon. This thought fills him with anxiety, fear, and regret and keeps his mind in ceaseless trepidation, which leads him perpetually to change his plans and his abode.

If in addition to the taste for physical well-being a social condition be added in which neither laws nor customs retain any person in his place, there is a great additional stimulant to this restlessness of temper. Men will then be seen continually to change their track for fear of missing the shortest cut to happiness.

It may readily be conceived that if men passionately bent upon physical gratifications desire eagerly, they are also easily discouraged; as their ultimate object is to enjoy, the means to reach that object must be prompt and easy or the trouble of acquiring the gratification would be greater than the gratification itself. Their prevailing frame of mind, then, is at once ardent and relaxed, violent and enervated. Death is often less dreaded by them than perseverance in continuous efforts to one end.

The equality of conditions leads by a still straighter road to several of the effects that I have here described. When all the privileges of birth and fortune are abolished, when all professions are accessible to all, and a man's own energies may place him at the top of any one of them, an easy and unbounded career seems open to his ambition and he will readily persuade himself that he is born to no common destinies. But this is an erroneous notion, which is corrected by daily experience. The same equality that allows every citizen to conceive these lofty hopes renders all the citizens less able to realize them; it circumscribes their powers on every side, while it gives freer scope to their desires. Not only are they themselves powerless, but they are met at every step by immense obstacles, which they did not at first perceive. They have swept away the privileges of some of their fellow creatures which stood in their way, but they have opened the door to universal competition; the barrier has changed its shape rather than its position. When men are nearly alike and all follow the same track, it is very difficult for any one individual to walk quickly and cleave a way through the dense throng that surrounds and presses on him. This constant strife between the inclination springing from the equality of condition and the means it supplies to satisfy them harasses and wearies the mind.

It is possible to conceive of men arrived at a degree of freedom that should completely content them; they would then enjoy their independence without anxiety and without impatience. But men will never establish any equality with which they can be contented. Whatever efforts a people may make, they will never succeed in reducing all the conditions of society to a perfect level; and even if they unhappily attained that absolute and complete equality of position, the inequality of minds would still remain, which, coming directly from the hand of God, will forever escape the laws of man. However democratic, then, the social state and the political constitution of a people may be, it is certain that every member of the community will always find out several points about him which overlook his own position; and we may foresee that his looks will be doggedly fixed in that direction. When inequality of conditions is the common law of society, the most marked inequalities do not strike the eye; when everything is nearly on the same level, the slightest are marked enough to hurt it. Hence the desire of equality always becomes more insatiable in proportion as equality is more complete.

Among democratic nations, men easily attain a certain equality of condition, but they can never attain as much as they desire. It perpetually retires from before them, yet without hiding itself from their sight, and in retiring draws them on. At every moment they think they are about to grasp it; it escapes at every moment from their hold. They are near enough to see its charms, but too far off to enjoy them; and before they have fully tasted its delights, they die.

To these causes must be attributed that strange melancholy which often haunts the inhabitants of democratic countries in the midst of their abundance, and that disgust at life which sometimes seizes upon them in the midst of calm and easy circumstances. Complaints are made in France that the number of suicides increases; in America suicide is rare, but insanity is said to be more common there than anywhere else. These are all different symptoms of the same disease. The Americans do not put an end to their lives, however disquieted they may be, because their religion forbids it; and among them materialism may be said hardly to exist, notwithstanding the general passion for physical gratification. The will resists, but reason frequently gives way.

In democratic times enjoyments are more intense than in the ages of aristocracy, and the number of those who partake in them is vastly larger: but, on the other hand, it must be admitted that man's hopes and desires are oftener blasted, the soul is more stricken and perturbed, and care itself more keen.

Source: https://www.gutenberg.org/files/816/816-h/816-h.htm

Document 1 Questions

Some answers may require more space than provided.

1. What contrast does Tocqueville see, writing in the 1830s, between the "ignorant and poor inhabitants" of remote Old World locations and the "free and enlightened" Americans? Why are the former so much happier than the latter?

2. What does Tocqueville place at the root of Americans' disquiet and restlessness?

3. How does Tocqueville relate this to democracy?

4. Tocqueville is often praised as a prophet, and his work often seems to describe the America of today. Does this reading describe features that you can see operating in present-day American life?

Document 2

DAVY CROCKETT, LETTER TO CHARLES SCHULTZ ON INDIAN REMOVAL, 1834

This is a portion of a letter from David Crockett to Charles Schultz, condemning the forced removal of the Cherokee from Georgia. A fierce opponent of Jackson on this issue, Crockett lost his reelection to Congress. As he threatened in this letter, he did leave the United States for Texas. He died at the Alamo in the fight for Texan independence from Mexico. Land of Hope *states that the policy of removal "was also in part a failure of imagination" (p. 116). Crockett may have had the imagination to see the possibility of sovereign tribes existing alongside citizens of the United States. His understanding, however, was not widely held.*

Crockett had a rudimentary education, as seen in the spelling and punctuation in this letter. But a lack of formal education did not dull his ability to think through important questions. The "little Vann" and "vanburen" mentioned in the letter refer to Jackson's vice president, Martin Van Buren.

Washington City 25 Decr 1834

… The time has Come that man is expected to be transfarable and as negotiable as a promisary note of hand, in those days of Glory and – Jackson & reform & co – little Vann Sets in his chair and [inserted: looks] as Sly as a red fox and I have no doubt but that he thinks Andrew Jackson has full power to transfer the people of these united States at his will, and I am truly afread that a majority of the free Citizens of these united States will Submit to it and Say amen Jackson done it. It is right If we Judge by the past we can make no other Calculations. I have almost given up the Ship as lost. I have gone So far as to declare that if he martin vanburen is elected that I will leave the united States for I never will live under his king dom before I will Submit to his Governmint I will go to the wildes of Texas, I will consider that government a Paridice to what this will be in fait at this time our Republican Governmint has dwindled almost into insignificancy our bosted land of liberty have almost Bowed to the yoke of of Bondage our happy days of Republican principles are near at an end when a few is to transfer the many.…

Source: © 2012 The Gilder Lehrman Institute of American History, https://www.gilderlehrman.org/sites/default/files/inline-pdfs/01162_FPS.pdf. For a contemporary glimpse at how the Chickasaw now see Crockett on this issue, see https://www.chickasaw.tv/videos/davy-crockett-an-early-supporter-of-tribal-sovereignty?ref=durl

Document 2 Questions

Some answers may require more space than provided.

1. What does Crockett mean when he says that "the time has Come that man is expected to be transfarable and as negotiable as a promisary note of hand"?

2. What sentences and phrases does Crockett use to indicate his pessimism regarding the republic?

3. What assumptions does Crockett seem to make in this letter?

4. What do you think the "republican principles" are that Crockett felt we were losing? Why?

CHAPTER SEVEN

THE CULTURE OF DEMOCRACY

Questions

Some answers may require more space than provided.

1. Is democracy merely a political system? Or an entire culture?

2. "The first thing to notice is that the remarkable partnership of _____ and _____ rationalism, that easy harmony of potential antagonists ... was beginning to fray." (p. 120)

3. Established churches were "increasingly drawn to more rational and Enlightened offshoots of Christianity, such as Deism and Unitarianism." How did these offshoots differ from orthodox Christianity?

4. Meanwhile, on "the other side of the religious divide, the _____ side, came the _____." Be able to write several paragraphs about the key persons, events, and institutions of this movement. (pp. 121–23)

5. Yet the two sides of this new religious divide were not so far apart when considered in light of the old Calvinist doctrine of _____. What important belief did Deists and followers of Charles Grandison Finney have in common?

6. The America of the Jacksonian years became a magnet for utopian political and social movements. What were the specific beliefs and practices of the Millerites? The Fox sisters? Brook Farm? Robert Owen? The French socialist Charles Fourier? The Rappites? The Shakers? The Oneida community?

7. Be able to write one or several paragraphs on the origin and history of the Mormons; why have they proven to be a permanent part of American society?

8. "Perhaps the most visible and popular of all these reform movements was _____." Why? (p. 126)

9. What was the average annual consumption of alcohol around the year 1830? How does that compare to today?

10. What reforms did each of the following promote: Horace Mann, Dorothea Dix, Thomas Gallaudet, Samuel Gridley Howe?

11. What was the greatest of all antebellum American reform causes? Was it primarily a secular or a religious cause?

12. Why did the early abolitionist movement lack political effectiveness?

13. Did the antislavery movement make things better or worse? Explain each side's argument.

14. Explain Max Weber's distinction between the ethic of moral conviction and the ethic of responsibility. Which did William Lloyd Garrison espouse? Which did Lincoln?

15. Why did *Uncle Tom's Cabin* have such an impact?

16. What did Tocqueville think of American high culture? Why was the freshness of America a disadvantage for writers?

17. How and why did American culture change between the 1830s and the 1850s?

18. "Both romanticism and religious piety and emotionalism derived from a shared suspicion of and weariness with the _____." (p. 131)

19. What are some key ideas associated with romanticism?

20. Emerson, Hawthorne, Thoreau, Alcott, and Fuller all knew one another, living in or near _____. They also shared a distinctive outlook called Transcendentalism. Describe it briefly. (p. 132)

21. How did the Transcendentalists view nature and subjective experience, and society?

22. "In Transcendentalism, the mysticism of _____ was turned loose.... Nature took the place of _____ and the sense of sin itself had begun to

evaporate. This sounds very much like a highbrow version of Finney's theology." (p. 133)

23. The specific establishment against which Transcendentalism was rebelling was _____, which was characterized by what?

24. Why was Emerson America's first great intellectual? His address "The American Scholar" was seen as America's _____. (pp. 134–35)

25. Be able to write a sentence or two about the work of Thoreau, Hawthorne, Melville, and Whitman. What similarities does their writing exhibit?

Objective Questions

Matching:

____ Emerson	A. *Moby Dick*
____ Hawthorne	B. *Leaves of Grass*
____ Melville	C. *The Scarlet Letter*
____ Thoreau	D. *Walden*
____ Whitman	E. "The American Scholar"

Matching:

____ Dorothea Dix	A. public education
____ Horace Mann	B. schools for the blind
____ Samuel Gridley Howe	C. schools for the deaf
____ Thomas Gallaudet	D. better treatment for the insane

Matching:

____ Brook Farm	A. multiple marriages
____ Charles Fourier	B. Joseph Smith
____ Fox sisters	C. predicted the end of the world
____ Millerites	D. spoke with the dead
____ Mormons	E. English socialist
____ Oneida community	F. French socialist
____ Robert Owen	G. practiced celibacy
____ Shakers	H. Transcendentalists

Document 1

RALPH WALDO EMERSON, *SELF-RELIANCE* (EXCERPT), FROM *ESSAYS: FIRST SERIES* (1847 EDITION)

I read the other day some verses written by an eminent painter which were original and not conventional. The soul always hears an admonition in such lines, let the subject be what it may. The sentiment they instill is of more value than any thought they may contain. **To believe your own thought, to believe that what is true for you in your private heart is true for all men, – that is genius.** Speak your latent conviction, and it shall be the universal sense; for the inmost in due time becomes the outmost, – and our first thought is rendered back to us by the trumpets of the Last Judgment. Familiar as the voice of the mind is to each, the highest merit we ascribe to Moses, Plato, and Milton is, that they set at naught books and traditions, and spoke not what men but what they thought. A man should learn to detect and watch that gleam of light which flashes across his mind from within, more than the lustre of the firmament of bards and sages. Yet he dismisses without notice his thought, because it is his. In every work of genius we recognize our own rejected thoughts: they come back to us with a certain alienated majesty. Great works of art have no more affecting lesson for us than this. They teach us to abide by our spontaneous impression with good-humored inflexibility than most when the whole cry of voices is on the other side. Else, to-morrow a stranger will say with masterly good sense precisely what we have thought and felt all the time, and we shall be forced to take with shame our own opinion from another.

  There is a time in every man's education when he arrives at the conviction that envy is ignorance; that imitation is suicide; that he must take himself for better, for worse, as his portion; that though the wide universe is full of good, no kernel of nourishing corn can come to him but through his toil bestowed on that plot of ground which is given to him to till. The power which resides in him is new in nature, and none but he knows what that is which he can do, nor does he know until he has tried. Not for nothing one face, one character, one fact, makes much impression on him, and another none. This sculpture in the memory is not without preestablished harmony. The eye was placed where one ray should fall, that it might testify of that particular ray. We but half express ourselves, and are ashamed of that divine idea which each of us represents. It may be safely trusted as proportionate and of good issues, so it be faithfully imparted, but God will not have his work made manifest by cowards. A man is relieved and gay when he has put his heart into his work and done his best; but what he has said or done otherwise, shall give him no peace. It is a deliverance which does not deliver. In the attempt his genius deserts him; no muse befriends; no invention, no hope.

Trust thyself: every heart vibrates to that iron string. Accept the place the divine providence has found for you, the society of your contemporaries, the connection of events. Great men have always done so, and confided themselves childlike to the genius of their age, betraying their perception that the absolutely trustworthy was seated at their heart, working through their hands, predominating in all their being. And we are now men, and must accept in the highest mind the same transcendent destiny; and not minors and invalids in a protected corner, not cowards fleeing before a revolution, but guides, redeemers, and benefactors, obeying the Almighty effort, and advancing on Chaos and the Dark.

What pretty oracles nature yields us on this text, in the face and behaviour of children, babes, and even brutes! That divided and rebel mind, that distrust of a sentiment because our arithmetic has computed the strength and means opposed to our purpose, these have not. Their mind being whole, their eye is as yet unconquered, and when we look in their faces, we are disconcerted. Infancy conforms to nobody: all conform to it, so that one babe commonly makes four or five out of the adults who prattle and play to it. So God has armed youth and puberty and manhood no less with its own piquancy and charm, and made it enviable and gracious and its claims not to be put by, if it will stand by itself. Do not think the youth has no force, because he cannot speak to you and me. Hark! in the next room his voice is sufficiently clear and emphatic. It seems he knows how to speak to his contemporaries. Bashful or bold, then, he will know how to make us seniors very unnecessary.

The nonchalance of boys who are sure of a dinner, and would disdain as much as a lord to do or say aught to conciliate one, is the healthy attitude of human nature. A boy is in the parlour what the pit is in the playhouse; independent, irresponsible, looking out from his corner on such people and facts as pass by, he tries and sentences them on their merits, in the swift, summary way of boys, as good, bad, interesting, silly, eloquent, troublesome. He cumbers himself never about consequences, about interests: he gives an independent, genuine verdict. You must court him: he does not court you. But the man is, as it were, clapped into jail by his consciousness. As soon as he has once acted or spoken with eclat, he is a committed person, watched by the sympathy or the hatred of hundreds, whose affections must now enter into his account. There is no Lethe for this. Ah, that he could pass again into his neutrality! Who can thus avoid all pledges, and having observed, observe again from the same unaffected, unbiased, unbribable, unaffrighted innocence, must always be formidable. He would utter opinions on all passing affairs, which being seen to be not private, but necessary, would sink like darts into the ear of men, and put them in fear.

These are the voices which we hear in solitude, but they grow faint and inaudible as we enter into the world. Society everywhere is in conspiracy against the manhood of every one of its members. Society is a joint-stock company, in which the members agree, for the better securing of his bread to each shareholder, to surrender the liberty and culture of the eater. The virtue in most request is conformity. Self-reliance is its aversion. It loves not realities and creators, but names and customs.

Whoso would be a man must be a nonconformist. He who would gather immortal palms must not be hindered by the name of goodness, but must explore if it be goodness. Nothing is at last sacred but the integrity of your own mind. Absolve you to yourself, and you shall have the suffrage of the world. I remember an answer which when quite young I was prompted to make to a valued adviser, who was wont to importune me with the dear old doctrines of the church. On my saying, What have I to do with the sacredness of traditions, if I live wholly from within? my friend suggested, – "But these impulses may be from below, not from above." I replied, "They do not seem to me to be such; but if I am the Devil's child, I will live then from the Devil." No law can be sacred to me but that of my nature. Good and bad are but names very readily transferable to that or this; the only right is what is after my constitution, the only wrong what is against it. A man is to carry himself in the presence of all opposition, as if every thing were titular and ephemeral but he. I am ashamed to think how easily we capitulate to badges and names, to large societies and dead institutions. Every decent and well-spoken individual affects and sways me more than is right. I ought to go upright and vital, and speak the rude truth in all ways. If malice and vanity wear the coat of philanthropy, shall that pass? If an angry bigot assumes this bountiful cause of Abolition, and comes to me with his last news from Barbadoes, why should I not say to him, "Go love thy infant; love thy wood-chopper: be good-natured and modest: have that grace; and never varnish your hard, uncharitable ambition with this incredible tenderness for black folk a thousand miles off. Thy love afar is spite at home." Rough and graceless would be such greeting, but truth is handsomer than the affectation of love. Your goodness must have some edge to it, – else it is none. The doctrine of hatred must be preached as the counteraction of the doctrine of love when that pules and whines. I shun father and mother and wife and brother, when my genius calls me. I would write on the lintels of the door-post, Whim. I hope it is somewhat better than whim at last, but we cannot spend the day in explanation. Expect me not to show cause why I seek or why I exclude company.

Then, again, do not tell me, as a good man did to-day, of my obligation to put all poor men in good situations. Are they my poor? I tell thee, thou foolish philanthropist, that I grudge the dollar, the dime, the cent, I give to such men as do not belong to me and to whom I do not belong. There is a class of persons to whom by all spiritual affinity I am bought and sold; for them I will go to prison, if need be; but your miscellaneous popular charities; the education at college of fools; the building of meeting-houses to the vain end to which many now stand; alms to sots; and the thousandfold Relief Societies; – though I confess with shame I sometimes succumb and give the dollar, it is a wicked dollar which by and by I shall have the manhood to withhold....

Source: https://en.wikisource.org/wiki/Essays:_First_Series/Self-Reliance

Document 1 Questions

Some answers may require more space than provided.

1. How does Emerson embody the culture of democracy?

2. So what does Emerson believe to be the source of all our problems?

3. Do you see a relationship between Emerson's style of writing (and speaking) and the ideas that he is trying to convey?

4. "Thy love afar is spite at home." What does Emerson mean by this?

Document 2

ELIZABETH CADY STANTON, DECLARATION OF SENTIMENTS, JULY 19, 1848

When, in the course of human events, it becomes necessary for one portion of the family of man to assume among the people of the earth a position different from that which they have hitherto occupied, but one to which the laws of nature and of nature's God entitle them, a decent respect to the opinions of mankind requires that they should declare the causes that impel them to such a course.

We hold these truths to be self-evident: that all men and women are created equal; that they are endowed by their Creator with certain inalienable rights; that among these are life, liberty, and the pursuit of happiness; that to secure these rights governments are instituted, deriving their just powers from the consent of the governed. Whenever any form of government becomes destructive of these ends, it is the right of those who suffer from it to refuse allegiance to it, and to insist upon the institution of a new government, laying its foundation on such principles, and organizing its powers in such form, as to them shall seem most likely to effect their safety and happiness. Prudence, indeed, will dictate that governments long established should not be changed for light and transient causes; and accordingly all experience hath shown that mankind are more disposed to suffer, while evils are sufferable, than to right themselves by abolishing the forms to which they were accustomed. But when a long train of abuses and usurpations, pursuing invariably the same object evinces a design to reduce them under absolute despotism, it is their duty to throw off such government, and to provide new guards for their future security. Such has been the patient sufferance of the women under this government, and such is now the necessity which constrains them to demand the equal station to which they are entitled.

The history of mankind is a history of repeated injuries and usurpations on the part of man toward woman, having in direct object the establishment of an absolute tyranny over her. To prove this, let facts be submitted to a candid world.

He has never permitted her to exercise her inalienable right to the elective franchise.

He has compelled her to submit to laws, in the formation of which she had no voice.

He has withheld from her rights which are given to the most ignorant and degraded men–both natives and foreigners.

Having deprived her of this first right of a citizen, the elective franchise, thereby leaving her without representation in the halls of legislation, he has oppressed her on all sides.

He has made her, if married, in the eye of the law, civilly dead.

He has taken from her all right in property, even to the wages she earns.

He has made her, morally, an irresponsible being, as she can commit many crimes with impunity, provided they be done in the presence of her husband. In the covenant of marriage, she is compelled to promise obedience to her husband, he becoming, to all intents and purposes, her master – the law giving him power to deprive her of her liberty, and to administer chastisement.

He has so framed the laws of divorce, as to what shall be the proper causes, and in case of separation, to whom the guardianship of the children shall be given, as to be wholly regardless of the happiness of women – the law, in all cases, going upon a false supposition of the supremacy of man, and giving all power into his hands.

After depriving her of all rights as a married woman, if single, and the owner of property, he has taxed her to support a government which recognizes her only when her property can be made profitable to it.

He has monopolized nearly all the profitable employments, and from those she is permitted to follow, she receives but a scanty remuneration. He closes against her all the avenues to wealth and distinction which he considers most honorable to himself. As a teacher of theology, medicine, or law, she is not known.

He has denied her the facilities for obtaining a thorough education, all colleges being closed against her.

He allows her in Church, as well as State, but a subordinate position, claiming Apostolic authority for her exclusion from the ministry, and, with some exceptions, from any public participation in the affairs of the Church.

He has created a false public sentiment by giving to the world a different code of morals for men and women, by which moral delinquencies which exclude women from society, are not only tolerated, but deemed of little account in man.

He has usurped the prerogative of Jehovah himself, claiming it as his right to assign for her a sphere of action, when that belongs to her conscience and to her God.

He has endeavored, in every way that he could, to destroy her confidence in her own powers, to lessen her self-respect, and to make her willing to lead a dependent and abject life.

Now, in view of this entire disfranchisement of one-half the people of this country, their social and religious degradation – in view of the unjust laws above mentioned, and because women do feel themselves aggrieved, oppressed, and fraudulently deprived of their most sacred rights, we insist that they have immediate admission to all the rights and privileges which belong to them as citizens of the United States.

In entering upon the great work before us, we anticipate no small amount of misconception, misrepresentation, and ridicule; but we shall use every instrumentality within our power to effect our object. We shall employ agents, circulate tracts, petition the State and National legislatures, and endeavor to enlist the pulpit and the press in our behalf. We hope this Convention will be followed by a series of Conventions embracing every part of the country.

Source: https://teachingamericanhistory.org/library/document/declaration-of-sentiments/

Document 2 Questions

Some answers may require more space than provided.

1. List some of the ways that this Declaration mimics the Declaration of Independence. Why did Stanton choose to pattern this document in this way? In your opinion, was this a wise choice? Do you think that she might, in part, have meant the document to be humorous?

2. What does she mean in saying that man "has made [woman], morally, an irresponsible being"?

3. How does Stanton's picture of the ideal social environment compare to Emerson's?

4. Stanton has almost nothing to say about the rights and responsibilities of mothers. Is this an important omission on her part? Or are such considerations irrelevant to her larger concerns?

CHAPTER EIGHT

THE OLD SOUTH AND SLAVERY

Questions

1. What factors of climate and geography caused the South to focus on commercial or staple crop agriculture?

2. How important to the U.S. and world economies was cotton? What were the requirements for successful mass production of this cash crop?

3. Unlike the North, the South attracted little immigration from Europe; why? What was the effect of this on southern demographics, society, and culture?

4. Southern society was biracial but also, paradoxically, characterized by a certain commonality of culture between whites and blacks. What were the causes and elements of this common culture?

5. Is the "Old South" myth or history? Yes. Explain your answer.

6. Why was the planter class so confident that cotton was king, even though it "placed the region on a collision course with changing moral sensibilities in the world, and with fundamental American ideals"?

7. "The majority of slave-holders were ordinary farmers who owned fewer than twenty slaves and worked in the field with their slaves." How many southern whites owned no slaves at all? How many were wealthy planters?

8. What characteristics of a medieval feudal society did the South exhibit – and embrace?

9. Why is it difficult to tell the story of black southerners under slavery?

10. How did Christianity shape, and how was it shaped by, the slave experience?

11. Why was the Underground Railroad successful in freeing many thousands of slaves, while slave revolts were rare and uniformly unsuccessful?

12. How and why did Nat Turner's revolt change slavery and the South? Include discussion of the debate in the Virginia General Assembly of 1831–32. What new laws did the assembly finally pass?

13. How did southerners like George Fitzhugh and John C. Calhoun defend slavery? How did this make civil war increasingly likely?

Objective Question

Put in order:

____ "Gag rule" in House prohibits discussion of slavery
____ Nat Turner's uprising
____ Virginia Assembly rejects plan for gradual emancipation

Document

THE SONGS OF AFRICAN AMERICAN SLAVERY

The African American scholar and activist W. E. B. Du Bois produced one of the most beautiful and most penetrating accounts of the songs from the days of slavery, often called "spirituals," in a chapter called "The Sorrow Songs," appearing in his 1903 book The Souls of Black Folk. *Interested students will want to read the whole chapter, which can be found at https://www.bartleby.com/114/14.html. But for our purposes, we will consider only a few small parts of the text:*

> *What are these songs, and what do they mean? I know little of music and can say nothing in technical phrase, but I know something of men, and knowing them, I know that these songs are the articulate message of the slave to the world. They tell us in these eager days that life was joyous to the black slave, careless and happy. I can easily believe this of some, of many. But not all the past South, though it rose from the dead, can gainsay the heart-touching witness of these songs. They are the music of an unhappy people, of the children of disappointment; they tell of death and suffering and unvoiced longing toward a truer world, of misty wanderings and hidden ways.*

Du Bois is warning us that surfaces can be deceiving, and the seeming joyfulness of the songs is always laced with deep currents of sadness and longing. The songs could serve many purposes; they could be work songs, celebratory songs, commemorative songs, the means by which a captive people unable to read or write managed nevertheless to communicate and share memories. Some songs contained coded information about means of escape, about safe houses. Many borrowed from the imagery of the Bible, comparing themselves to the enslaved Israelites who were bound, eventually, for the Promised Land of freedom.

The lyrics are, of course, much diminished when presented without the music. But here are a few of the more famous songs; lyrics are taken from the website Negrospirituals.com.

Sometimes I Feel Like a Motherless Child

The profound sadness and uprootedness of slavery are captured in a "relatable" way by being compared to the experience of a homeless orphan.

Sometimes I feel like a motherless child
Sometimes I feel like a motherless child
Sometimes I feel like a motherless child
A long ways from home
A long ways from home
True believer
A long ways from home
Along ways from home

Sometimes I feel like I'm almos' gone
Sometimes I feel like I'm almos' gone
Sometimes I feel like I'm almos' gone
Way up in de heab'nly land
Way up in de heab'nly land
True believer
Way up in de heab'nly land
Way up in de heab'nly land

Sometimes I feel like a motherless child
Sometimes I feel like a motherless child
Sometimes I feel like a motherless child
A long ways from home
There's praying everywhere

WADE IN THE WATER

Harriet Tubman used "Wade in the Water" to tell escaping slaves that they could get into the water to avoid being apprehended.

> *Chorus:* Wade in the Water, wade in the water children.

> Wade in the Water. God's gonna trouble the water.
> Who are those children all dressed in Red?
> God's gonna trouble the water.
> Must be the ones that Moses led.
> God's gonna trouble the water.

> *Chorus*

> Who are those children all dressed in White?
> God's gonna trouble the water.
> Must be the ones of the Israelites.
> God's gonna trouble the water.

> *Chorus*

> Who are those children all dressed in Blue?
> God's gonna trouble the water.
> Must be the ones that made it through.
> God's gonna trouble the water.

> *Chorus*

STEAL AWAY

This song has an overtly religious message but also a more worldly undercurrent: the person singing it is planning to escape.

> *Chorus:* Steal away, steal away!

> Steal away to Jesus?
> Steal away, steal away home!
> I ain't got long to stay here!

My Lord calls me!
He calls me by the thunder!
The trumpet sound it in my soul!
I ain't got long to stay here!

Chorus

My Lord calls me!
He calls me by the lighting!
The trumpet sound it in my soul!
I ain't got long to stay here!

Chorus

GO DOWN MOSES

Here, too, the enslaved singers found a precedent and a hope in the story of ancient Israel.

When Israel was in Egypt's land
Let my people go
Oppressed so hard they could not stand
Let my people go

Go down Moses
Way down in Egypt land
Tell old Pharaoh
"Let my people go"

"Thus spoke the Lord" bold Moses said
Let my people go
"If not I'll smite your first born dead
Let my people go

No more in bondage shall they toil
Let my people go
Let them come out with Egypt's spoil"
Let my people go

A slave hearing this song would ready himself to escape – a band of angels is coming to take him to freedom. The Underground Railroad (the sweet chariot) was coming South (swing low) to take the slave to the North or freedom (carry me home).

> Swing low, sweet chariot,
> Coming for to carry me home,
> Swing low, sweet chariot,
> Coming for to carry me home.
>
> I looked over Jordan and what did I see
> Coming for to carry me home,
> A band of angels coming after me,
> Coming for to carry me home.
>
> If you get there before I do,
> Coming for to carry me home,
> Tell all my friends that I'm coming, too,
> Coming for to carry me home.

Returning to Du Bois's essay, he argues that hope was an animating force in the hearts of even those to whom the Land of Hope had given little reason for hope – indeed, he argues that those hearts had made an inestimable contribution to what is best in America.

> *Through all the sorrow of the Sorrow Songs there breathes a hope – a faith in the ultimate justice of things. The minor cadences of despair change often to triumph and calm confidence. Sometimes it is faith in life, sometimes a faith in death, sometimes assurance of boundless justice in some fair world beyond. But whichever it is, the meaning is always clear: that sometime, somewhere, men will judge men by their souls and not by their skins. Is such a hope justified? Do the Sorrow Songs sing true?*
>
> *.... Your country? How came it yours? Before the Pilgrims landed we were here. Here we have brought our three gifts and mingled them with yours: a gift of story and song – soft, stirring melody in an ill-harmonized and unmelodious land; the gift of sweat and brawn to beat back the wilderness, conquer the soil, and lay the foundations of this vast economic empire two hundred years earlier than your weak hands could have done it; the third, a gift of the Spirit. Around us the history of the land has centred for thrice a hundred years; out of the*

nation's heart we have called all that was best to throttle and subdue all that was worst; fire and blood, prayer and sacrifice, have billowed over this people, and they have found peace only in the altars of the God of Right. Nor has our gift of the Spirit been merely passive. Actively we have woven ourselves with the very warp and woof of this nation, – we fought their battles, shared their sorrow, mingled our blood with theirs, and generation after generation have pleaded with a headstrong, careless people to despise not Justice, Mercy, and Truth, lest the nation be smitten with a curse. Our song, our toil, our cheer, and warning have been given to this nation in blood-brotherhood. Are not these gifts worth the giving? Is not this work and striving? Would America have been America without her Negro people?

Document Questions

Some answers may require more space than provided.

1. What were the multiple uses of their songs for African American slaves?

2. How do the songs borrow from the Bible?

3. Where and how does Du Bois find hope emerging in the Sorrow Songs? Does he share this hope?

4. Du Bois seems to be insisting at the end that America would not have been America without her "Negro people," her African Americans. What does he mean by that? What are the "three gifts" to which he refers earlier in the paragraph?

5. Why is the image of feeling like a "motherless child, a long ways from home" so piercing?

CHAPTER NINE

THE GATHERING STORM

Questions

Some answers may require more space than provided.

1. What is the problem with historical hindsight?

2. "History is only rarely the story of _____, and it almost never appears in that form to its participants. It is more often a story of _____ and _____." (p. 151)

3. "What we can say, though, is that there were landmark moments in which a blood-stained outcome became much more likely." At *what point* do you think civil war became all but unavoidable? Be prepared to defend your answer in class or in writing.

4. What were the consequences of the Mexican War?

5. Be able to write a short description of the role and significance of Stephen F. Austin, Antonio Lopez de Santa Anna, the Mexican Constitution of 1824, Sam Houston, and the battles of the Alamo, Goliad, and San Jacinto.

6. The Texans wanted to become part of the United States. Why did this not happen for ten years?

7. Why did the British want Texas to remain an independent republic?

8. Annexation of Texas by the United States seems to be the first occasion for the use of the term *Manifest Destiny* (by journalist John L. O'Sullivan). What did Americans of the 1840s mean by that term?

9. Mexico still refused to recognize Texan independence in 1845. Could war with the United States, following annexation, have been avoided? Did either side try very hard?

10. Although most Americans supported the Mexican War, there was some opposition. From whom, and why?

11. What and where are the "halls of Montezuma"?

12. By how much, and how, did the United States grow between 1846 and 1848? How was the event at Sutter's Mill the icing on the cake?

13. How did the growth of the United States in 1846–48 upset the delicate political balance of the nation?

14. What antithetical positions were argued by David Wilmot and John C. Calhoun? A possible solution was the idea of _____ offered by Lewis Cass. Explain that idea.

15. Who was the main architect of the Compromise of 1850? What were its elements? What did it settle? What did it *not* settle?

16. We tend to think primarily of the South as appealing to states' rights and nullification, and even secession, though those ideas had been espoused in New England in opposition to the War of 1812. How did northern states react to the new Fugitive Slave Law?

17. Did the rise of antislavery as a moral crusade rather than a political cause make compromise more difficult? Impossible? Was this a good thing or a bad thing? Be prepared to discuss in class or on paper.

18. Debate over the possible route of a _____ led to the Kansas–Nebraska Act of 1854, which showed the weakness of popular sovereignty and led to _____, where deadly violence first erupted between pro- and anti-slavery forces. (p. 162)

19. What and when were John Brown's two acts of violence?

20. How did violence spread to the halls of Congress?

21. When and why did the Republican Party emerge? Why was it unique in American history to that point?

22. President Buchanan was ineffective in dealing with the crisis in Kansas, but the Supreme Court made things far worse with the _____ decision. What was its effect?

23. If your opponents have an intense and irrational fear of you, how can you reassure them of your good intentions? What happens if both sides have similarly intense and irrational ideas about the other? Is that what happened in pre–Civil War America?

24. Why were the Lincoln–Douglas debates important? Who won the election?

25. Were Lincoln's objections to slavery moral or political? Was he an abolitionist?

26. Be able to describe the election of 1860. Who ran? Who won? Why?

27. How did the southern states respond to Lincoln's election?

28. It is widely and (for the most part) correctly argued that slavery caused the Civil War. Yet how, then, does one explain support by Lincoln and other Republicans for the Corwin Amendment? And how does one explain the southern states' clinging to secession if they had such a guarantee of protection of slavery where it already existed?

Objective Questions

Put in order:

____ "Bleeding Kansas"
____ Kansas–Nebraska Act
____ John Brown's raid on Harpers Ferry

Put in order:

    ____ *Dred Scott* decision
    ____ Missouri Compromise
    ____ Lincoln–Douglas debates

Put in order:

    ____ Corwin Amendment passes Congress
    ____ Lincoln is elected
    ____ South Carolina secedes

Put in order:

    ____ Alamo battle
    ____ San Jacinto battle
    ____ Santa Anna overthrows Mexican Constitution

Put in order:

    ____ caning of Sumner
    ____ Compromise of 1850
    ____ Kansas–Nebraska Act

Document

LINCOLN'S SPEECH ON THE *DRED SCOTT* DECISION, JUNE 26, 1857 (ABRIDGED)

FELLOW CITIZENS: I am here to-night, partly by the invitation of some of you, and partly by my own inclination. Two weeks ago Judge Douglas spoke here on the several subjects of Kansas, the Dred Scott decision, and Utah. I listened to the speech at the time, and have read the report of it since. It was intended to controvert opinions which I think just, and to assail (politically, not personally,) those men who, in common with me, entertain those opinions. For this reason I wished then, and still wish, to make some answer to it, which I now take the opportunity of doing.

    .... And now as to the Dred Scott decision. That decision declares two propositions – first, that a negro cannot sue in the U.S. Courts; and secondly, that Congress cannot prohibit slavery in the Territories. It was made by a divided court-dividing differently on the different points. Judge Douglas does not discuss the merits of the decision; and, in that respect, I shall follow his example, believing I could no more improve on McLean and Curtis, than he could on Taney.

He denounces all who question the correctness of that decision, as offering violent resistance to it. But who resists it? Who has, in spite of the decision, declared Dred Scott free, and resisted the authority of his master over him?

Judicial decisions have two uses – first, to absolutely determine the case decided, and secondly, to indicate to the public how other similar cases will be decided when they arise. For the latter use, they are called "precedents" and "authorities."

We believe, as much as Judge Douglas, (perhaps more) in obedience to, and respect for the judicial department of government. We think its decisions on Constitutional questions, when fully settled, should control, not only the particular cases decided, but the general policy of the country, subject to be disturbed only by amendments of the Constitution as provided in that instrument itself. More than this would be revolution. But we think the Dred Scott decision is erroneous. We know the court that made it, has often over-ruled its own decisions, and we shall do what we can to have it to over-rule this. We offer no resistance to it.

Judicial decisions are of greater or less authority as precedents, according to circumstances. That this should be so, accords both with common sense, and the customary understanding of the legal profession.

If this important decision had been made by the unanimous concurrence of the judges, and without any apparent partisan bias, and in accordance with legal public expectation, and with the steady practice of the departments throughout our history, and had been in no part, based on assumed historical facts which are not really true; or, if wanting in some of these, it had been before the court more than once, and had there been affirmed and re-affirmed through a course of years, it then might be, perhaps would be, factious, nay, even revolutionary, to not acquiesce in it as a precedent.

But when, as it is true we find it wanting in all these claims to the public confidence, it is not resistance, it is not factious, it is not even disrespectful, to treat it as not having yet quite established a settled doctrine for the country – But Judge Douglas considers this view awful. Hear him:

> "The courts are the tribunals prescribed by the Constitution and created by the authority of the people to determine, expound and enforce the law. Hence, whoever resists the final decision of the highest judicial tribunal, aims a deadly blow to our whole Republican system of government – a blow, which if successful would place all our rights and liberties at the mercy of passion, anarchy and violence. I repeat, therefore, that if

resistance to the decisions of the Supreme Court of the United States, in a matter like the points decided in the Dred Scott case, clearly within their jurisdiction as defined by the Constitution, shall be forced upon the country as a political issue, it will become a distinct and naked issue between the friends and the enemies of the Constitution – the friends and the enemies of the supremacy of the laws."

Why this same Supreme court once decided a national bank to be constitutional; but Gen. Jackson, as President of the United States, disregarded the decision, and vetoed a bill for a re-charter, partly on constitutional ground, declaring that each public functionary must support the Constitution, "as he understands it." But hear the General's own words. Here they are, taken from his veto message:

"It is maintained by the advocates of the bank, that its constitutionality, in all its features, ought to be considered as settled by precedent, and by the decision of the Supreme Court. To this conclusion I cannot assent. Mere precedent is a dangerous source of authority, and should not be regarded as deciding questions of constitutional power, except where the acquiescence of the people and the States can be considered as well settled. So far from this being the case on this subject, an argument against the bank might be based on precedent. One Congress in 1791, decided in favor of a bank; another in 1811, decided against it. One Congress in 1815 decided against a bank; another in 1816 decided in its favor. Prior to the present Congress, therefore the precedents drawn from that source were equal. If we resort to the States, the expressions of legislative, judicial and executive opinions against the bank have been probably to those in its favor as four to one. There is nothing in precedent, therefore, which if its authority were admitted, ought to weigh in favor of the act before me."

I drop the quotations merely to remark that all there ever was, in the way of precedent up to the Dred Scott decision, on the points therein decided, had been against that decision. But hear Gen. Jackson further –

"If the opinion of the Supreme court covered the whole ground of this act, it ought not to control the co-ordinate authorities of this Government. The Congress, the executive and the court, must each for itself be guided by its own opinion of the Constitution. Each public officer, who takes an oath to support the Constitution, swears that he will support it as he understands it, and not as it is understood by others."

Again and again have I heard Judge Douglas denounce that bank decision, and applaud Gen. Jackson for disregarding it. It would be interesting for him to look over his recent speech, and see how exactly his fierce philippics against us for resisting Supreme Court decisions, fall upon his own head. It will call to his mind a long and fierce political war in this country, upon an issue which, in his own language, and, of course, in his own changeless estimation, was "a distinct and naked issue between the friends and the enemies of the Constitution," and in which war he fought in the ranks of the enemies of the Constitution.

I have said, in substance, that the Dred Scott decision was, in part, based on assumed historical facts which were not really true; and I ought not to leave the subject without giving some reasons for saying this; I therefore give an instance or two, which I think fully sustain me. Chief Justice Taney, in delivering the opinion of the majority of the Court, insists at great length that negroes were no part of the people who made, or for whom was made, the Declaration of Independence, or the Constitution of the United States.

On the contrary, Judge Curtis, in his dissenting opinion, shows that in five of the then thirteen states, to wit, New Hampshire, Massachusetts, New York, New Jersey and North Carolina, free negroes were voters, and, in proportion to their numbers, had the same part in making the Constitution that the white people had. He shows this with so much particularity as to leave no doubt of its truth; and, as a sort of conclusion on that point, holds the following language:

"The Constitution was ordained and established by the people of the United States, through the action, in each State, of those persons who were qualified by its laws to act thereon in behalf of themselves and all other citizens of the State. In some of the States, as we have seen, colored persons were among those qualified by law to act on the subject. These colored persons were not only included in the body of 'the people of the United States' – by whom the Constitution was ordained and established; but in at least five of the States they had the power to act, and, doubtless, did act, by their suffrages, upon the question of its adoption."

Again, Chief Justice Taney says: "It is difficult, at this day to realize the state of public opinion in relation to that unfortunate race, which prevailed in the civilized and enlightened portions of the world at the time of the Declaration of Independence, and when the Constitution of the United States was framed and adopted." And again, after quoting from the Declaration, he says: "The general words above quoted would seem to include the whole human family, and if they were used in a similar instrument at this day, would be so understood."

In these the Chief Justice does not directly assert, but plainly assumes, as a fact, that the public estimate of the black man is more favorable now than it was in the days of the Revolution. This assumption is a mistake. In some trifling particulars, the condition of that race has been ameliorated; but, as a whole, in this country, the change between then and now is decidedly the other way; and their ultimate destiny has never appeared so hopeless as in the last three or four years. In two of the five States – New Jersey and North Carolina – that then gave the free negro the right of voting, the right has since been taken away; and in a third – New York – it has been greatly abridged; while it has not been extended, so far as I know, to a single additional State, though the number of the States has more than doubled. In those days, as I understand, masters could, at their own pleasure, emancipate their slaves; but since then, such legal restraints have been made upon emancipation, as to amount almost to prohibition. In those days, Legislatures held the unquestioned power to abolish slavery in their respective States; but now it is becoming quite fashionable for State Constitutions to withhold that power from the Legislatures. In those days, by common consent, the spread of the black man's bondage to new countries was prohibited; but now, Congress decides that it will not continue the prohibition, and the Supreme Court decides that it could not if it would. In those days, our Declaration of Independence was held sacred by all, and thought to include all; but now, to aid in making the bondage of the negro universal and eternal, it is assailed, and sneered at, and construed, and hawked at, and torn, till, if its framers could rise from their graves, they could not at all recognize it. All the powers of earth seem rapidly combining against him. Mammon is after him; ambition follows, and philosophy follows, and the Theology of the day is fast joining the cry. They have him in his prison house; they have searched his person, and left no prying instrument with him. One after another they have closed the heavy iron doors upon him, and now they have him, as it were, bolted in with a lock of a hundred keys, which can never be unlocked without the concurrence of every key; the keys in the hands of a hundred different men, and they scattered to a hundred different and distant places; and they stand musing as to what invention, in all the dominions of mind and matter, can be produced to make the impossibility of his escape more complete than it is.

It is grossly incorrect to say or assume, that the public estimate of the negro is more favorable now than it was at the origin of the government.

Three years and a half ago, Judge Douglas brought forward his famous Nebraska bill. The country was at once in a blaze. He scorned all opposition, and carried it through Congress. Since then he has seen himself superseded in a Presidential nomination, by one indorsing the general doctrine of his measure, but at the same time standing clear of the odium of its untimely agitation, and its gross breach of national faith; and he has seen that successful rival

Constitutionally elected, not by the strength of friends, but by the division of adversaries, being in a popular minority of nearly four hundred thousand votes. He has seen his chief aids in his own State, Shields and Richardson, politically speaking, successively tried, convicted, and executed, for an offense not their own, but his. And now he sees his own case, standing next on the docket for trial.

There is a natural disgust in the minds of nearly all white people, to the idea of an indiscriminate amalgamation of the white and black races; and Judge Douglas evidently is basing his chief hope, upon the chances of being able to appropriate the benefit of this disgust to himself. If he can, by much drumming and repeating, fasten the odium of that idea upon his adversaries, he thinks he can struggle through the storm. He therefore clings to this hope, as a drowning man to the last plank. He makes an occasion for lugging it in from the opposition to the Dred Scott decision. He finds the Republicans insisting that the Declaration of Independence includes ALL men, black as well as white; and forth-with he boldly denies that it includes negroes at all, and proceeds to argue gravely that all who contend it does, do so only because they want to vote, and eat, and sleep, and marry with negroes! He will have it that they cannot be consistent else. Now I protest against that counterfeit logic which concludes that, because I do not want a black woman for a slave I must necessarily want her for a wife. I need not have her for either, I can just leave her alone. In some respects she certainly is not my equal; but in her natural right to eat the bread she earns with her own hands without asking leave of any one else, she is my equal, and the equal of all others.

Chief Justice Taney, in his opinion in the Dred Scott case, admits that the language of the Declaration is broad enough to include the whole human family, but he and Judge Douglas argue that the authors of that instrument did not intend to include negroes, by the fact that they did not at once, actually place them on an equality with the whites. Now this grave argument comes to just nothing at all, by the other fact, that they did not at once, or ever afterwards, actually place all white people on an equality with one or another. And this is the staple argument of both the Chief Justice and the Senator, for doing this obvious violence to the plain unmistakable language of the Declaration. I think the authors of that notable instrument intended to include all men, but they did not intend to declare all men equal in all respects. They did not mean to say all were equal in color, size, intellect, moral developments, or social capacity. They defined with tolerable distinctness, in what respects they did consider all men created equal – equal in "certain inalienable rights, among which are life, liberty, and the pursuit of happiness." This they said, and this meant. They did not mean to assert the obvious untruth, that all were then actually enjoying that equality, nor yet, that they were about to confer it immediately upon them.

In fact they had no power to confer such a boon. They meant simply to declare the right, so that the enforcement of it might follow as fast as circumstances should permit. They meant to set up a standard maxim for free society, which should be familiar to all, and revered by all; constantly looked to, constantly labored for, and even though never perfectly attained, constantly approximated, and thereby constantly spreading and deepening its influence, and augmenting the happiness and value of life to all people of all colors everywhere. The assertion that "all men are created equal" was of no practical use in effecting our separation from Great Britain; and it was placed in the Declaration, nor for that, but for future use. Its authors meant it to be, thank God, it is now proving itself, a stumbling block to those who in after times might seek to turn a free people back into the hateful paths of despotism. They knew the proneness of prosperity to breed tyrants, and they meant when such should re-appear in this fair land and commence their vocation they should find left for them at least one hard nut to crack.

I have now briefly expressed my view of the meaning and objects of that part of the Declaration of Independence which declares that "all men are created equal."

Now let us hear Judge Douglas's view of the same subject, as I find it in the printed report of his late speech. Here it is:

> "No man can vindicate the character, motives and conduct of the signers of the Declaration of Independence except upon the hypothesis that they referred to the white race alone, and not to the African, when they declared all men to have been created equal – that they were speaking of British subjects on this continent being equal to British subjects born and residing in Great Britain – that they were entitled to the same inalienable rights, and among them were enumerated life, liberty and the pursuit of happiness. The Declaration was adopted for the purpose of justifying the colonists in the eyes of the civilized world in withdrawing their allegiance from the British crown, and dissolving their connection with the mother country."

My good friends, read that carefully over some leisure hour, and ponder well upon it – see what a mere wreck – mangled ruin – it makes of our once glorious Declaration.

"They were speaking of British subjects on this continent being equal to British subjects born and residing in Great Britain!" Why, according to this, not only negroes but white people outside of Great Britain and America are not spoken of in that instrument. The English, Irish and Scotch, along with white

Americans, were included to be sure, but the French, Germans and other white people of the world are all gone to pot along with the Judge's inferior races. I had thought the Declaration promised something better than the condition of British subjects; but no, it only meant that we should be equal to them in their own oppressed and unequal condition. According to that, it gave no promise that having kicked off the King and Lords of Great Britain, we should not at once be saddled with a King and Lords of our own.

I had thought the Declaration contemplated the progressive improvement in the condition of all men everywhere; but no, it merely "was adopted for the purpose of justifying the colonists in the eyes of the civilized world in withdrawing their allegiance from the British crown, and dissolving their connection with the mother country." Why, that object having been effected some eighty years ago, the Declaration is of no practical use now – mere rubbish – old wadding left to rot on the battle-field after the victory is won.

I understand you are preparing to celebrate the "Fourth," tomorrow week. What for? The doings of that day had no reference to the present; and quite half of you are not even descendants of those who were referred to at that day. But I suppose you will celebrate; and will even go so far as to read the Declaration. Suppose after you read it once in the old fashioned way, you read it once more with Judge Douglas's version. It will then run thus: "We hold these truths to be self-evident that all British subjects who were on this continent eighty-one years ago, were created equal to all British subjects born and then residing in Great Britain."

And now I appeal to all – to Democrats as well as others, – are you really willing that the Declaration shall be thus frittered away? – thus left no more at most, than an interesting memorial of the dead past? thus shorn of its vitality, and practical value; and left without the germ or even the suggestion of the individual rights of man in it?

But Judge Douglas is especially horrified at the thought of the mixing blood by the white and black races: agreed for once – a thousand times agreed. There are white men enough to marry all the white women, and black men enough to marry all the black women; and so let them be married. On this point we fully agree with the Judge; and when he shall show that his policy is better adapted to prevent amalgamation than ours we shall drop ours, and adopt his. Let us see. In 1850 there were in the United States, 405,751, mulattoes. Very few of these are the offspring of whites and free blacks; nearly all have sprung from black slaves and white masters. A separation of the races is the only perfect preventive of amalgamation but as an immediate separation is impossible the next best thing is to keep them apart where they are not already together. If white and black people never get together in Kansas, they will never mix blood in Kansas. That is at least one self-evident truth. A few free colored persons may get into the free States, in any event; but their number is too insignificant to amount to much in the way of mixing blood. In 1850 there were in the free states, 56,649 mulattoes; but for the most part they were not born there – they came from the slave States, ready made up. In the same year the slave States had 348,874 mulattoes all of home production. The proportion of free mulattoes to free blacks – the only colored classes in the free states – is much greater in the slave than in the free states. It is worthy of note too, that among the free states those which make the colored man the nearest to equal the white, have, proportionably the fewest mulattoes the least of amalgamation. In New Hampshire, the State which goes farthest towards equality between the races, there are just 184 Mulattoes while there are in Virginia – how many do you think? 79,775, being 23,126 more than in all the free States together. These statistics show that slavery is the greatest source of amalgamation; and next to it, not the elevation, but the degeneration of the free blacks. Yet Judge Douglas dreads the slightest restraints on the spread of slavery, and the slightest human recognition of the negro, as tending horribly to amalgamation.

This very Dred Scott case affords a strong test as to which party most favors amalgamation, the Republicans or the dear Union-saving Democracy. Dred Scott, his wife and two daughters were all involved in the suit. We desired the court to have held that they were citizens so far at least as to entitle them to a hearing as to whether they were free or not; and then, also, that they were in fact and in law really free. Could we have had our way, the chances of these black girls, ever mixing their blood with that of white people, would have been diminished at least to the extent that it could not have been without their consent. But Judge Douglas is delighted to have them decided to be slaves, and not human enough to have a hearing, even if they were free, and thus left subject to the forced concubinage of their masters, and liable to become the mothers of mulattoes in spite of themselves – the very state of case that produces nine tenths of all the mulattoes – all the mixing of blood in the nation.

Of course, I state this case as an illustration only, not meaning to say or intimate that the master of Dred Scott and his family, or any more than a percentage of masters generally, are inclined to exercise this particular power which they hold over their female slaves.

I have said that the separation of the races is the only perfect preventive of amalgamation. I have no right to say all the members of the Republican party are in favor of this, nor to say that as a party they are in favor of it. There is nothing in their platform directly on the subject. But I can say a very large proportion of its members are for it, and that the chief plank in their platform – opposition to the spread of slavery – is most favorable to that separation.

Such separation, if ever effected at all, must be effected by colonization; and no political party, as such, is now doing anything directly for colonization. Party operations at present only favor or retard colonization incidentally. The enterprise is a difficult one; but "when there is a will there is a way"; and what colonization needs most is a hearty will. Will springs from the two elements of moral sense and self-interest. Let us be brought to believe it is morally right, and, at the same time, favorable to, or, at least, not against, our interest, to transfer the African to his native clime, and we shall find a way to do it, however great the task may be. The children of Israel, to such numbers as to include four hundred thousand fighting men, went out of Egyptian bondage in a body.

How differently the respective courses of the Democratic and Republican parties incidentally bear on the question of forming a will – a public sentiment – for colonization, is easy to see. The Republicans inculcate, with whatever of ability they can, that the negro is a man; that his bondage is cruelly wrong, and that the field of his oppression ought not to be enlarged. The Democrats deny his manhood; deny, or dwarf to insignificance, the wrong of his bondage; so far as possible, crush all sympathy for him, and cultivate and excite hatred and disgust against him; compliment themselves as Union-savers for doing so; and call the indefinite outspreading of his bondage "a sacred right of self-government."

The plainest print cannot be read through a gold eagle; and it will be ever hard to find many men who will send a slave to Liberia, and pay his passage while they can send him to a new country, Kansas for instance, and sell him for fifteen hundred dollars, and the rise.

Document Questions

Some answers may require more space than provided.

1. What are two uses for judicial decisions, according to Lincoln?

2. Why does Lincoln argue that the *Dred Scott* decision should not be considered as having set a legitimate precedent?

3. Why does Lincoln quote at length arguments that Andrew Jackson made when Jackson vetoed a renewal of the charter for the Bank of the United States?

4. Why does Lincoln say that the decision was based on faulty history?

5. What can be understood as Lincoln's view of equality?

CHAPTER TEN

THE HOUSE DIVIDES

Questions

Some answers may require more space than provided.

1. How did President-Elect Lincoln spend the four months between his election and his inauguration?

2. What were Lincoln's goals in his first inaugural address? What was his tone?

3. How did Lincoln handle the crisis of Fort Sumter? What resulted?

4. What, and which, were the "border states"? How important were they to Lincoln? (see Question 11)

5. What was Lincoln's chief objective in launching a war against the Confederacy?

6. What were the relative advantages of North and South in the war? Which side would win a draw?

7. How important were military victories to Lincoln politically?

8. At the start of the war, the United States had no true national army. That is the context for what image in the gallery following p. 224?

9. Trace the course of the war in the east from First Bull Run through Appomattox. How many of Lincoln's generals did Robert E. Lee defeat before Lincoln found Grant?

10. Describe Grant's background, character, and methods as a commander.

11. Explain the political, military, and diplomatic context of the Emancipation Proclamation. What did it do? What did it not do?

12. What was the constitutional status of slavery? How did Lincoln accommodate this?

13. For all of its problematical nature, the Emancipation Proclamation did enlarge the war's purpose; it was no longer just about the _____ of the _____. (p. 180)

14. What happened during the first four days of July 1863?

15. What did Lincoln achieve in the very short Gettysburg Address?

16. Modern war is characterized by the full mobilization of each society's resources, so the goal must be to destroy the enemy's _____ to fight, and to break the _____ of enemy civilians in the ability of their own government to protect them. (p. 183)

17. Why did General Sherman come to be hated in the postwar South?

18. What did it take for Lincoln to win reelection in 1864?

19. How was Lincoln perceived by his contemporaries?

20. How did Lincoln see the hand of God in the war and its outcome?

21. Lincoln's goal at the end of the war was not to punish the wicked but to _____. (p. 187)

22. How did Grant deal with Lee's army after the surrender at Appomattox?

23. What was the death toll of the war? In proportion to population, what would such a war cost today?

24. Why was Lincoln's assassination such a tragedy for the defeated South?

Objective Questions

In the blank beside each name, Put a U if he served the Union or a C if he served the Confederacy:

____ Robert E. Lee
____ Stonewall Jackson
____ U. S. Grant
____ William T. Sherman

Put in order:

____ Battle of Antietam
____ Battle of Gettysburg
____ Emancipation Proclamation

Put in order:

____ Lincoln calls for militia volunteers
____ South Carolina bombards Fort Sumter
____ Virginia secedes

Put in order:

____ Grant captures Richmond
____ Grant captures Vicksburg
____ Sherman captures Atlanta

Document

LINCOLN, THE GETTYSBURG ADDRESS, NOVEMBER 19, 1863

Four score and seven years ago our fathers brought forth on this continent, a new nation, conceived in Liberty, and dedicated to the proposition that all men are created equal.

Now we are engaged in a great civil war, testing whether that nation, or any nation so conceived and so dedicated, can long endure. We are met on a great battle-field of that war. We have come to dedicate a portion of that field, as a final resting place for those who here gave their lives that that nation might live. It is altogether fitting and proper that we should do this.

But, in a larger sense, we can not dedicate – we can not consecrate – we can not hallow – this ground. The brave men, living and dead, who struggled here, have consecrated it, far above our poor power to add or detract. The world will little note, nor long remember what we say here, but it can never forget what they did here. It is for us the living, rather, to be dedicated here to the unfinished work which they who fought here have thus far so nobly advanced. It is rather for us to be here dedicated to the great task remaining before us – that from these honored dead we take increased devotion to that cause for which they gave the last full measure of devotion – that we here highly resolve that these dead shall not have died in vain – that this nation, under God, shall have a new birth of freedom – and that government of the people, by the people, for the people, shall not perish from the earth.

Document Questions

Some answers may require more space than provided.

1. Why does Lincoln begin his speech with the archaic numbering "four score and seven years" rather than saying "in 1776"?

2. In what way is the Civil War a "testing"?

3. Why does Lincoln insist that "we cannot dedicate … consecrate … hallow this ground"?

4. What is that "great task"?

CHAPTER ELEVEN

THE ORDEAL OF RECONSTRUCTION

Questions

Some answers may require more space than provided.

1. What was the condition of the South when the war ended? What was the situation of the freedmen?

2. How had the North fared during the war? Why?

3. Why did Charles A. Beard call the war a "second American revolution"? What is the weakness of Beard's argument?

4. What questions did the victorious North have to answer in dealing with the defeated South?

5. Was the South to be treated as _____ or as _____? (The first gave them many rights, including representation in Congress; the second subjected them to being ruled *by* Congress.) (p. 192)

6. What was Lincoln's plan for Reconstruction? How far was he able to go in implementing it before his death?

7. How did the Republicans in Congress feel about Lincoln's policy?

8. Why was Lincoln's assassination such a disaster for the South?

9. How did Andrew Johnson become vice president and then, on Lincoln's death, president? What were his goals? Why was he unable to achieve them?

10. What was the situation in the South when Congress reconvened in December 1865?

11. How did the Radical Republicans take control of Reconstruction policy? What policy did they impose on the South?

12. In what two ways did Johnson try to oppose Congress in this? How successful was he?

13. Why was Johnson impeached? Why was he not convicted?

14. There are three "Reconstruction amendments" to the Constitution: the Thirteenth, Fourteenth, and Fifteenth. Describe when each was passed and what each said or did.

15. The First Amendment begins "Congress shall make no law" and so did not apply to the states. Today it *does* apply. Why?

16. What was Johnson's last official act as president?

17. What were the problems facing Reconstruction governments in southern states? How successful were they in addressing those problems?

18. What replaced slavery as a labor system in much of the South?

19. How did the South resist Reconstruction?

20. Why was Grant ineffective as president?

21. Be able to define *carpetbaggers*, *scalawags*, and *redeemers*. What do these terms imply about who was setting the terms of the controversies over Reconstruction?

22. Why did the North lose much of its prewar zeal for reform?

23. Recount the story of the election of 1876 and the compromise that settled it.

24. Be able to assess the degree of success and failure of Reconstruction.

Objective Questions

Put in order:

_____ Johnson is impeached
_____ Johnson pardons Jefferson Davis
_____ Johnson vetoes the Tenure in Office Act

Put in order:

_____ Fourteenth Amendment is proposed
_____ Lincoln is assassinated
_____ Wade–Davis Bill

Put in order:

_____ Compromise of 1877
_____ Hayes becomes president
_____ U.S. troops withdrawn from the South

Document

THE FOURTEENTH AMENDMENT

Amendment XIV

Section 1.

All persons born or naturalized in the United States, and subject to the jurisdiction thereof, are citizens of the United States and of the state wherein they reside. No state shall make or enforce any law which shall abridge the privileges or immunities of citizens of the United States; nor shall any state deprive any person of life, liberty, or property, without due process of law; nor deny to any person within its jurisdiction the equal protection of the laws.

Section 2.

Representatives shall be apportioned among the several states according to their respective numbers, counting the whole number of persons in each state, excluding Indians not taxed. But when the right to vote at any election for the choice of electors for President and Vice President of the United States, Representatives in Congress, the executive and judicial officers of a state, or the members of the legislature thereof, is denied to any of the male inhabitants of such state, being twenty-one years of age, and citizens of the United States, or in any way abridged, except for participation in rebellion, or other crime, the basis of representation therein shall be reduced in the proportion which the number of such male citizens shall bear to the whole number of male citizens twenty-one years of age in such state.

Section 3.

No person shall be a Senator or Representative in Congress, or elector of President and Vice President, or hold any office, civil or military, under the United States, or under any state, who, having previously taken an oath, as a member of Congress, or as an officer of the United States, or as a member of any state legislature, or as an executive or judicial officer of any state, to support the Constitution of the United States, shall have engaged in insurrection or rebellion against the same, or given aid or comfort to the enemies thereof. But Congress may by a vote of two-thirds of each House, remove such disability.

Section 4.

The validity of the public debt of the United States, authorized by law, including debts incurred for payment of pensions and bounties for services in suppressing insurrection or rebellion, shall not be questioned. But neither the United States nor any state shall assume or pay any debt or obligation incurred in aid of insurrection or rebellion against the United States, or any claim for the loss or emancipation of any slave; but all such debts, obligations and claims shall be held illegal and void.

Section 5.
      The Congress shall have power to enforce, by appropriate legislation, the provisions of this article.

Document Questions

Some answers may require more space than provided.

1. How is U.S. citizenship defined in Section 1? Why is this important?

2. According to Section 1, what may states not do?

3. Why was this amendment directed at the states?

4. What about the actions of private (nonstate) individuals?

5. What else did the Fourteenth Amendment do?

CHAPTER TWELVE

A NATION TRANSFORMED

Questions

Some answers may require more space than provided.

1. The Civil War marks the boundary between the earlier _____ republic and a larger, more _____, more _____, and more _____ nation-state. (p. 205)

2. What did the Grand Review symbolize?

3. What were the great constitutional questions following the war?

4. How, why, and when did the United States become the world's leading industrial power?

5. How important were railroads after the war?

6. How did business organization change after the war?

7. Be able to describe the careers and impact of Cornelius Vanderbilt, Andrew Carnegie, John D. Rockefeller, and J. Pierpont Morgan. Why were political leaders, including presidents, relatively insignificant in comparison?

8. Big business might be perceived as a threat to democracy or republican government, but it also provided great prosperity, which was widely enjoyed. The best example of this is the _____ business pioneered by _____ and then by _____ Company. (p. 213)

9. What are *communities of consumption*? How do they contrast with *island communities*?

10. How did the lives of workers change?

11. Why were labor unions weak and often ineffective?

12. What did Thomas Jefferson think of cities and farmers?

13. Before roughly 1870, the American city was a _____ with a compact urban core. Suburbs did not exist. People needed to live near to where they worked. Technological innovations like streetcars changed this, and the urban core deteriorated as more people lived farther out. (p. 217)

14. Why were cities so dreadful?

15. How did immigration change after the Civil War? What technological innovation contributed by making ocean voyages faster and cheaper?

16. "Thus did the three great -*ations* converge – _____, _____, and _____." (p. 220)

17. Most of these people were _____ immigrants, moving from Europe to America and from rural to city life. No wonder they are called the "_____." (pp. 220–21)

18. What is a better metaphor than "_____ pot"?

19. In 1890, four out of _____ residents of New York City were foreign born.

20. Why were native Americans suspicious and fearful of these immigrants?

21. How much of the West does the U.S. government own?

22. How did the U.S. government deal with 250,000 Plains Indians?

23. What was Frederick Jackson Turner's thesis about America?

Objective Question

Matching:

____ Andrew Carnegie   A. banking
____ John D. Rockefeller   B. oil
____ J. Pierpont Morgan   C. railroads
____ Cornelius Vanderbilt   D. steel

Document

EMMA LAZARUS, "THE NEW COLOSSUS," 1883

"The New Colossus" is a Petrarchan sonnet by American poet Emma Lazarus (1849–87), who wrote the poem in 1883 to raise money for the construction of a pedestal for the Statue of Liberty. In 1903, the poem was cast onto a bronze plaque and mounted inside the pedestal's lower level. The great statue, a gift from the people of France to the people of the United States, was originally meant to symbolize the international spirit of enlightened republicanism; indeed, its name was Liberty Enlightening the World. *Emma Lazarus's poem had the effect of transforming the statue's meaning into a symbol of America's openness to immigrants.*

THE NEW COLOSSUS

Not like the brazen giant of Greek fame,
With conquering limbs astride from land to land;
Here at our sea-washed, sunset gates shall stand
A mighty woman with a torch, whose flame
Is the imprisoned lightning, and her name
Mother of Exiles. From her beacon-hand
Glows world-wide welcome; her mild eyes command
The air-bridged harbor that twin cities frame.
"Keep, ancient lands, your storied pomp!" cries she
With silent lips. "Give me your tired, your poor,
Your huddled masses yearning to breathe free,

The wretched refuse of your teeming shore.
Send these, the homeless, tempest-tost to me,
I lift my lamp beside the golden door!"

Document Questions

Some answers may require more space than provided.

1. What do you think Lazarus is getting at with the contrast that she makes in the first four lines between the "brazen giant" of antiquity (probably referring to the Colossus of Rhodes) and the "mighty woman with a torch" who is Mother of Exiles?

2. Why is she the "Mother of Exiles"?

3. Why does she invite "the wretched refuse" and the "homeless, tempest-tost" to be sent to her?

4. In what ways is the poem consistent with the original concept of the sculpture, and in what ways is it inconsistent?

CHAPTER THIRTEEN

BECOMING A WORLD POWER

Questions

Some answers may require more space than provided.

1. From the end of the War of 1812 through the rest of the nineteenth century, the United States "enjoyed a long _____ from any major involvement in _____." (p. 225)

2. Why is it not exactly accurate to call America isolationist during this time?

3. America "goes not abroad in search of monsters to destroy. She is the well-wisher to the freedom and independence of all. She is the champion and vindicator _____." – John Quincy Adams, July 4, 1821 (pp. 226–27)

4. Yet Adams also was responsible two years later for the _____, declaring that the United States would not accept any further colonization by Europe of the western hemisphere. The United States lacked the power to enforce this doctrine, but it was consistent with _____ interests, who wanted to see Latin America independent and so open to _____ trade. (pp. 227–28)

5. "In very rough terms, *imperial* tends to refer to the activity of _____, while *colonial* tends to refer to the activity of _____." (p. 229)

6. European nations had practiced imperialism since the sixteenth century, but a new form of more paternalistic imperialism developed based to an extent on

_____'s notion of the "_____." "Superior" races were meant to rule; other races were meant to follow. But imperial rule might also be seen partly as a "civilizing mission" to uplift the "less advanced" cultures. (pp. 229–30)

7. Who was Alfred T. Mahan?

8. Mahan argued that sea power was not just a matter of the projection of power through battleships and the like. He believed it was as much an economic as a military concept. Explain what he meant by that. You may want to consult Beveridge's speech "The March of the Flag" (pp. 135–40), which touches on all of those points.

9. How did America first grow into the Pacific?

10. Why was America sympathetic to the Cuban revolution against Spain?

11. How was McKinley forced into war?

12. The war started with two spectacular American _____, at Manila in the Philippines and at Santiago, the Spanish naval base in Cuba. American troops then occupied Cuba as well as Puerto Rico, Guam, and the Philippines. Suddenly the United States had a _____ and status as a _____. (pp. 233–34)

13. Who opposed American imperialism? Why?

14. What was the problem in the Philippines? How was it eventually solved?

15. How was Cuba dealt with?

16. What was the Roosevelt Corollary to the Monroe Doctrine?

17. How did American imperialism contrast with that of European powers (and increasingly also Japan)?

18. Theodore Roosevelt's secretary of war, Elihu Root, summed it up: "We do not want _____. We do not want _____. We want to help them." But helping people is generally more complicated than it first seems. How was that true in this case? (p. 239)

Objective Questions

Put in order:

____ Mahan writes *Influence of Seapower*
____ Monroe Doctrine
____ Roosevelt Corollary

Put in order:

____ battle of Santiago
____ *Maine* explodes
____ Platt Amendment

Document 1

JOHN QUINCY ADAMS, AN ADDRESS CELEBRATING THE DECLARATION OF INDEPENDENCE, JULY 4, 1821

Fellow Citizens,

Until within a few days before that which we have again assembled to commemorate, our fathers, the people of this Union, had constituted a portion of the British nation; a nation, renowned in arts and arms, who, from a small Island in the Atlantic ocean, had extended their dominion over considerable parts of every quarter of the globe. Governed themselves by a race of kings, whose title to sovereignty had originally been founded on conquest, spellbound, for a succession of ages, under that portentous system of despotism and of superstition which, in the name of the meek and humble Jesus, had been spread over the Christian world, the history of this nation had, for a period of seven hundred years, from the days of the conquest till our own, exhibited a conflict almost continued, between the oppressions of power and the claims of right. In the theories of the crown and the mitre, man had no rights. Neither the body nor the soul of the individual was his own....

The religious reformation was an improvement in the science of mind; an improvement in the intercourse of man with his Creator, and in his acquaintance with himself. It was an advance in the knowledge of his duties and his rights. It was a step in the progress of man, in comparison with which the magnet and gunpowder, the wonders of either India, nay the printing press itself, were but as the paces of a pigmy to the stride of a giant....

The corruptions and usurpations of the church were the immediate objects of these reformers; but at the foundation of all their exertions there was a single plain and almost self-evident principle – that man has a right to the exercise of his own reason. It was this principle which the sophistry and rapacity of the church had obscured and obliterated, and which the intestine divisions of that same church itself first restored. The triumph of reason was the result of inquiry and discussion. Centuries of desolating wars have succeeded and oceans of human blood have flowed, for the final establishment of this principle; but it was from the darkness of the cloister that the first spark was emitted, and from the arches of a university that it first kindled into day. From the discussion of religious rights and duties, the transition to that of the political and civil relations of men with one another was natural and unavoidable; in both, the reformers were met by the weapons of temporal power. At the same glance of reason, the tiara would have fallen from the brow of priesthood, and the despotic scepter would have departed from the hand of royalty, but for the sword, by which they were protected; that sword which, like the flaming sword of the Cherubims, turned every way to debar access to the tree of life.

The double contest against the oppressors of church and state was too appalling for the vigor, or too comprehensive for the faculties of the reformers of the European continent. In Britain alone was it undertaken, and in Britain but partially succeeded.

It was in the midst of that fermentation of the human intellect, which brought right and power in direct and deadly conflict with each other, that the rival crowns of the two portions of the British Island were united on the same head. It was then, that, released from the fetters of ecclesiastical domination, the minds of men began to investigate the foundations of civil government. But the mass of the nation surveyed the fabric of their Institutions as it existed in fact. It had been founded in conquest; it had been cemented in servitude; and so broken and molded had been the minds of this brave and intelligent people to their actual conditions, that instead of solving civil society into its first elements in search of their rights, they looked back only to conquest as the origin of their liberties, and claimed their rights but as donations from their kings. This faltering assertion of freedom is not chargeable indeed upon the whole nation. There were spirits capable of tracing civil government to its first foundation in the moral and physical nature of man: but conquest and servitude were so mingled up in every particle of the social existence of the nation, that they had become vitally necessary to them, as a portion of the fluid, itself destructive of life, is indispensably blended with the atmosphere in which we live.

Fellow citizens, it was in the heat of this war of moral elements, which brought one Stuart to the block and hurled another from his throne, that our forefathers sought refuge from its fury, in the then wilderness of this Western World. They were willing exiles from a country dearer to them than life. But they were the exiles of liberty and of conscience: dearer to them even than their country. They came too, with charters from their kings; for even in removing to another hemisphere, they "cast longing, lingering looks behind," and were anxiously desirous of retaining ties of connection with their country, which, in the solemn compact of a charter, they hoped by the corresponding links of allegiance and protection to preserve. But to their sense of right, the charter was only the ligament between them, their country, and their king. Transported to a new world, they had relations with one another, and relations with the aboriginal inhabitants of the country to which they came; for which no royal charter could provide. The first settlers of the Plymouth colony, at the eve of landing from their ship, therefore, bound themselves together by a written covenant; and immediately after landing, purchased from the Indian natives the right of settlement upon the soil.

Thus was a social compact formed upon the elementary principles of civil society, in which conquest and servitude had no part. The slough of brutal force was entirely cast off; all was voluntary; all was unbiased consent; all was the agreement of soul with soul.

Other colonies were successively founded, and other charters granted, until in the compass of a century and a half, thirteen distinct British provinces peopled the Atlantic shores of the North American continent with two millions of freemen; possessing by their charters the rights of British subjects, and nurtured by their position and education, in the more comprehensive and original doctrines of human rights. From their infancy they had been treated by the parent state with neglect, harshness and injustice. Their charters had often been disregarded and violated; their commerce restricted and shackled; their interest wantonly or spitefully sacrificed; so that the hand of the parent had been scarcely ever felt, but in the alternate application of whips and scorpions.

When in spite of all these persecutions, by the natural vigor of their constitution, they were just attaining the maturity of political manhood, a British parliament, in contempt of the clearest maxims of natural equity, in defiance of the fundamental principle upon which British freedom itself had been cemented with British blood; on the naked, unblushing allegation of absolute and uncontrollable power, undertook by their act to levy, without representation and without consent, taxes upon the people of America for the benefit of the people of Britain. This enormous project of public robbery was no sooner made known, than it excited, throughout the colonies, one general burst of indignant resistance. It was abandoned, reasserted and resumed, until fleets and armies were transported, to record in the characters of fire, famine, and desolation, the transatlantic wisdom of British legislation, and the tender mercies of British consanguinity....

For the independence of North America, there were ample and sufficient causes in the laws of moral and physical nature. The tie of colonial subjection is compatible with the essential purposes of civil government, only when the condition of the subordinate state is from its weakness incompetent to its own protection. Is the greatest moral purpose of civil government, the administration of justice? And if justice has been truly defined, the constant and perpetual will of securing to every one his right, how absurd and impracticable is that form of polity, in which the dispenser of justice is in one quarter of the globe, and he to whom justice is to be dispensed is in another.... Are the essential purposes of civil government, to administer to the wants, and to fortify the infirmities of solitary man? To unite the sinews of numberless arms, and combine the councils of multitudes of minds, for the promotion of the well-being of all? The first moral element then of this composition is sympathy between the members of which it consists; the second is sympathy between the giver and the receiver of the law. The sympathies of men begin with the relations of domestic life. They are rooted in the natural relations of domestic life. They are rooted in the natural relations of husband and wife, of parent and child, of brother and sister; thence they spread through the social and moral propinquities of neighbor and friend, to the broader and more complicated relations of countryman and fellow-citizens; terminating only with the circumference of the globe which we inhabit, in the co-extensive charities incident to the common nature of man. To each of these relations, different degrees of sympathy are allotted by the ordinances of nature. The sympathies of domestic life are not more sacred and obligatory, but closer and more powerful, than those of neighborhood and friendship. The tie which binds us to our country is not more holy in the sight of God, but it is more deeply seated in our nature, more tender and endearing, than that common link which merely connects us with our fellow-mortal, man. It is a common government that constitutes our country. But in that association, all the sympathies of domestic life and kindred blood, all the moral ligatures of friendship and of neighborhood, are combined with that instinctive and mysterious connection between man and physical nature, which binds the first perceptions of childhood in a chain of sympathy with the last gasp of expiring age, to the spot of our nativity, and the natural objects by which it is surrounded. These sympathies belong and are indispensable to the relations ordained by nature between the individual and his country. They dwell in the memory and are indelible in the hearts of the first settlers of a distant colony. These are the feelings under which the children of Israel "sat down by the rivers of Babylon, and wept when they remembered Zion." These are the sympathies under which they "hung their harps upon the willow," and instead of songs of mirth, exclaimed, "If I forget thee, O Jerusalem, let my right hand forget her cunning." But these sympathies can never exist for a country, which we have never seen. They are transferred in the hearts of succeeding generations, from the country of human institution, to the country of their birth; from the land of which they have only heard, to the land where their eyes first opened to the day. The ties of neighborhood are broken up, those of friendship can never be formed, with an intervening ocean; and the natural ties of domestic life, the all-subduing sympathies of love, the indissoluble bonds of marriage, the heart-riveted kindliness of consanguinity, gradually wither and perish in the lapse of a few generations. All the elements, which form the basis of that sympathy between the individual and his country, are dissolved.

Long before the Declaration of Independence, the great mass of the people of America and of the people of Britain had become total strangers to each other.... The sympathies therefore most essential to the communion of country were, between the British and American people, extinct. Those most indispensable to the just relation between sovereign and subject, had never existed and could not exist between the British government and the American people. The connection was unnatural; and it was in the moral order no less than in the positive decrees of Providence, that it should be dissolved.

Yet, fellow-citizens, these are not the causes of the separation assigned in the paper which I am about to read. The connection between different portions of the same people and between a people and their government, is a connection of duties as well as rights. In the long conflict of twelve years which had preceded and led to the Declaration of Independence, our fathers had been not less faithful to their duties, than tenacious of their rights. Their resistance had not been rebellion. It was not a restive and ungovernable spirit of ambition, bursting from the bonds of colonial subjection; it was the deep and wounded sense of successive wrongs, upon which complaint had been only answered by aggravation, and petition repelled with contumely, which had driven them to their last stand upon the adamantine rock of human rights.

It was then fifteen months after the blood of Lexington and Bunker's hill, after Charlestown and Falmouth, fired by British hands, were but heaps of ashes, after the ear of the adder had been turned to two successive supplications to the throne; after two successive appeals to the people of Britain, as friends, countrymen, and brethren, to which no responsive voice of sympathetic tenderness had been returned.... Then it was that the thirteen United Colonies of North America, by their delegates in Congress assembled, exercising the first act of sovereignty by a right ever inherent in the people, but never to be resorted to, save at the awful crisis when civil society is solved into its first elements, declared themselves free and independent states; and two days afterwards, in justification of that act, issued this [Declaration].

[*Adams here read the Declaration of Independence*]

...The interest, which in this paper has survived the occasion upon which it was issued; the interest which is of every age and every clime; the interest which quickens with the lapse of years, spreads as it grows old, and brightens as it recedes, is in the principles which it proclaims. It was the first solemn declaration by a nation of the only legitimate foundation of civil government. It was the corner stone of a new fabric, destined to cover the surface of the globe. It demolished at a stroke the lawfulness of all governments founded upon conquest. It swept away all the rubbish of accumulated centuries of servitude. It announced in practical form to the world the transcendent truth of the unalienable sovereignty of the people. It proved that the social compact was no figment of the imagination; but a real, solid, and sacred bond of the social union. From the day of this declaration, the people of North America were no longer the fragment of a distant empire, imploring justice and mercy from an inexorable master in another hemisphere. They were no longer children appealing in vain to the sympathies of a heartless mother; no longer subjects leaning upon the shattered columns of royal promises, and invoking the faith of parchment to secure their rights. They were a nation, asserting as of right, and maintaining by war, its own existence. A nation was born in a day.

How many ages hence
Shall this their lofty scene be acted o'er
In states unborn, and accents yet unknown?

It will be acted o'er, fellow-citizens, but it can never be repeated. It stands, and must forever stand alone, a beacon on the summit of the mountain, to which all the inhabitants of the earth may turn their eyes for a genial and saving light, till time shall be lost in eternity, and this globe itself dissolve, nor leave a wreck behind. It stands forever, a light of admonition to the rulers of men; a light of salvation and redemption to the oppressed. So long as this planet shall be inhabited by human beings, so long as man shall be of social nature, so long as government shall be necessary to the great moral purposes of society, and so long as it shall be abused to the purposes of oppression, so long shall this declaration hold out to the sovereign and to the subject the extent and the boundaries of their respective rights and duties; founded in the laws of nature and of nature's God. Five and forty years have passed away since this Declaration was issued by our fathers; and here are we, fellow-citizens, assembled in the full enjoyment of its fruits, to bless the Author of our being for the bounties of his providence, in casting our lot in this favored land; to remember with effusions of gratitude the sages who put forth, and the heroes who bled for the establishment of this Declaration; and, by the communion of soul in the re-perusal and hearing of this instrument, to renew the genuine Holy Alliance of its principles, to recognize them as eternal truths, and to pledge ourselves and bind our posterity to a faithful and undeviating adherence to them....

...AND NOW, FRIENDS AND COUNTRYMEN, if the wise and learned philosophers of the elder world, the first observers of nutation and aberration, the discoverers of maddening ether and invisible planets, the inventors of Congreve rockets and Shrapnel shells, should find their hearts disposed to enquire what has America done for the benefit of mankind?

Let our answer be this: America, with the same voice which spoke herself into existence as a nation, proclaimed to mankind the inextinguishable rights of human nature, and the only lawful foundations of government. America, in the assembly of nations, since her admission among them, has invariably, though often fruitlessly, held forth to them the hand of honest friendship, of equal freedom, of generous reciprocity.

She has uniformly spoken among them, though often to heedless and often to disdainful ears, the language of equal liberty, of equal justice, and of equal rights.

She has, in the lapse of nearly half a century, without a single exception, respected the independence of other nations while asserting and maintaining her own.

She has abstained from interference in the concerns of others, even when conflict has been for principles to which she clings, as to the last vital drop that visits the heart.

She has seen that probably for centuries to come, all the contests of that Aceldama the European world, will be contests of inveterate power, and emerging right.

Wherever the standard of freedom and Independence has been or shall be unfurled, there will her heart, her benedictions and her prayers be.

But she goes not abroad, in search of monsters to destroy.

She is the well-wisher to the freedom and independence of all.

She is the champion and vindicator only of her own.

She will commend the general cause by the countenance of her voice, and the benignant sympathy of her example.

She well knows that by once enlisting under other banners than her own, were they even the banners of foreign independence, she would involve herself beyond the power of extrication, in all the wars of interest and intrigue, of individual avarice, envy, and ambition, which assume the colors and usurp the standard of freedom.

The fundamental maxims of her policy would insensibly change from liberty to force....

She might become the dictatress of the world. She would be no longer the ruler of her own spirit....

[America's] glory is not dominion, but liberty. Her march is the march of the mind. She has a spear and a shield: but the motto upon her shield is, Freedom, Independence, Peace. This has been her Declaration: this has been, as far as her necessary intercourse with the rest of mankind would permit, her practice.

Some answers may require more space than provided.

1. How does Adams feel about kings?

2. What about the Reformation?

3. How did his era's forefathers come to America?

4. How did the American Revolution come about, according to Adams?

5. How was the Declaration unique in his eyes?

6. What in Adams's view is the best thing that America has done for the world? How might it spoil that?

Document 2

ALBERT BEVERIDGE, "MARCH OF THE FLAG," 1898

It is a noble land that God has given us; a land that can feed and clothe the world; a land whose coastlines would inclose half the countries of Europe; a land set like a sentinel between the two imperial oceans of the globe, a greater England with a nobler destiny.

It is a mighty people that He has planted on this soil; a people sprung from the most masterful blood of history; a people perpetually revitalized by the virile, man-producing working-folk of all the earth; a people imperial by virtue of their power, by right of their institutions, by authority of their Heaven-directed purposes – the propagandists and not the misers of liberty.

It is a glorious history our God has bestowed upon His chosen people; a history heroic with faith in our mission and our future; a history of statesmen who flung the boundaries of the Republic out into unexplored lands and savage wilderness; a history of soldiers who carried the flag across blazing deserts and through the ranks of hostile mountains, even to the gates of sunset; a history of a multiplying people who overran a continent in half a century; a history of prophets who saw the consequences of evils inherited from the past and of martyrs who died to save us from them; a history divinely logical, in the process of whose tremendous reasoning we find ourselves today.

Therefore, in this campaign, the question is larger than a party question. It is an American question. It is a world question. Shall the American people continue their march toward the commercial supremacy of the world? Shall free institutions broaden their blessed reign as the children of liberty wax in strength, until the empire of our principles is established over the hearts of all mankind?

Have we no mission to perform, no duty to discharge to our fellow man? Has God endowed us with gifts beyond our deserts and marked us as the people of His peculiar favor, merely to rot in our own selfishness, as men and nations must, who take cowardice for their companion and self for their deity – as China has, as India has, as Egypt has?

Shall we be as the man who had one talent and hid it, or as he who had ten talents and used them until they grew to riches? And shall we reap the reward that waits on our discharge of our high duty; shall we occupy new markets for what our farmers raise, our factories make, our merchants sell-aye, and please God, new markets for what our ships shall carry?

Hawaii is ours; Porto Rico is to be ours; at the prayer of her people Cuba finally will be ours; in the islands of the East, even to the gates of Asia, coaling stations are to be ours at the very least; the flag of a liberal government is to float over the Philippines, and may it be the banner that Taylor unfurled in Texas and Fremont carried to the coast.

The Opposition tells us that we ought not to govern a people without their consent. I answer, The rule of liberty that all just government derives its authority from the consent of the governed, applies only to those who are capable of selfgovernment. We govern the Indians without their consent, we govern our territories without their consent, we govern our children without their consent. How do they know what our government would be without their consent? Would not the people of the Philippines prefer the just, humane, civilizing government of this Republic to the savage, bloody rule of pillage and extortion from which we have rescued them?

And, regardless of this formula of words made only for enlightened, self-governing people, do we owe no duty to the world? Shall we turn these peoples back to the reeking hands from which we have taken them? Shall we abandon them, with Germany, England, Japan, hungering for them? Shall we save them from those nations, to give them a selfrule of tragedy?

They ask us how we shall govern these new possessions. I answer: Out of local conditions and the necessities of the case methods of government will grow. If England can govern foreign lands, so can America. If Germany can govern foreign lands, so can America. If they can supervise protectorates, so can America. Why is it more difficult to administer Hawaii than New Mexico or California? Both had a savage and an alien population: both were more remote from the seat of government when they came under our dominion than the Philippines are today.

Will you say by your vote that American ability to govern has decayed, that a century's experience in selfrule has failed of a result? Will you affirm by your vote that you are an infidel to American power and practical sense? Or will you say that ours is the blood of government; ours the heart of dominion; ours the brain and genius of administration? Will you remember that we do but what our fathers did – we but pitch the tents of liberty farther westward, farther southward-we only continue the march of the flag?

The march of the flag! In 1789 the flag of the Republic waved over 4,000,000 souls in thirteen states, and their savage territory which stretched to the Mississippi, to Canada, to the Floridas. The timid minds of that day said that no new territory was needed, and, for the hour, they were right. But Jefferson, through whose intellect the centuries marched; Jefferson, who dreamed of Cuba as an American state, Jefferson, the first Imperialist of the Republic – Jefferson acquired that imperial territory which swept from the Mississippi to the mountains, from Texas to the British possessions, and the march of the flag began!

The infidels to the gospel of liberty raved, but the flag swept on! The title to that noble land out of which Oregon, Washington, Idaho and Montana have been carved was uncertain: Jefferson, strict constructionist of constitutional power though he was, obeyed the AngloSaxon impulse within him, whose watchword is, "Forward!": another empire was added to the Republic, and the march of the flag went on!

Those who deny the power of free institutions to expand urged every argument, and more, that we hear, today; but the people's judgment approved the command of their blood, and the march of the flag went on!

A screen of land from New Orleans to Florida shut us from the Gulf, and over this and the Everglade Peninsula waved the saffron flag of Spain; Andrew Jackson seized both, the American people stood at his back, and, under Monroe, the Floridas came under the dominion of the Republic, and the march of the flag went on! The Cassandras prophesied every prophecy of despair we hear, today, but the march of the flag went on!

Then Texas responded to the bugle calls of liberty, and the march of the flag went on! And, at last, we waged war with Mexico, and the flag swept over the southwest, over peerless California, past the Gate of Gold to Oregon on the north, and from ocean to ocean its folds of glory blazed.

And, now, obeying the same voice that Jefferson heard and obeyed, that Jackson heard and obeyed, that Monroe heard and obeyed, that Seward heard and obeyed, that Grant heard and obeyed, that Harrison heard and obeyed, our President today plants the flag over the islands of the seas, outposts of commerce, citadels of national security, and the march of the flag goes on!

Distance and oceans are no arguments. The fact that all the territory our fathers bought and seized is contiguous, is no argument. In 1819 Florida was farther from New York than Porto Rico is from Chicago today; Texas, farther from Washington in 1845 than Hawaii is from Boston in 1898; California, more inaccessible in 1847 than the Philippines are now. Gibraltar is farther from London than Havana is from Washington; Melbourne is farther from Liverpool than Manila is from San Francisco.

The ocean does not separate us from lands of our duty and desire – the oceans join us, rivers never to be dredged, canals never to be repaired. Steam joins us; electricity joins us – the very elements are in league with our destiny. Cuba not contiguous? Porto Rico not contiguous! Hawaii and the Philippines not contiguous! The oceans make them contiguous. And our navy will make them contiguous.

But the Opposition is right – there is a difference. We did not need the western Mississippi Valley when we acquired it, nor Florida, nor Texas, nor California, nor the royal provinces of the far northwest. We had no emigrants to people this imperial wilderness, no money to develop it, even no highways to cover it. No trade awaited us in its savage fastnesses. Our productions were not greater than our trade There was not one reason for the landlust of our statesmen from Jefferson to Grant, other than the prophet and the Saxon within them. But, today, we are raising more than we can consume, making more than we can use. Therefore we must find new markets for our produce.

And so, while we did not need the territory taken during the past century at the time it was acquired, we do need what we have taken and we need it now. The resources and the commerce of the immensely rich dominions will be increased as much as American energy is greater than Spanish sloth.

In Cuba, alone, there are 15,000,000 acres of forest unacquainted with the ax, exhaustless mines of iron, priceless deposits of manganese, millions of dollars' worth of which we must buy, today, from the Black Sea districts. There are millions of acres yet unexplored.

The resources of Porto Rico have only been trifled with. The riches of the Philippines have hardly been touched by the fingertips of modern methods. And they produce what we consume, and consume what we produce – the very predestination of reciprocity – a reciprocity "not made with hands, eternal in the heavens." They sell hemp, sugar, cocoanuts, fruits of the tropics, timber of price like mahogany; they buy flour, clothing, tools, implements, machinery and all that we can raise and make. Their trade will be ours in time. Do you indorse that policy with your vote?

Cuba is as large as Pennsylvania, and is the richest spot on the globe. Hawaii is as large as New Jersey; Porto Rico half as large as Hawaii; the Philippines larger than all New England, New York, New Jersey, and Delaware combined. Together they are larger than the British Isles, larger than France, larger than Germany, larger than Japan.

If any man tells you that trade depends on cheapness and not on government influence, ask him why England does not abandon South Africa, Egypt, India. Why does France seize South China, Germany, the vast region whose port is Kaouchou?

Our trade with Porto Rico, Hawaii and the Philippines must be as free as between the states of the Union, because they are American territory, while every other nation on earth must pay our tariff before they can compete with us. Until Cuba shall ask for annexation, our trade with her will, at the very least, be like the preferential trade of Canada with England. That, and the excellence of our goods and products; that, and the convenience of traffic; that, and the kinship of interests and destiny, will give the monopoly of these markets to the American people.

The commercial supremacy of the Republic means that this Nation is to be the sovereign factor in the peace of the world. For the conflicts of the future are to be conflicts of trade – struggles for markets – commercial wars for existence. And the golden rule of peace is impregnability of position and invincibility of preparedness. So, we see England, the greatest strategist of history, plant her flag and her cannon on Gibraltar, at Quebec, in the Bermudas, at Vancouver, everywhere.

So Hawaii furnishes us a naval base in the heart of the Pacific; the Ladrones another, a voyage further on; Manila another, at the gates of Asia – Asia, to the trade of whose hundreds of millions American merchants, manufacturers, farmers, have as good right as those of Germany or France or Russia or England; Asia, whose commerce with the United Kingdom alone amounts to hundreds of millions of dollars every year; Asia, to whom Germany looks to take her surplus products; Asia, whose doors must not be shut against American trade. Within five decades the bulk of Oriental commerce will be ours.

No wonder that, in the shadows of coming events so great, free-silver is already a memory. The current of history has swept past that episode. Men understand, today, the greatest commerce of the world must be conducted with the steadiest standard of value and most convenient medium of exchange human ingenuity can devise. Time, that unerring reasoner, has settled the silver question. The American people are tired of talking about money-they want to make it....

There are so many real things to be done – canals to be dug, railways to be laid, forests to be felled, cities to be builded, fields to be tilled, markets to be won, ships to be launched, peoples to be saved, civilization to be proclaimed and the Rag of liberty Hung to the eager air of every sea. Is this an hour to waste upon triflers with nature's laws? Is this a season to give our destiny over to wordmongers and prosperity-wreckers? No! It is an hour to remember our duty to our homes. It is a moment to realize the opportunities fate has opened to us. And so is all hour for us to stand by the Government.

Wonderfully has God guided us Yonder at Bunker Hill and Yorktown. His providence was above us at New Orleans and on ensanguined seas His hand sustained us. Abraham Lincoln was His minister and His was the altar of freedom the Nation's soldiers set up on a hundred battlefields. His power directed Dewey in the East and delivered the Spanish fleet into our hands, as He delivered the elder Armada into the hands of our English sires two centuries ago [actually in 1588]. The American people can not use a dishonest medium of exchange; it is ours to set the world its example of right and honor. We can not fly from our world duties; it is ours to execute the purpose of a fate that has driven us to be greater than our small intentions. We can not retreat from any soil where Providence has unfurled our banner; it is ours to save that soil for liberty and civilization.

Document 2 Questions

Some answers may require more space than provided.

1. How would you contrast Beveridge's view of America with John Quincy Adams's?

2. On what grounds does Beveridge arrive at his conclusions?

3. How does he justify governing without the consent of the governed?

4. What does he mean by the "march of the flag"?

5. For all their manifest differences, what do Adams's and Beveridge's views have in common?

CHAPTER FOURTEEN

THE PROGRESSIVE ERA

Questions

Some answers may require more space than provided.

1. Why can the term "Progressive Era" for the period 1898 to 1917 easily mislead?

2. Who was Henry George? How are his ideas a precursor to Progressivism?

3. Who was Edward Bellamy?

4. What was the "Social Gospel"?

5. How did the lives of farmers change in the decades after the Civil War?

6. Who were the Populists? What did they want?

7. Who was William Jennings Bryan? (His image is in the portrait gallery following p. 224.)

8. What was the relationship between Populists and Progressives?

9. Who were the "muckrakers"?

10. At what level of government did Progressivism have its first and greatest successes?

11. Progressives professed _____, avowing to be working for the "public interest" and not from self-interest. "This was admirable; it could also be annoyingly _____." (p. 245)

12. At the state level, Progressives changed the legislative process to include _____, _____, _____, and the party _____ – all increasing direct popular influence. (p. 245)

13. One of the paradoxes of the Progressive view of things was that they were skeptical of _____ and preferred the rule of experts, yet they had expansive faith in the people and their ability to initiate positive change in the public interest, operating outside the legislative process. They had great faith in _____ but far less faith in _____. (p. 246)

14. What was the basis for Progressives' support of prohibition?

15. "The Progressive view of human nature saw humans as _____ and evil as a function of _____ not something irremediably wrong or sinful deep in the soul of individual persons." (p. 247)

16. John Dewey's philosophy saw the old "_____" as a thing of the past; Progressivism "cared deeply about the common people _____." (p. 248)

17. Condescension was not the worst of the Progressives' blind spots; _____ was. _____ was "not a fringe phenomenon in its time, and it was not confined to the most reactionary elements; it was endorsed by leading scientists and scientific organizations as well as figures such as the feminist Margaret Sanger [and] the African American scholar W. E. B. Du Bois." (p. 248)

18. Eugenics, and the "_____" in the workplace, clashed with Christian values, such as the dignity and worth of every human as made in _____. (pp. 248–49)

19. What two ways did Progressives answer the question of how best to control and direct big business, made to serve the public interest?

20. What was Theodore Roosevelt's background?

21. What was TR's political style?

22. Was TR more a trust buster or a consolidator?

23. TR's lasting achievement is his focus on _____ and the establishment of _____ and the U.S. _____. (p. 252)

24. TR chose his own successor, William Howard Taft, then went off to Africa. But Taft was less a Progressive, and TR was still quite young; he decided in 1912 that he was not through being president. What happened in the election of 1912?

25. Wilson was a convert to Progressivism, of the antitrust variety. He called his program "_____" to contrast with TR's "_____." (p. 255)

26. What was Woodrow Wilson's academic and intellectual background?

27. What did Wilson accomplish during his first term?

28. How did Wilson differ from TR on racial matters?

29. The Progressives were always tempted to cast off constitutional restrictions. But what did G. K. Chesterton say about fences?

Objective Question

Put TR or WW in the blank according to whether Theodore Roosevelt or Woodrow Wilson is described:

_____ New Freedom
_____ New Nationalism
_____ president of Princeton
_____ wrote naval history of the War of 1812
_____ welcomed Booker T. Washington to the White House
_____ was a strong supporter of racial segregation

Document

WOODROW WILSON, "WHAT IS PROGRESS?," 1913

In that sage and veracious chronicle, "Alice Through the Looking-Glass," it is recounted how, on a noteworthy occasion, the little heroine is seized by the Red Chess Queen, who races her off at a terrific pace. They run until both of them are out of breath; then they stop, and Alice looks around her and says, "Why, we are just where we were when we started!" "Oh, yes," says the Red Queen; "you have to run twice as fast as that to get anywhere else."

That is a parable of progress. The laws of this country have not kept up with the change of political circumstances in this country; and therefore we are not even where we were when we started. We shall have to run, not until we are out of breath, but until we have caught up with our own conditions, before we shall be where we were when we started; when we started this great experiment which has been the hope and the beacon of the world. And we should have to run twice as fast as any rational program I have seen in order to get anywhere else.

I am, therefore, forced to be a progressive, if for no other reason, because we have not kept up with our changes of conditions, either in the economic field or in the political field. We have not kept up as well as other nations have. We have not kept our practices adjusted to the facts of the case, and until we do, and unless we do, the facts of the case will always have the better of the argument; because if you do not adjust your laws to the facts, so much the worse for the laws, not for the facts, because law trails along after the facts. Only that law is unsafe which runs ahead of the facts and beckons to it and makes it follow the will-o'-the-wisps of imaginative projects.

Business is in a situation in America which it was never in before; it is in a situation to which we have not adjusted our laws. Our laws are still meant for business done by individuals; they have not been satisfactorily adjusted to business done by great combinations, and we have got to adjust them. I do not say we may or may not; I say we must; there is no choice. If your laws do not fit your facts, the facts are not injured, the law is damaged; because the law, unless I have studied it amiss, is the expression of the facts in legal relationships. Laws have never altered the facts; laws have always necessarily expressed the facts; adjusted interest as they have arisen and have changed toward one another.

Politics in America is in a case which sadly requires attention. The system set up by our law and our usage doesn't work, – or at least it can't be depended on; it is made to work only by a most unreasonable expenditure of labor and pains. The government, which was designed for the people, has got into the hands of bosses and their employers, the special interests. An invisible empire has been set up above the forms of democracy.

There are serious things to do. Does any man doubt the great discontent in this country? Does any man doubt that there are grounds and justifications for discontent? Do we dare stand still? Within the past few months we have witnessed (along with other strange political phenomena, eloquently significant of popular uneasiness) on one side a doubling of the Socialist vote and on the other the posting on dead walls and hoardings all over the country of certain very attractive and diverting bills warning citizens that it was "better to be safe than sorry" and advising them to "let well enough alone." Apparently a good many citizens doubted whether the situation they were advised to let alone was really well enough, and concluded that they would take a chance of being sorry. To me, these counsels of do-nothingism, these counsels of sitting still for fear something would happen, these counsels addressed to the hopeful, energetic people of the United States, telling them that they are not wise enough to touch their own affairs without marring them, constitute the most extraordinary argument of fatuous ignorance I ever heard. Americans are not yet cowards. True, their self-reliance has been sapped by years of submission to the doctrine that prosperity is something that benevolent magnates provide for them with the aid of the government; their self-reliance has been weakened, but not so utterly destroyed that you can twit them about it. The American people are not naturally stand-patters. Progress is the word that charms their ears and stirs their hearts.

There are, of course, Americans who have not yet heard that anything is going on. The circus might come to town, have the big parade and go, without their catching a sight of the camels or a note of the calliope. There are people, even Americans, who never move themselves or know that anything else is moving.

A friend of mind who had heard of the Florida "cracker," as they call a certain ne'er-do-well portion of the population down there, when passing through the State in a train, asked some one to point out a "cracker" to him. The man asked replied, "Well, if you see something off in the woods that looks brown, like a stump, you will know it is either a stump or a cracker; if it moves, it is a stump."

Now, movement has no virtue in itself. Change is not worth while for its own sake. I am not one of those who love variety for its own sake. If a thing is good today, I should like to have it stay that way tomorrow. Most of our calculations in life are dependent upon things staying the way they are. For example, if, when you got up this morning, you had forgotten how to dress, if you had forgotten all about those ordinary things which you do almost automatically, which you can almost do half awake, you would have to find out what you did yesterday. I am told by the psychologists that if I did not remember who I was yesterday, I should not know who I am today, and that, there fore, my very identity depends upon my being able to tally today with yesterday. If they do not tally, then I am confused; I do not know who I am, and I have to go around and ask somebody to tell me my name and where I came from.

I am not one of those who wish to break connection with the past; I am not one of those who wish to change for the mere sake of variety. The only men who do that are the men who want to forget something, the men who filled yesterday with something they would rather not recollect today, and so go about seeking diversion, seeking abstraction in something that will blot out recollection, or seeking to put something into them which will blot out all recollection. Change is not worth while unless it is improvement. If I move out of my present house because I do not like it, then I have got to choose a better house, or build a better house, to justify the change.

It would seem a waste of time to point out that ancient distinction, – between mere change and improvement. Yet there is a class of mind that is prone to confuse them. We have had political leaders whose conception of greatness was to be forever frantically doing something, – it mattered little what; restless, vociferous men, without sense of the energy of concentration, knowing only the energy of succession. Now, life does not consist of eternally running to a fire. There is no virtue in going anywhere unless you will gain something by being there. The direction is just as important as the impetus of motion.

All progress depends on how fast you are going, and where you are going, and I fear there has been too much of this thing of knowing neither how fast we were going or where we were going. I have my private belief that we have been doing most of our progressiveness after the fashion of those things that in my boyhood days we called "treadmills," a treadmill being a moving platform, with cleats on it, on which some poor devil of a mule was forced to walk forever without getting anywhere. Elephants and even other animals have been known to turn treadmills, making a good deal of noise, and causing certain wheels to go round, and I daresay grinding out some sort of product for somebody, but without achieving much progress. Lately, in an effort to persuade the elephant to move, really, his friends tried dynamite. It moved, – in separate and scattered parts, but it moved.

A cynical but witty Englishman said, in a book, not long ago, that it was a mistake to say of a conspicuously successful man, eminent in his line of business, that you could not bribe a man like that, because, he said, the point about such men is that they have been bribed – not in the ordinary meaning of that word, not in any gross, corrupt sense, but they have achieved their great success by means of the existing order of things and therefore they have been put under bonds to see that that existing order of things is not change; they are bribed to maintain the *status quo*.

It was for that reason that I used to say, when I had to do with the administration of an educational institution, that I should like to make the young gentlemen of the rising generation as unlike their fathers as possible. Not because their fathers lacked character or intelligence or knowledge or patriotism, but because their fathers, by reason of their advancing years and their established position in society, had lost touch with the processes of life; they had forgotten what it was to begin; they had forgotten what it was to rise; they had forgotten what it was to be dominated by the circumstances of their life on their way up from the bottom to the top, and, therefore, they were out of sympathy with the creative, formative and progressive forces of society.

Progress! Did you ever reflect that that word is almost a new one? No word comes more often or more naturally to the lips of modern man, as if the thing it stands for were almost synonymous with life itself, and yet men through many thousand years never talked or thought of progress. They thought in the other direction. Their stories of heroisms and glory were tales of the past. The ancestor wore the heavier armor and carried the larger spear. "There were giants in those days." Now all that has altered. We think of the future, not the past, as the more glorious time in comparison with which the present is nothing. Progress, development, – those are modern words. The modern idea is to leave the past and press onward to something new.

But what is progress going to do with the past, and with the present? How is it going to treat them? With ignominy, or respect? Should it break with them altogether, or rise out of them, with its roots still deep in the older time? What attitude shall progressives take toward the existing order, toward those institutions of conservatism, the Constitution, the laws, and the courts?

Are those thoughtful men who fear that we are now about to disturb the ancient foundations of our institutions justified in their fear? If they are, we ought to go very slowly about the processes of change. If it is indeed true that we have grown tired of the institutions which we have so carefully and sedulously built up, then we ought to go very slowly and very carefully about the very dangerous task of altering them. We ought, therefore, to ask ourselves, first of all, whether thought in this country is tending to do anything by which we shall retrace our steps, or by which we shall change the whole direction of our development?

I believe, for one, that you cannot tear up ancient rootages and safely plant the tree of liberty in soil which is not native to it. I believe that the ancient traditions of a people are its ballast; you cannot make a *tabula rasa* upon which to write a political program. You cannot take a new sheet of paper and determine what your life shall be tomorrow. You must knit the new into the old. You cannot put a new patch on an old garment without ruining it; it must be not a patch, but something woven into the old fabric, of practically the same pattern, of the same texture and intention. If I did not believe that to be progressive was to preserve the essentials of our institutions, I for one could not be a progressive.

One of the chief benefits I used to derive from being president of a university was that I had the pleasure of entertaining thoughtful men from all over the world. I cannot tell you how much has dropped into my granary by their presence. I had been casting around in my mind for something by which to draw several parts of my political thought together when it was my good fortune to entertain a very interesting Scotsman who had been devoting himself to the philosophical thought of the seventeenth century. His talk was so engaging that it was delightful to hear him speak of anything, and presently there came out of the unexpected region of his thought the thing I had been waiting for. He called my attention to the fact that in every generation all sorts of speculation and thinking tend to fall under the formula of the dominant thought of the age. For example, after the Newtonian Theory of the universe had been developed, almost all thinking tended to express itself in the analogies of the Newtonian Theory, and since the Darwinian Theory has reigned amongst us, everybody is likely to express whatever he wishes to expound in terms of development and accommodation to environment.

Now, it came to me, as this interesting man talked, that the Constitution of the United States had been made under the dominion of the Newtonian Theory. You have only to read the papers of the *The Federalist* to see that fact written on every page. They speak of the "checks and balances" of the Constitution, and use to express their idea the simile of the organization of the universe, and particularly of the solar system, – how by the attraction of gravitation the various parts are held in their orbits; and then they proceed to represent Congress, the Judiciary, and the President as a sort of imitation of the solar system.

They were only following the English Whigs, who gave Great Britain its modern constitution. Not that those Englishmen analyzed the matter, or had any theory about it; Englishmen care little for theories. It was a Frenchman, Montesquieu, who pointed out to them how faithfully they had copied Newton's description of the mechanism of the heavens.

The makers of our Federal Constitution read Montesquieu with true scientific enthusiasm. They were scientists in their way – the best way of their age – those fathers of the nation. Jefferson wrote of "the laws of Nature" – and then by way of afterthought – "and of Nature's God." And they constructed a government as they would have constructed an orrery – to display the laws of nature. Politics in their thought was a variety of mechanics. The Constitution was founded on the law of gravitation. The government was to exist and move by virtue of the efficacy of "checks and balances."

The trouble with the theory is that government is not a machine, but a living thing. It falls, not under the theory of the universe, but under the theory of organic life. It is accountable to Darwin, not to Newton. It is modified by its environment, necessitated by its tasks, shaped to its functions by the sheer pressure of life. No living thing can have its organs offset against each other, as checks, and live. On the contrary, its life is dependent upon their quick cooperation, their ready response to the commands of instinct or intelligence, their amicable community of purpose. Government is not a body of blind forces; it is a body of men, with highly differentiated functions, no doubt, in our modern day, of specialization, with a common task and purpose. Their cooperation is indispensable, their warfare fatal. There can be no successful government without the intimate, instinctive coordination of the organs of life and action. This is not theory, but fact, and displays its force as fact, whatever theories may be thrown across its track. Living political constitutions must be Darwinian in structure and in practice. Society is a living organism and must obey the laws of life, not of mechanics; it must develop.

All that progressives ask or desire is permission – in an era when "development" "evolution," is the scientific word – to interpret the Constitution according to the Darwinian principle; all they ask is recognition of the fact that a nation is a living thing and not a machine.

Some citizens of this country have never got beyond the Declaration of Independence, signed in Philadelphia, July 4th, 1776. Their bosoms swell against George III, but they have no consciousness of the war for freedom that is going on today.

The Declaration of Independence did not mention the questions of our day. It is of no consequence to us unless we can translate its general terms into examples of the present day and substitute them in some vital way for the examples it itself gives, so concrete, so intimately involved in the circumstances of the day in which it was conceived and written. It is an eminently practical document, meant for the use of practical men; not a thesis for philosophers, but a whip for tyrants; not a theory for government, but a program of action. Unless we can translate it into the questions of our own day, we are not worthy of it, we are not the sons of the sires who acted in response to its challenge.

What form does the contest between tyranny and freedom take to-day? What is the special form of tyranny we now fight? How does it endanger the rights of the people, and what do we mean to do in order to make our contest against it effectual? What are to be the items of our new declaration of independence?

By tyranny, as we now fight it, we mean control of the law, of legislation and adjudication, by organizations which do not represent the people, by means which are private and selfish. We mean, specifically, the conduct of our affairs and the shaping of our legislation in the interest of special bodies of capital and those who organize their use. We mean the alliance, for this purpose, of political machines with selfish business. We mean the exploitation of the people by legal and political means. We have seen many governments under these influences cease to be representative governments, cease to be governments representative of the people, and become governments representative of special interests, controlled by machines, which in their turn are not controlled by the people.

Sometimes, when I think of the growth of our economic system, it seems to me as if, leaving our law just about where it was before any of the modern inventions or developments took place, we had simply at haphazard extended the family residence, added an office here and a workroom there, and a new set of sleeping rooms there, built up higher on our foundations, and put out little lean-tos on the side, until we have a structure that has no character whatever. Now, the problem is to continue to live in the house and yet change it.

Well, we are architects in our time, and our architects are also engineers. We don't have to stop using a railroad terminal because a new station is being built. We don't have to stop any of the processes of our lives because we are rearranging the structures in which we conduct those processes. What we have to undertake is to systematize the foundations of the house, then to thread all the old parts of the structure with the steel which will be laced together in modern fashion, accommodated to all the modern knowledge of structural strength and elasticity, and then slowly change the partitions, relay the walls, let in the light through new apertures, improve the ventilation; until finally, a generation or two from now, the scaffolding will be taken away, and there will be the family in a great building whose noble architecture will at last be disclosed, where men can live as a single community, cooperative as in a perfected, coordinated beehive, not afraid of any storm of nature, not afraid of any artificial storm, any imitation of thunder and lightning, knowing that the foundations go down to the bedrock of principle, and knowing that whenever they please they can change that plan again and accommodate it as they please to the altering necessities of their lives.

But there are a great many men who don't like the idea. Some wit recently said, in view of the fact that most of our American architects are trained in a certain *Ecole* in Paris, that all American architecture in recent years was either bizarre or "Beaux Arts." I think that our economic architecture is decidedly bizarre; and I am afraid that there is a good deal to learn about matters other than architecture from the other side of the water. Men can now hold up against us the reproach that we have not adjusted our lives to modern conditions to the same extent that they have adjusted theirs. I was very much interested in some of the reasons given by our friends across the Canadian border for being very shy about the reciprocity arrangements. They said: "We are not sure whither these arrangements will lead, and we don't care to associate too closely with the economic conditions of the United States until those conditions are as modern as ours." And when I resented it, and asked for particulars, I had, in regard to many matters, to retire from the debate because I found that they had adjusted their regulations of economic development to conditions we had not yet found a way to meet in the United States.

Well, we have started now at all events. The procession is under way. The stand-patter doesn't know there is a procession. He is asleep in the back part of his house. He doesn't know that the road is resounding with the tramp of men going to the front. And when he wakes up, the country will be empty. He will be deserted, and he will wonder what has happened. Nothing has happened. The world has been going on. The world has a habit of going on. The world has a habit of leaving those behind who won't go with it. The world has always neglected stand-patters. And, therefore, the stand-patter does not excite my indignation; he excited my sympathy. He is going to be so lonely before it is all over. And we are good fellows, we are good company; why doesn't he come along? We are not going to do him any harm. We are going to show him a good time. We are going to climb the slow road until it reaches some upland where the air is fresher, where the whole talk of mere politicians is stilled, where men can look in each other's faces and see that there is nothing to conceal, that all they have to talk about they are willing to talk about in the open and talk about with each other; and whence, looking back over the road, we shall see at last that we have fulfilled our promise to mankind. We had said to all the world, "America was created to break every kind of monopoly, and to set men free, upon a footing of equality, upon a footing of opportunity, to match their brains and their energies." And now we have proved that we meant it.

Source: https://teachingamericanhistory.org/library/document/what-is-progress/

Document Questions

Some answers may require more space than provided.

1. Why does Wilson say that "I am forced to be a progressive"?

2. What are some examples of this obsolescence in our national life?

3. Why does Wilson say that when he was president of Princeton University, he wanted "to make the young gentlemen of the rising generation as unlike their fathers as possible"?

4. What is Wilson's problem with the Declaration of Independence and the Constitution as political guides?

CHAPTER FIFTEEN

WOODROW WILSON AND THE GREAT WAR

Questions

Some answers may require more space than provided.

1. Why was what we now call World War I such a shock to Americans?

2. "Some of the greatest events in human history are also among the most unfathomable." Explain.

3. The war "changed Europe and the world forever, ending a long period of _____ and _____ and replacing it with persistent _____ and _____ about the very idea of _____ itself." (p. 259)

4. How did the unification of Germany upset the balance of power? What two alliances resulted?

5. "It was a royal mess, like a game of toppling and exploding dominoes." How did an act of terrorism in the periphery of Europe lead to general war?

6. What was the response by President Wilson to the outbreak of war?

7. Why did the war not end quickly? Why was the slaughter unparalleled? (And why did this shatter optimism based on scientific and technological progress?)

8. What was the human cost of the Battle of the Somme? What resulted from the battle?

9. Where did Americans' sympathies lie? Was there a united national sentiment? Why or why not?

10. Germany had the strongest army, while Britain had the strongest navy. How did this asymmetry affect America's desire to remain neutral?

11. How did Wilson respond to German submarine warfare?

12. Why was Wilson's reelection in 1916 not easy? (Recall how he was elected in 1912.) How strong was the United States militarily? What slogan did Wilson run on? Why did he manage to win his second term?

13. How did Wilson try to restore peace? Whom did he address in his speech of January 22, 1917? What ideals did he proclaim?

14. Why did the Germans decide to "roll the dice" by resuming submarine warfare in February 1917?

15. After the U.S. declaration of war, "the race was on between American _____ and _____ Germany hoped to administer."

16. The Progressive Wilson "proved to be an excellent wartime leader, once he _____." How did Wilson's government respond to the needs of mobilization? (p. 265)

17. How did America fill the need for workers as four million men entered the military?

18. What was the Creel Committee? What were the long-term consequences of its work?

19. How did civil liberties fare under Wilson's wartime administration?

20. "Wilson seemed to have an impatience with _____ and a reluctance to _____." (p. 267)

21. How did the Progressive movement change as a result of the war?

22. "How can a liberal political culture, one grounded ultimately in the _____ of _____, nevertheless be capable of purposeful _____ when circumstances call for it?" (p. 268)

23. What is the fundamental conflict between Progressivism and the structures of the U.S. Constitution, such as checks and balances? What opposing views of human nature are involved?

24. How close did Germany come to winning in 1917? How did American participation in the war turn it around?

25. How did American deaths compare to those of other nations?

26. Besides wiping out 10 percent of Europe's population, what else did the war destroy?

27. What was Wilson's vision for the world, expressed in the Fourteen Points?

28. How did the Fourteen Points help end the war? What were their internal contradictions? How realistic were they?

29. "The idea of _____ inevitably fired the growth of _____ – the very same force that Wilson felt needed to be tamped down." (pp. 271–72)

30. How did the Allies respond to Wilson's idealism?

31. Why did Wilson decide to go to Paris to lead the American peace delegation? Why – and there are several reasons – did this turn out to be a very bad idea?

32. Wilson's decision to go to Paris "proceeded from a mixture of _____ _____." (p. 272)

33. What was the result of the 1918 midterm elections?

34. Wilson's biggest blunder was failing to take any _____ along with him. (p. 272)

35. Germany had surrendered in part as a result of Wilson's implied promise that they would not be punished by a "victors' peace." How was Germany in fact treated by the treaty? How did this lay the foundation for World War II twenty years later?

36. What one Point of the Fourteen was most important to Wilson?

37. How and why did the Republicans led by Senator Henry Cabot Lodge oppose the treaty and the League? Who refused to delink the two? What resulted?

38. How did Wilson twice appeal to public opinion against Lodge and the Senate Republicans? What resulted?

39. Harding was the first presidential candidate to receive more than 60 percent of the popular vote. What was the significance of such a sweeping victory?

Put in order:

____ Germany asks for armistice
____ Versailles Peace Conference
____ Wilson issues the Fourteen Points

Document

WOODROW WILSON, FOURTEEN POINTS, JANUARY 8, 1918

Gentlemen of the Congress, –

Once more, as repeatedly before, the spokesmen of the Central Empires have indicated their desire to discuss the objects of the war and the possible basis of a general peace. Parleys have been in progress at Brest-Litovsk between representatives of the Central Powers to which the attention of all the belligerents has been invited for the purpose of ascertaining whether it may be possible to extend these parleys into a general conference with regard to terms of peace and settlement.

The Russian representatives presented not only a perfectly definite statement of the principles upon which they would be willing to conclude peace, but also an equally definite program of the concrete application of those principles. The representatives of the Central Powers, on their part, presented an outline of settlement which, if much less definite, seemed susceptible of liberal interpretation until their specific program of practical terms was added. That program proposed no concessions at all either to the sovereignty of Russia or to the preferences of the populations with whose fortunes it dealt, but meant, in a word, that the Central Empires were to keep every foot of territory their armed forces had occupied, – every province, every city, every point of vantage, – as a permanent addition to their territories and their power. It is a reasonable conjecture that the general principles of settlement which they at first suggested originated with the more liberal statesmen of Germany and Austria, the men who have begun to feel the force of their own peoples' thought and purpose, while the concrete terms of actual settlement came from the military leaders who have no thought but to keep what they have got. The negotiations have been broken off. The Russian representatives were sincere and in earnest. They cannot entertain such proposals of conquest and domination.

The whole incident is full of significance. It is also full of perplexity. With whom are the Russian representatives dealing? For whom are the representatives of the Central Empires speaking? Are they speaking for the majorities of their respective parliaments or for the minority parties, that military and imperialistic minority which has so far dominated their whole policy and controlled the affairs of Turkey and of the Balkan states which have felt obliged to become their associates in this war? The Russian representatives have insisted, very justly, very wisely, and in the true spirit of modern democracy, that the conferences they have been holding with the Teutonic and Turkish statesmen should be held within open, not closed doors, and all the world has been audience, as was desired.

To whom have we been listening, then? To those who speak the spirit and intention of the Resolutions of the German Reichstag on the 9th of July last, the spirit and intention of the liberal leaders and parties of Germany, or to those who resist and defy that spirit and intention and insist upon conquest and subjugation? Or are we listening, in fact, to both, unreconciled and in open and hopeless contradiction? These are very serious and pregnant questions. Upon the answer to them depends the peace of the world. But, whatever the results of the parleys at Brest-Litovsk, whatever the confusions of counsel and of purpose in the utterances of the spokesmen of the Central Empires, they have again attempted to acquaint the world with their objects in the war and have again challenged their adversaries to say what their objects are and what sort of settlement they would deem just and satisfactory. There is no good reason why that challenge should not be responded to, and responded to with the utmost candor. We did not wait for it. Not once, but again and again, we have laid our whole thought and purpose before the world, not in general terms only, but each time with sufficient definition to make it clear what sort of definitive terms of settlement must necessarily spring out of them.

Within the last week Mr. Lloyd George has spoken with admirable candor and in admirable spirit for the people and Government of Great Britain. There is no confusion of counsel among the adversaries of the Central Powers, no uncertainty of principle, no vagueness of detail. The only secrecy of counsel, the only lack of fearless frankness, the only failure to make definite statement of the objects of the war, lies with Germany and her Allies. The issues of life and death hang upon these definitions. No statesman who has the least conception of his responsibility ought for a moment to permit himself to continue this tragical and appalling outpouring of blood and treasure unless he is sure beyond a peradventure that the objects of the vital sacrifice are part and parcel of the very life of Society and that the people for whom he speaks think them right and imperative as he does.

There is, moreover, a voice calling for these definitions of principle and of purpose which is, it seems to me, more thrilling and more compelling than any of the many moving voices with which the troubled air of the world is filled. It is the voice of the Russian people. They are prostrate and all but helpless, it would seem, before the grim power of Germany, which has hitherto known no relenting and no pity. Their power, apparently, is shattered. And yet their soul is not subservient. They will not yield either in principle or in action. Their conception of what is right, of what is humane and honorable for them to accept, has been stated with a frankness, a largeness of view, a generosity of spirit, and a universal human sympathy which must challenge the admiration of every friend of mankind; and they have refused to compound their ideals or desert others that they themselves may be safe.

They call to us to say what it is that we desire, – in what, if in anything, our purpose and our spirit differ from theirs; and I believe that the people of the United States would wish me to respond, with utter simplicity and frankness. Whether their present leaders believe it or not, it is our heartfelt desire and hope that some way may be opened whereby we may be privileged to assist the people of Russia to attain their utmost hope of liberty and ordered peace.

It will be our wish and purpose that the processes of peace, when they are begun, shall be absolutely open and that they shall involve and permit henceforth no secret understandings of any kind. The day of conquest and aggrandizement is gone by; so is also the day of secret covenants entered into in the interest of particular governments and likely at some unlooked-for moment to upset the peace of the world. It is this happy fact, now clear to the view of every public man whose thoughts do not still linger in an age that is dead and gone, which makes it possible for every nation whose purposes are consistent with justice and the peace of the world to avow now or at any other time the objects it has in view.

We entered this war because violations of right had occurred which touched us to the quick and made the life of our own people impossible unless they were corrected and the world secured once for all against their recurrence. What we demand in this war, therefore, is nothing peculiar to ourselves. It is that the world be made fit and safe to live in; and particularly that it be made safe for every peace-loving nation which, like our own, wishes to live its own life, determine its own institutions, be assured of justice and fair dealing by the other peoples of the world as against force and selfish aggression. All the peoples of the world are in effect partners in this interest, and for our own part we see very clearly that unless justice be done to others it will not be done to us.

The program of the world's peace, therefore, is our program; and that program, the only possible program, as we see it, is this:

1. Open covenants of peace, openly arrived at, after which there shall be no private international understandings of any kind but diplomacy shall proceed always frankly and in the public view.

2. Absolute freedom of navigation upon the seas, outside territorial waters, alike in peace and in war, except as the seas may be closed in whole or in part by international action for the enforcement of international covenants.

3. The removal, so far as possible, of all economic barriers and the establishment of an equality of trade conditions among all the nations consenting to the peace and associating themselves for its maintenance.

4. Adequate guarantees given and taken that national armaments will be reduced to the lowest point consistent with domestic safety.

5. A free, open-minded, and absolutely impartial adjustment of all colonial claims, based upon a strict observance of the principle that in determining all such questions of sovereignty the interests of the populations concerned must have equal weight with the equitable claims of the government whose title is to be determined.

6. The evacuation of all Russian territory and such a settlement of all questions affecting Russia as will secure the best and freest cooperation of the other nations of the world in obtaining for her an unhampered and unembarrassed opportunity for the independent determination of her own political development and national policy and assure her of a sincere welcome into the society of free nations under institutions of her own choosing; and, more than a welcome, assistance also of every kind that she may need and may herself desire. The treatment accorded Russia by her sister nations in the months to come will be the acid test of their good will, of their comprehension of her needs as distinguished from their own interests, and of their intelligent and unselfish sympathy.

7. Belgium, the whole world will agree, must be evacuated and restored, without any attempt to limit the sovereignty which she enjoys in common with all other free nations. No other single act will serve as this will serve to restore confidence among the nations in the laws which they have themselves set

and determined for the government of their relations with one another. Without this healing act the whole structure and validity of international law is forever impaired.

8. All French territory should be freed and the invaded portions restored, and the wrong done to France by Prussia in 1871 in the matter of Alsace-Lorraine, which has unsettled the peace of the world for nearly fifty years, should be righted, in order that peace may once more be made secure in the interests of all.

9. A readjustment of the frontiers of Italy should be effected along clearly recognizable lines of nationality.

10. The peoples of Austria-Hungary, whose place among the nations we wish to see safeguarded and assured, should be accorded the freest opportunity of autonomous development.

11. Rumania, Serbia, and Montenegro should be evacuated; occupied territories restored; Serbia accorded free and secure access to the sea; and the relations of the several Balkan states to one another determined by friendly counsel along historically established lines of allegiance and nationality; and international guarantees of the political and economic independence and territorial integrity of the several Balkan states should be entered into.

12. The Turkish portions of the present Ottoman Empire should be assured a secure sovereignty, but the other nationalities which are now under Turkish rule should be assured an undoubted security of life and an absolutely unmolested opportunity of autonomous development, and the Dardanelles should be permanently opened as a free passage to the ships and commerce of all nations under international guarantees.

13. An independent Polish state should be erected which should include the territories inhabited by indisputably Polish populations, which should be assured a free and secure access to the sea, and whose political and economic independence and territorial integrity should be guaranteed by international covenant.

14. A general association of nations must be formed under specific covenants for the purpose of affording mutual guarantees of political independence and territorial integrity to great and small states alike.

In regard to these essential rectifications of wrong and assertions of right we feel ourselves to be intimate partners of all the governments and peoples associated together against the Imperialists. We cannot be separated in interest or divided in purpose. We stand together until the end.

For such arrangements and covenants we are willing to fight and to continue to fight until they are achieved; but only because we wish the right to prevail and desire a just and stable peace such as can be secured only by removing the chief provocations to war, which this program does remove. We have no jealousy of German greatness, and there is nothing in this program that impairs it. We grudge her no achievement or distinction of learning or of pacific enterprise, such as have made her record very bright and very enviable. We do not wish to injure her or to block in any way her legitimate influence or power. We do not wish to fight her either with arms or with hostile arrangements of trade if she is willing to associate herself with us and the other peace-loving nations of the world in covenants of justice and law and fair dealing. We wish her only to accept a place of equality among the peoples of the world, – the new world in which we now live, – instead of a place of mastery.

Neither do we presume to suggest to her any alteration or modification of her institutions. But it is necessary, we must frankly say, and necessary as a preliminary to any intelligent dealings with her on our part, that we should know whom her spokesmen speak for when they speak to us, whether for the Reichstag majority or for the military party and the men whose creed is imperial domination.

We have spoken now, surely, in terms too concrete to admit of any further doubt or question. An evident principle runs through the whole program I have outlined. It is the principle of justice to all peoples and nationalities, and their right to live on equal terms of liberty and safety with one another, whether they be strong or weak.

Unless this principle be made its foundation no part of the structure of international justice can stand. The people of the United States could act upon no other principle; and to the vindication of this principle they are ready to devote their lives, their honor, and everything they possess. The moral climax of this the culminating and final war for human liberty has come, and they are ready to put their own strength, their own highest purpose, their own integrity and devotion to the test.

Source: https://teachingamericanhistory.org/library/document/fourteen-points/

Document Questions

Some answers may require more space than provided.

1. Note how many times Wilson distinguishes between governments and peoples. In which does he seem to have more faith, and with whose welfare is he most concerned? Does the overall tendency of this speech tend to undermine the legitimacy of the international political system?

2. What political entities does Wilson envision ending? What new nations and governments does he wish to create?

3. What territory does Wilson envision changing hands?

4. Which of the Fourteen Points seem realistic, and which seem idealistic?

5. What assurances did Wilson offer Germany, which at this point had not yet surrendered?

CHAPTER SIXTEEN

FROM BOOM TO BUST

Questions

Some answers may require more space than provided.

1. What did Harding mean by a "return to normalcy," and why did his words resonate with voters?

2. What did economist John Maynard Keynes think of the peace treaty and its likely consequences?

3. All of Wilson's grand rhetoric now "_____." (p. 277)

4. What motives did Americans suspect were really behind the American entry into war?

5. How well planned was demobilization and the reduction of wartime economic regulations? What happened to the cost of living?

6. What different types of violent unrest erupted during 1919?

7. What did the Spanish flu do to the world? To America?

8. What events led to the Palmer raids? (Palmer was Woodrow Wilson's attorney general.) Why did support for them finally stop?

9. Why did politicians now loom less large in the American story? What group takes their places?

10. How did Andrew Mellon advise President Harding to deal with the economic crisis created by the end of the war? What resulted?

11. How did Harding improve the government's attitude toward and treatment of African Americans?

12. By how much did the economy grow under the Harding/Mellon policies?

13. We know what Henry Ford did; *how* did he do it?

14. _____became the centrally important industry that was not only a big business in its own right but also a powerful economic multiplier that gave rise to important by-products, which included additional big businesses, subsidiary industries, and various other ripple effects. Explain. (p. 282)

15. How did automobiles transform the American landscape and American life in general?

16. Why did Ford pay his workers so well? (Provide at least two reasons.)

17. What contradictions and complexities did Ford's personality contain?

18. The 1920s were the first decade of "our times," in which the basic structures of life are essentially like what we have today. Explain.

19. How did American culture develop during the 1920s?

20. _____became a model of how the new mass communications not only reflected events but _____ them. (p. 285)

21. How and why did Charles Lindbergh become an American hero?

22. "These events became elements of a shared national experience," but "there was always the danger" that what? (Can you think of people who are "famous for being famous," whose fame does not seem to rest on any genuine achievement?)

23. Is it true that journalism is the "_____ of history"? (pp. 286–87)

24. "_____ is believing." But "things _____." What peace-time industry is based on the same manipulative techniques used by the Creel Committee? (p. 287)

25. Frederick Lewis Allen's influential 1931 book *Only Yesterday* was "in many respects a summation of the journalistic images of the Roaring Twenties." But was Allen's judgment correct that the Twenties saw a "revolution in manners and morals"?

26. What is the risk in generalizing about culture based on only a small part of society – especially on the rich and famous? (p. 288)

27. Many of Fitzgerald's characters "are _____ Midwesterners filled with _____ and foreboding about the possible moral consequences of the very prosperity their characters were craving and enjoying." (p. 288)

28. What does it mean to say that the Twenties were a time of cultural bifurcation? Explain.

29. How did American Christianity split during the Twenties?

30. For William Jennings Bryan, Darwinism was to be resisted because _____ _____. (p. 289)

31. The textbook Scopes taught from "was indeed an openly and unapologetically _____ text, in line with Bryan's claims." (p. 289)

32. Who supported Prohibition? Why? Who opposed it? Why?

33. How did the "noble experiment" of Prohibition turn out?

34. Despite some excellent appointments like Mellon, Taft, and Hoover, Harding's administration was rife with corruption. Discuss the story of Teapot Dome and why it was a scandal.

35. How did Calvin Coolidge become president? What were his personality and style?

36. Why was Coolidge's Philadelphia address in July 1926 "a speech for the ages"? "If all men are created equal, that is _____. If they are endowed with inalienable rights, that is _____. If governments derive their just powers from the consent of the governed, that is _____." (p. 292)

37. Describe Herbert Hoover's early life and career.

38. Why was the Democratic Party much stronger than it seemed during the Republican decade of the 1920s?

39. Why was the stock market a bubble? When and why did it burst?

40. Was the stock market crash the main cause of the Great Depression? If not, what was?

41. What are the two schools of thought about the causes of the Great Depression?

42. "But the truth of the matter is that, as with the origins of the First World War, so with the Great Depression, we live in the immense shadow of a great event that remains, in some crucial aspects, a _____." (p. 296)

Objective Question

Put in order:

____ Lindbergh's flight
____ Mellon tax cuts
____ Palmer raids

Document

CALVIN COOLIDGE, SPEECH ON THE 150TH ANNIVERSARY OF THE DECLARATION OF INDEPENDENCE, JULY 5, 1926

We meet to celebrate the birthday of America. The coming of a new life always excites our interest. Although we know in the case of the individual that it has been an infinite repetition reaching back beyond our vision, that only makes it the more wonderful. But how our interest and wonder increase when we behold the miracle of the birth of a new nation. It is to pay our tribute of reverence and respect to those who participated in such a mighty event that we annually observe the fourth day of July. Whatever may have been the impression created by the news which went out from this city on that summer day in 1776, there can be no doubt as to the estimate which is now placed upon it. At the end of 150 years the four corners of the earth unite in coming to Philadelphia as to a holy shrine in grateful acknowledgement of a service so great, which a few inspired men here rendered to humanity, that it is still the preeminent support of free government throughout the world.

Although a century and a half measured in comparison with the length of human experience is but a short time, yet measured in the life of governments and nations it ranks as a very respectable period. Certainly enough time has elapsed to demonstrate with a great deal of thoroughness the value of our institutions and their dependability as rules for the regulation of human conduct and the advancement of civilization. They have been in existence long enough to become very well seasoned. They have met, and met successfully, the test of experience.

It is not so much, then, for the purpose of undertaking to proclaim new theories and principles that this annual celebration is maintained, but rather to reaffirm and reestablish those old theories and principles which time and the unerring logic of events have demonstrated to be sound. Amid all the clash of conflicting interests, amid all the welter of partisan politics, every American can turn for solace and consolation to the Declaration of Independence and the Constitution of the United States with the assurance and confidence that those two great charters of freedom and justice remain firm and unshaken. Whatever perils appear, whatever dangers threaten, the Nation remains secure in the knowledge that the ultimate application of the law of the land will provide an adequate defense and protection.

It is little wonder that people at home and abroad consider Independence Hall as hallowed ground and revere the Liberty Bell as a sacred relic. That pile of bricks and mortar, that mass of metal, might appear to the uninstructed as only the outgrown meeting place and the shattered bell of a former time, useless now because of more modern conveniences, but to those who know they have become consecrated by the use which men have made of them. They have long been identified with a great cause. They are the framework of a spiritual event. The world looks upon them, because of their associations of one hundred and fifty years ago, as it looks upon the Holy Land because of what took place there nineteen hundred years ago. Through use for a righteous purpose they have become sanctified.

It is not here necessary to examine in detail the causes which led to the American Revolution. In their immediate occasion they were largely economic. The colonists objected to the navigation laws which interfered with their trade, they denied the power of Parliament to impose taxes which they were obliged to pay, and they therefore resisted the royal governors and the royal forces which were sent to secure obedience to these laws. But the conviction is inescapable that a new civilization had come, a new spirit had arisen on this side of the Atlantic more advanced and more developed in its regard for the rights of the individual than that which characterized the Old World. Life in a new and open country had aspirations which could not be realized in any subordinate position. A separate establishment was ultimately inevitable. It had been decreed by the very laws of human nature. Man everywhere has an unconquerable desire to be the master of his own destiny.

We are obliged to conclude that the Declaration of Independence represented the movement of a people. It was not, of course, a movement from the top. Revolutions do not come from that direction. It was not without the support of many of the most respectable people in the Colonies, who were entitled to all the consideration that is given to breeding, education, and possessions. It had the support of another element of great significance and importance to which I shall later refer. But the preponderance of all those who occupied a position which took on the aspect of aristocracy did not approve of the Revolution and held toward it an attitude either of neutrality or open hostility. It was in no sense a rising of the oppressed and downtrodden. It brought no scum to the surface, for the reason that colonial society had developed no scum. The great body of the people were accustomed to privations, but they were free from depravity. If they had poverty, it was not of the hopeless kind that afflicts great cities, but the inspiring kind that marks the spirit of the pioneer. The American Revolution represented the informed and mature convictions of a great mass of independent, liberty-loving, God-fearing people who knew their rights, and possessed the courage to dare to maintain them.

The Continental Congress was not only composed of great men, but it represented a great people. While its Members did not fail to exercise a remarkable leadership, they were equally observant of their representative capacity. They were industrious in encouraging their constituents to instruct them to support independence. But until such instructions were given they were inclined to withhold action.

While North Carolina has the honor of first authorizing its delegates to concur with other Colonies in declaring independence, it was quickly followed by South Carolina and Georgia, which also gave general instructions broad enough to include such action. But the first instructions which unconditionally directed its delegates to declare for independence came from the great Commonwealth of Virginia. These were immediately followed by Rhode Island and Massachusetts, while the other Colonies, with the exception of New York, soon adopted a like course.

This obedience of the delegates to the wishes of their constituents, which in some cases caused them to modify their previous positions, is a matter of great significance. It reveals an orderly process of government in the first place; but more than that, it demonstrates that the Declaration of Independence was the result of the seasoned and deliberate thought of the dominant portion of the people of the Colonies. Adopted after long discussion and as the result of the duly authorized expression of the preponderance of public opinion, it did not partake of dark intrigue or hidden conspiracy. It was well advised. It had about it nothing of the lawless and disordered nature of a riotous insurrection.

It was maintained on a plane which rises above the ordinary conception of rebellion. It was in no sense a radical movement but took on the dignity of a resistance to illegal usurpations. It was conservative and represented the action of the colonists to maintain their constitutional rights which from time immemorial had been guaranteed to them under the law of the land.

When we come to examine the action of the Continental Congress in adopting the Declaration of Independence in the light of what was set out in that great document and in the light of succeeding events, we can not escape the conclusion that it had a much broader and deeper significance than a mere secession of territory and the establishment of a new nation. Events of that nature have been taking place since the dawn of history. One empire after another has arisen, only to crumble away as its constituent parts separated from each other and set up independent governments of their own. Such actions long ago became commonplace. They have occurred too often to hold the attention of the world and command the admiration and reverence of humanity. There is something beyond the establishment of a new nation, great as that event would be, in the Declaration of Independence which has ever since caused it to be regarded as one of the great charters that not only was to liberate America but was everywhere to ennoble humanity.

It was not because it was proposed to establish a new nation, but because it was proposed to establish a nation on new principles, that July 4, 1776, has come to be regarded as one of the greatest days in history. Great ideas do not burst upon the world unannounced. They are reached by a gradual development over a length of time usually proportionate to their importance. This is especially true of the principles laid down in the Declaration of Independence. Three very definite propositions were set out in its preamble regarding the nature of mankind and therefore of government. These were the doctrine that all men are created equal, that they are endowed with certain inalienable rights, and that therefore the source of the just powers of government must be derived from the consent of the governed.

If no one is to be accounted as born into a superior station, if there is to be no ruling class, and if all possess rights which can neither be bartered away nor taken from them by any earthly power, it follows as a matter of course that the practical authority of the Government has to rest on the consent of the governed. While these principles were not altogether new in political action, and were very far from new in political speculation, they had never been assembled before and declared in such a combination. But remarkable as this may be, it is not the chief distinction of the Declaration of Independence. The importance of political speculation is not to be underestimated, as I shall presently disclose. Until the idea is developed and the plan made there can be no action.

It was the fact that our Declaration of Independence containing these immortal truths was the political action of a duly authorized and constituted representative public body in its sovereign capacity, supported by the force of general opinion and by the armies of Washington already in the field, which makes it the most important civil document in the world. It was not only the principles declared, but the fact that therewith a new nation was born which was to be founded upon those principles and which from that time forth in its development has actually maintained those principles, that makes this pronouncement an incomparable event in the history of government. It was an assertion that a people had arisen determined to make every necessary sacrifice for the support of these truths and by their practical application bring the War of Independence to a successful conclusion and adopt the Constitution of the United States with all that it has meant to civilization.

The idea that the people have a right to choose their own rulers was not new in political history. It was the foundation of every popular attempt to depose an undesirable king. This right was set out with a good deal of detail by the Dutch when as early as July 26, 1581, they declared their independence of Philip of Spain. In their long struggle with the Stuarts the British people asserted the same principles, which finally culminated in the Bill of Rights deposing the last of that house and placing William and Mary on the throne. In each of these cases sovereignty through divine right was displaced by sovereignty through the consent of the people. Running through the same documents, though expressed in different terms, is the clear inference of inalienable rights. But we should search these charters in vain for an assertion of the doctrine of equality. This principle had not before appeared as an official political declaration of any nation. It was profoundly revolutionary. It is one of the corner stones of American institutions.

But if these truths to which the Declaration refers have not before been adopted in their combined entirety by national authority, it is a fact that they had been long pondered and often expressed in political speculation. It is generally assumed that French thought had some effect upon our public mind during Revolutionary days. This may have been true. But the principles of our Declaration had been under discussion in the Colonies for nearly two generations before the advent of the French political philosophy that characterized the middle of the eighteenth century. In fact, they come from an earlier date. A very positive echo of what the Dutch had done in 1581, and what the English were preparing to do, appears in the assertion of the Rev. Thomas Hooker, of Connecticut, as early as 1638, when he said in a sermon before the General Court that –

"The foundation of authority is laid in the free consent of the people."

"The choice of public magistrates belongs unto the people by God's own allowance."

This doctrine found wide acceptance among the nonconformist clergy who later made up the Congregational Church. The great apostle of this movement was the Rev. John Wise, of Massachusetts. He was one of the leaders of the revolt against the royal governor Andros in 1687, for which he suffered imprisonment. He was a liberal in ecclesiastical controversies. He appears to have been familiar with the writings of the political scientist, Samuel Pufendorf, who was born in Saxony in 1632. Wise published a treatise, entitled "The Church's Quarrel Espoused," in 1710, which was amplified in another publication in 1717. In it he dealt with the principles of civil government. His works were reprinted in 1772 and have been declared to have been nothing less than a textbook of liberty for our Revolutionary fathers.

While the written word was the foundation, it is apparent that the spoken word was the vehicle for convincing the people. This came with great force and wide range from the successors of Hooker and Wise. It was carried on with a missionary spirit which did not fail to reach the Scotch-Irish of North Carolina, showing its influence by significantly making that Colony the first to give instructions to its delegates looking to independence. This preaching reached the neighborhood of Thomas Jefferson, who acknowledged that his "best ideas of democracy" had been secured at church meetings.

That these ideas were prevalent in Virginia is further revealed by the Declaration of Rights, which was prepared by George Mason and presented to the general assembly on May 27, 1776. This document asserted popular sovereignty and inherent natural rights, but confined the doctrine of equality to the assertion that "All men are created equally free and independent." It can scarcely be imagined that Jefferson was unacquainted with what had been done in his own Commonwealth of Virginia when he took up the task of drafting the Declaration of Independence. But these thoughts can very largely be traced back to what John Wise was writing in 1710. He said, "Every man must be acknowledged equal to every man." Again, "The end of all good government is to cultivate humanity and promote the happiness of all and the good of every man in all his rights, his life, liberty, estate, honor, and so forth…." And again, "For as they have a power every man in his natural state, so upon combination they can and do bequeath this power to others and settle it according as their united discretion shall determine." And still again, "Democracy is Christ's government in church and state." Here was the doctrine of equality, popular sovereignty, and the substance of the theory of inalienable rights clearly asserted by Wise at the opening of the eighteenth century, just as we have the principle of the consent of the governed stated by Hooker as early as 1638.

When we take all these circumstances into consideration, it is but natural that the first paragraph of the Declaration of Independence should open with a reference to Nature's God and should close in the final paragraphs with an appeal to the Supreme Judge of the world and an assertion of a firm reliance on Divine Providence. Coming from these sources, having as it did this background, it is no wonder that Samuel Adams could say "The people seem to recognize this resolution as though it were a decree promulgated from heaven."

No one can examine this record and escape the conclusion that in the great outline of its principles the Declaration was the result of the religious teachings of the preceding period. The profound philosophy which Jonathan Edwards applied to theology, the popular preaching of George Whitefield, had aroused the thought and stirred the people of the Colonies in preparation for this great event. No doubt the speculations which had been going on in England, and especially on the Continent, lent their influence to the general sentiment of the times. Of course, the world is always influenced by all the experience and all the thought of the past. But when we come to a contemplation of the immediate conception of the principles of human relationship which went into the Declaration of Independence we are not required to extend our search beyond our own shores. They are found in the texts, the sermons, and the writings of the early colonial clergy who were earnestly undertaking to instruct their congregations in the great mystery of how to live. They preached equality because they believed in the fatherhood of God and the brotherhood of man. They justified freedom by the text that we are all created in the divine image, all partakers of the divine spirit.

Placing every man on a plane where he acknowledged no superiors, where no one possessed any right to rule over him, he must inevitably choose his own rulers through a system of self-government. This was their theory of democracy. In those days such doctrines would scarcely have been permitted to flourish and spread in any other country. This was the purpose which the fathers cherished. In order that they might have freedom to express these thoughts and opportunity to put them into action, whole congregations with their pastors had migrated to the Colonies. These great truths were in the air that our people breathed. Whatever else we may say of it, the Declaration of Independence was profoundly American.

If this apprehension of the facts be correct, and the documentary evidence would appear to verify it, then certain conclusions are bound to follow. A spring will cease to flow if its source be dried up; a tree will wither if its roots be destroyed. In its main features the Declaration of Independence is a great spiritual document. It is a declaration not of material but of spiritual conceptions. Equality, liberty, popular sovereignty, the rights of man – these are not elements which we can see and touch. They are ideals. They have their source and their roots in the religious convictions. They belong to the unseen world. Unless the faith of the American people in these religious convictions is to endure, the principles of our Declaration will perish. We can not continue to enjoy the result if we neglect and abandon the cause.

We are too prone to overlook another conclusion. Governments do not make ideals, but ideals make governments. This is both historically and logically true. Of course the government can help to sustain ideals and can create institutions through which they can be the better observed, but their source by their very nature is in the people. The people have to bear their own responsibilities. There is no method by which that burden can be shifted to the government. It is not the enactment, but the observance of laws, that creates the character of a nation.

About the Declaration there is a finality that is exceedingly restful. It is often asserted that the world has made a great deal of progress since 1776, that we have had new thoughts and new experiences which have given us a great advance over the people of that day, and that we may therefore very well discard their conclusions for something more modern. But that reasoning can not be applied to this great charter. If all men are created equal, that is final. If they are endowed with inalienable rights, that is final. If governments derive their just powers from the consent of the governed, that is final. No advance, no progress can be made beyond these propositions. If anyone wishes to deny their truth or their soundness, the only direction in which he can proceed historically is not forward, but backward toward the time when there was no equality, no rights of the individual, no rule of the people. Those who wish to proceed in that direction can not lay claim to progress. They are reactionary. Their ideas are not more modern, but more ancient, than those of the Revolutionary fathers.

In the development of its institutions America can fairly claim that it has remained true to the principles which were declared 150 years ago. In all the essentials we have achieved an equality which was never possessed by any other people. Even in the less important matter of material possessions we have secured a wider and wider distribution of wealth. The rights of the individual are held sacred and protected by constitutional guaranties, which even the Government itself is bound not to violate. If there is any one thing among us that is established beyond question, it is self-government – the right of the people to rule. If there is any failure in respect to any of these principles, it is because there is a failure on the part of individuals to observe them. We hold that the duly authorized expression of the will of the people has a divine sanction. But even in that we come back to the theory of John Wise that "Democracy is Christ's government." The ultimate sanction of law rests on the righteous authority of the Almighty.

On an occasion like this a great temptation exists to present evidence of the practical success of our form of democratic republic at home and the ever-broadening acceptance it is securing abroad. Although these things are well known, their frequent consideration is an encouragement and an inspiration. But it is not results and effects so much as sources and causes that I believe it is even more necessary constantly to contemplate. Ours is a government of the people. It represents their will. Its officers may sometimes go astray, but that is not a reason for criticizing the principles of our institutions. The real heart of the American Government depends upon the heart of the people. It is from that source that we must look for all genuine reform. It is to that cause that we must ascribe all our results.

It was in the contemplation of these truths that the fathers made their declaration and adopted their Constitution. It was to establish a free government, which must not be permitted to degenerate into the unrestrained authority of a mere majority or the unbridled weight of a mere influential few. They undertook the balance of these interests against each other and provide the three separate independent branches, the executive, the legislative, and the judicial departments of the Government, with checks against each other in order that neither one might encroach upon the other. These are our guaranties of liberty. As a result of these methods enterprise has been duly protected from confiscation, the people have been free from oppression, and there has been an ever-broadening and deepening of the humanities of life.

Under a system of popular government there will always be those who will seek for political preferment by clamoring for reform. While there is very little of this which is not sincere, there is a large portion that is not well informed. In my opinion very little of just criticism can attach to the theories and principles of our institutions. There is far more danger of harm than there is hope of good in any radical changes. We do need a better understanding and comprehension of them and a better knowledge of the foundations of government in general. Our forefathers came to certain conclusions and decided upon certain courses of action which have been a great blessing to the world. Before we can understand their conclusions we must go back and review the course which they followed. We must think the thoughts which they thought. Their intellectual life centered around the meeting-house. They were intent upon religious worship. While there were always among them men of deep learning, and later those who had comparatively large possessions, the mind of the people was not so much engrossed in how much they knew, or how much they had, as in how they were going to live. While scantily provided with other literature, there was a wide acquaintance with the Scriptures. Over a period as great as that which measures the existence of our independence they were subject to this discipline not only in their religious life and educational training, but also in their political thought. They were a people who came under the influence of a great spiritual development and acquired a great moral power.

No other theory is adequate to explain or comprehend the Declaration of Independence. It is the product of the spiritual insight of the people. We live in an age of science and of abounding accumulation of material things. These did not create our Declaration. Our Declaration created them. The things of the spirit come first. Unless we cling to that, all our material prosperity, overwhelming though it may appear, will turn to a barren sceptre in our grasp. If we are to maintain the great heritage which has been bequeathed to us, we must be like-minded as the fathers who created it. We must not sink into a pagan materialism. We must cultivate the reverence which they had for the things that are holy. We must follow the spiritual and moral leadership which they showed. We must keep replenished, that they may glow with a more compelling flame, the altar fires before which they worshiped.

Source: https://teachingamericanhistory.org/library/document/speech-on-the-occasion-of-the-one-hundred-and-fiftieth-anniversary-of-the-declaration-of-independence/

Document Questions

Some answers may require more space than provided.

1. What does Coolidge see as the purpose of the annual celebration of national independence (the Fourth of July)?

2. How have the Liberty Bell and Independence Hall become "consecrated" objects? Does this resemble Lincoln's words about the "consecration" of Gettysburg's battlefield?

3. Why does Coolidge say that the Declaration was not "a movement from the top"?

4. Why is July 4, 1776, regarded as one of the great days of history?

5. In what way was the Declaration a product of the religious teachings of the times?

6. What does Coolidge mean by the "finality" of the Declaration? Are his words an answer to Wilson and other critics of the Founding?

CHAPTER SEVENTEEN

THE NEW DEAL

Questions

Some answers may require more space than provided.

1. How might Calvin Coolidge have responded to the stock market crash had he still been president?

2. Hoover's views "reflected the can-do problem-solving spirit of his own profession of engineering, and his activist tendencies were far closer to the _____ tradition than to the _____ tradition embraced by Harding and Coolidge." (pp. 297–98)

3. What was associationalism?

4. "Like the Progressives, Hoover was quite comfortable with the idea that government should play an active role in fostering a _____." (p. 298)

5. How did the economy spiral downward between 1929 and 1932?

6. What were Hoovervilles?

7. How did Hoover go about trying to restore prosperity?

8. Why was the Smoot–Hawley Tariff such a disaster?

9. How successful was the Reconstruction Finance Corporation (RFC)? What phrase did Will Rogers coin about it?

10. What part of federal government emergency relief did Hoover adamantly oppose? Why? How did the public perceive this? How did Democrats in Congress take advantage of it?

11. What is the tragedy (and irony) of Herbert Hoover's policies toward the Great Depression and their effect on his reputation?

12. What was the Bonus Expeditionary Force? What happened to it?

13. The Republicans were resigned to defeat in 1932. Who did the Democrats pick to win?

14. Describe FDR's background and personality.

15. FDR possessed "a second-class _____ but a first-class _____." (p. 303)

16. The term "new deal" was not carefully thought out but proved to resonate with voters. Why?

17. What sort of campaign did FDR run and win on?

18. What happened to the economy between the election and FDR's inauguration?

19. What were the tone and the content of FDR's inaugural address?

20. What did Congress do during the Hundred Days? Why (two reasons) was the result a "hodgepodge of conflicting tendencies"?

21. How did FDR deal with the bank crisis?

22. What were the "fireside chats"? How important were they?

23. What were the main elements of FDR's relief program? How effective were they? Was the effect more psychological than real?

24. The key program of the first New Deal was the NIRA that created the NRA. Describe the plan. What happened to it? Why was it an anticlimax when the Supreme Court declared the NRA unconstitutional?

25. The AAA was "somewhat more successful." Explain. Who benefited most? What happened to the AAA?

26. What were the TVA, the SEC, and the FHA?

27. Although the Democrats prevailed in the midterm elections of 1934 (an unusual event, as the party in power normally loses seats in Congress in midterms), FDR faced increasing criticism both from the Republicans and from within his own party – from the Left and the Right alike. Who led the American Liberty League? Who was Huey P. Long? Who was Francis Townsend? Charles Coughlin?

28. The centerpiece of the Second New Deal was _____. (p. 312)

29. How did Social Security "follow a very American pattern"?

30. What did the Wagner Act do?

31. What did the Revenue Act of 1935 do? How effective was it?

32. By how much did FDR and the Democrats win in 1936?

33. Why was there no Third New Deal?

34. Why did the court-packing plan fail? How was FDR seen by the public in the wake of it? (pp. 313–14)

35. What happened to the economy in 1937?

36. What happened to the Executive Reorganization Act? Why?

37. What happened in the midterm elections of 1938?

38. "Roosevelt's New Deal had made _____ in the landscape of American life and had eased the effects of _____. His spirit and his words had restored the _____. But his policies had not solved the problems of the economy and had not returned the country to full employment." (p. 315)

Objective Questions

Put in order:

_____ National Recovery Administration
_____ Reconstruction Finance Corporation
_____ Wagner Act

Put in order:

_____ Executive Reorganization Act
_____ Smoot–Hawley Tariff
_____ Civilian Conservation Corps

Matching:

_____ AAA	A.	Made work to increase employment
_____ FHA	B.	Dams and flood control and electricity
_____ NRA	C.	Regulated stock market
_____ SEC	D.	Industry councils to fix prices
_____ TVA	E.	Reduced crop production to raise prices
_____ WPA	F.	Insured bank loans for housing construction

FRANKLIN ROOSEVELT, COMMONWEALTH CLUB
ADDRESS, SEPTEMBER 23, 1932

The issue of Government has always been whether individual men and women will have to serve some system of Government or economics, or whether a system of Government and economics exists to serve individual men and women. This question has persistently dominated the discussion of government for many generations. On questions relating to these things men have differed, and for time immemorial it is probable that honest men will continue to differ.

The final word belongs to no man; yet we can still believe in change and in progress. Democracy, as a dear old friend of mine in Indiana, Meredith Nicholson, has called it, is a quest, a never-ending seeking for better things, and in the seeking for these things and the striving for them, there are many roads to follow. But, if we map the course of these roads, we find that there are only two general directions.

When we look about us, we are likely to forget how hard people have worked to win the privilege of government. The growth of the national Governments of Europe was a struggle for the development of a centralized force in the Nation, strong enough to impose peace upon ruling barons. In many instances the victory of the central Government, the creation of a strong central Government, was a haven of refuge to the individual. The people preferred the master far away to the exploitation and cruelty of the smaller master near at hand.

But the creators of national Government were perforce ruthless men. They were often cruel in their methods, but they did strive steadily toward something that society needed and very much wanted, a strong central State able to keep the peace, to stamp out civil war, to put the unruly nobleman in his place, and to permit the bulk of individuals to live safely. The man of ruthless force had his place in developing a pioneer country, just as he did in fixing the power of the central Government in the development of Nations. Society paid him well for his services and its development. When the development among the Nations of Europe, however, had been completed, ambition and ruthlessness, having served their term, tended to overstep their mark.

There came a growing feeling that Government was conducted for the benefit of a few who thrived unduly at the expense of all. The people sought a balancing – a limiting force. There came gradually, through town councils, trade guilds, national parliaments, by constitution and by popular participation and control, limitations on arbitrary power.

Another factor that tended to limit the power of those who ruled, was the rise of the ethical conception that a ruler bore a responsibility for the welfare of his subjects.

The American colonies were born in this struggle. The American Revolution was a turning point in it. After the Revolution the struggle continued and shaped itself in the public life of the country. There were those who because they had seen the confusion which attended the years of war for American independence surrendered to the belief that popular Government was essentially dangerous and essentially unworkable. They were honest people, my friends, and we cannot deny that their experience had warranted some measure of fear. The most brilliant, honest and able exponent of this point of view was Hamilton. He was too impatient of slow-moving methods. Fundamentally he believed that the safety of the republic lay in the autocratic strength of its Government, that the destiny of individuals was to serve that Government, and that fundamentally a great and strong group of central institutions, guided by a small group of able and public spirited citizens, could best direct all Government.

But Mr. Jefferson, in the summer of 1776, after drafting the Declaration of Independence turned his mind to the same problem and took a different view. He did not deceive himself with outward forms. Government to him was a means to an end, not an end in itself; it might be either a refuge and a help or a threat and a danger, depending on the circumstances. We find him carefully analyzing the society for which he was to organize a Government. "We have no paupers. The great mass of our population is of laborers, our rich who cannot live without labor, either manual or professional, being few and of moderate wealth. Most of the laboring class possess property, cultivate their own lands, have families and from the demand for their labor, are enabled to exact from the rich and the competent such prices as enable them to feed abundantly, clothe above mere decency, to labor moderately and raise their families."

These people, he considered, had two sets of rights, those of "personal competency" and those involved in acquiring and possessing property. By "personal competency" he meant the right of free thinking, freedom of forming and expressing opinions, and freedom of personal living, each man according to his own Rights. To insure the first set of rights, a Government must so order its functions as not to interfere with the individual. But even Jefferson realized that the exercise of the property rights might so interfere with the rights of the individual that the Government, without whose assistance the property rights could not exist, must intervene, not to destroy individualism, but to protect it.

You are familiar with the great political duel which followed; and how Hamilton, and his friends, building toward a dominant centralized power were at length defeated in the great election of 1800, by Mr. Jefferson's party. Out of that duel came the two parties, Republican and Democratic, as we know them today.

So began, in American political life, the new day, the day of the individual against the system, the day in which individualism was made the great watchword of American life. The happiest of economic conditions made that day long and splendid. On the Western frontier, land was substantially free. No one, who did not shirk the task of earning a living, was entirely without opportunity to do so. Depressions could, and did, come and go; but they could not alter the fundamental fact that most of the people lived partly by selling their labor and partly by extracting their livelihood from the soil, so that starvation and dislocation were practically impossible. At the very worst there was always the possibility of climbing into a covered wagon and moving west where the untilled prairies afforded a haven for men to whom the East did not provide a place. So great were our natural resources that we could offer this relief not only to our own people, but to the distressed of all the world; we could invite immigration from Europe, and welcome it with open arms. Traditionally, when a depression came a new section of land was opened in the West; and even our temporary misfortune served our manifest destiny.

It was in the middle of the nineteenth century that a new force was released and a new dream created. The force was what is called the industrial revolution, the advance of steam and machinery and the rise of the forerunners of the modern industrial plant. The dream was the dream of an economic machine, able to raise the standard of living for everyone; to bring luxury within the reach of the humblest; to annihilate distance by steam power and later by electricity, and to release everyone from the drudgery of the heaviest manual toil. It was to be expected that this would necessarily affect Government. Heretofore, Government had merely been called upon to produce conditions within which people could live happily, labor peacefully, and rest secure. Now it was called upon to aid in the consummation of this new dream. There was, however, a shadow over the dream. To be made real, it required use of the talents of men of tremendous will and tremendous ambition, since by no other force could the problems of financing and engineering and new developments be brought to a consummation.

So manifest were the advantages of the machine age, however, that the United States fearlessly, cheerfully, and, I think, rightly, accepted the bitter with the sweet. It was thought that no price was too high to pay for the advantages which we could draw from a finished industrial system. This history of the last half century is accordingly in large measure a history of a group of financial Titans, whose methods were not scrutinized with too much care and who were honored in proportion as they produced the results, irrespective of the means they used. The financiers who pushed the railroads to the Pacific were always ruthless, often wasteful, and frequently corrupt; but they did build railroads, and we have them today. It has been estimated that the American investor paid for the American railway system more than three times over in the process; but despite this fact the net advantage was to the United States. As long as we had free land; as long as population was growing by leaps and bounds; as long as our industrial plants were insufficient to supply our own needs, society chose to give the ambitious man free play and unlimited reward provided only that he produced the economic plant so much desired.

During this period of expansion, there was equal opportunity for all and the business of Government was not to interfere but to assist in the development of industry. This was done at the request of business men themselves. The tariff was originally imposed for the purpose of "fostering our infant industry," a phrase I think the older among you will remember as a political issue not so long ago. The railroads were subsidized, sometimes by grants of money, oftener by grants of land; some of the most valuable oil lands in the United States were granted to assist the financing of the railroad which pushed through the Southwest. A nascent merchant marine was assisted by grants of money, or by mail subsidies, so that our steam shipping might ply the seven seas. Some of my friends tell me that they do not want the Government in business. With this I agree; but I wonder whether they realize the implications of the past. For while it has been American doctrine that the Government must not go into business in competition with private enterprises, still it has been traditional, particularly in Republican administrations, for business urgently to ask the Government to put at private disposal all kinds of Government assistance. The same man who tells you that he does not want to see the Government interfere in business – and he means it, and has plenty of good reasons for saying so – is the first to go to Washington and ask the Government for a prohibitory tariff on his product. When things get just bad enough as they did two years ago, he will go with equal speed to the United States Government and ask for a loan; and the Reconstruction Finance Corporation is the outcome of it. Each group has sought protection from the Government for its own special interests, without realizing that the function of Government must be to favor no small group at the expense of its duty to protect the rights of personal freedom and of private property of all its citizens.

In retrospect we can now see that the turn of the tide came with the turn of the century. We were reaching our last frontier; there was no more free land

and our industrial combinations had become great uncontrolled and irresponsible units of power within the State. Clear-sighted men saw with fear the danger that opportunity would no longer be equal; that the growing corporation, like the feudal baron of old, might threaten the economic freedom of individuals to earn a living. In that hour, our antitrust laws were born. The cry was raised against the great corporations. Theodore Roosevelt, the first great Republican Progressive, fought a Presidential campaign on the issue of "trust busting" and talked freely about malefactors of great wealth. If the government had a policy it was rather to turn the clock back, to destroy the large combinations and to return to the time when every man owned his individual small business.

This was impossible; Theodore Roosevelt, abandoning the idea of "trust busting," was forced to work out a difference between "good" trusts and "bad" trusts. The Supreme Court set forth the famous "rule of reason" by which it seems to have meant that a concentration of industrial power was permissible if the method by which it got its power, and the use it made of that power, were reasonable.

Woodrow Wilson, elected in 1912, saw the situation more clearly. Where Jefferson had feared the encroachment of political power on the lives of individuals, Wilson knew that the new power was financial. He saw, in the highly centralized economic system, the despot of the twentieth century, on whom great masses of individuals relied for their safety and their livelihood, and whose irresponsibility and greed (if they were not controlled) would reduce them to starvation and penury. The concentration of financial power had not proceeded so far in 1912 as it has today; but it had grown far enough for Mr. Wilson to realize fully its implications. It is interesting, now, to read his speeches. What is called "radical" today (and I have reason to know whereof I speak) is mild compared to the campaign of Mr. Wilson. "No man can deny," he said, "that the lines of endeavor have more and more narrowed and stiffened; no man who knows anything about the development of industry in this country can have failed to observe that the larger kinds of credit are more and more difficult to obtain unless you obtain them upon terms of uniting your efforts with those who already control the industry of the country, and nobody can fail to observe that every man who tries to set himself up in competition with any process of manufacture which has taken place under the control of large combinations of capital will presently find himself either squeezed out or obliged to sell and allow himself to be absorbed." Had there been no World War – had Mr. Wilson been able to devote eight years to domestic instead of to international affairs – we might have had a wholly different situation at the present time. However, the then distant roar of European cannon, growing ever louder, forced him to abandon the study of this issue. The problem he saw so clearly is left with us as a legacy; and no one of us on either side of the political controversy can deny that it is a matter of grave concern to the Government.

A glance at the situation today only too clearly indicates that equality of opportunity as we have known it no longer exists. Our industrial plant is built; the problem just now is whether under existing conditions it is not overbuilt. Our last frontier has long since been reached, and there is practically no more free land. More than half of our people do not live on the farms or on lands and cannot derive a living by cultivating their own property. There is no safety valve in the form of a Western prairie to which those thrown out of work by the Eastern economic machines can go for a new start. We are not able to invite the immigration from Europe to share our endless plenty. We are now providing a drab living for our own people.

Our system of constantly rising tariffs has at last reacted against us to the point of closing our Canadian frontier on the north, our European markets on the east, many of our Latin-American markets to the south, and a goodly proportion of our Pacific markets on the west, through the retaliatory tariffs of those countries. It has forced many of our great industrial institutions which exported their surplus production to such countries, to establish plants in such countries, within the tariff walls. This has resulted in the reduction of the operation of their American plants, and opportunity for employment.

Just as freedom to farm has ceased, so also the opportunity in business has narrowed. It still is true that men can start small enterprises, trusting to native shrewdness and ability to keep abreast of competitors; but area after area has been pre-empted altogether by the great corporations, and even in the fields which still have no great concerns, the small man starts under a handicap. The unfeeling statistics of the past three decades show that the independent business man is running a losing race. Perhaps he is forced to the wall; perhaps he cannot command credit; perhaps he is "squeezed out," in Mr. Wilson's words, by highly organized corporate competitors, as your corner grocery man can tell you. Recently a careful study was made of the concentration of business in the United States. It showed that our economic life was dominated by some six hundred odd corporations who controlled two-thirds of American industry. Ten million small business men divided the other third. More striking still, it appeared that if the process of concentration goes on at the same rate, at the end of another century we shall have all American industry controlled by a dozen corporations, and run by perhaps a hundred men. Put plainly, we are steering a steady course toward economic oligarchy, if we are not there lready.

Clearly, all this calls for a re-appraisal of values. A mere builder of more industrial plants, a creator of more railroad systems, an organizer of more corporations, is as likely to be a danger as a help. The day of the great promoter or the financial Titan, to whom we granted anything if only he would build, or develop, is over. Our task now is not discovery or exploitation of natural resources, or necessarily producing more goods. It is the soberer, less dramatic business of administering resources and plants already in hand, of seeking to reestablish foreign markets for our surplus production, of meeting the problem of under-consumption, of adjusting production to consumption, of distributing wealth and products more equitably, of adapting existing economic organizations to the service of the people. The day of enlightened administration has come.

Just as in older times the central Government was first a haven of refuge, and then a threat, so now in a closer economic system the central and ambitious financial unit is no longer a servant of national desire, but a danger. I would draw the parallel one step farther. We did not think because national Government had become a threat in the 18th century that therefore we should abandon the principle of national Government. Nor today should we abandon the principle of strong economic units called corporations, merely because their power is susceptible of easy abuse. In other times we dealt with the problem of an unduly ambitious central Government by modifying it gradually into a constitutional democratic Government. So today we are modifying and controlling our economic units.

As I see it, the task of Government in its relation to business is to assist the development of an economic declaration of rights, an economic constitutional order. This is the common task of statesman and business man. It is the minimum requirement of a more permanently safe order of things.

Happily, the times indicate that to create such an order not only is the proper policy of Government, but it is the only line of safety for our economic structures as well. We know, now, that these economic units cannot exist unless prosperity is uniform, that is, unless purchasing power is well distributed throughout every group in the Nation. That is why even the most selfish of corporations for its own interest would be glad to see wages restored and unemployment ended and to bring the Western farmer back to his accustomed level of prosperity and to assure a permanent safety to both groups. That is why some enlightened industries themselves endeavor to limit the freedom of action of each man and business group within the industry in the common interest of all; why business men everywhere are asking a form of organization which will bring the scheme into balance, even though it may in some measure qualify the freedom of action of individual units within the business.

The exposition need not further be elaborated. It is brief and incomplete, but you will be able to expand it in terms of your own business or occupation without difficulty. I think everyone who has actually entered the economic struggle – which means everyone who was not born to safe wealth – knows in his own experience and his own life that we have now to apply the earlier concepts of American Government to the conditions of today.

The Declaration of Independence discusses the problem of Government in terms of a contract. Government is a relation of give and take, a contract, perforce, if we would follow the thinking out of which it grew. Under such a contract rulers were accorded power, and the people consented to that power on consideration that they be accorded certain rights. The task of statesmanship has always been the re-definition of these rights in terms of a changing and growing social order. New conditions impose new requirements upon Government and those who conduct Government.

I held, for example, in proceedings before me as Governor, the purpose of which was the removal of the Sheriff of New York, that under modern conditions it was not enough for a public official merely to evade the legal terms of official wrongdoing. He owned a positive duty as well. I said in substance that if he had acquired large sums of money, he was when accused required to explain the sources of such wealth. To that extent this wealth was colored with a public interest. I said that in financial matters, public servants should, even beyond private citizens, be held to a stern and uncompromising rectitude.

I feel that we are coming to a view through the drift of our legislation and our public thinking in the past quarter century that private economic power is, to enlarge an old phrase, a public trust as well. I hold that continued enjoyment of that power by any individual or group must depend upon the fulfillment of that trust. The men who have reached the summit of American business life know this best; happily, many of these urge the binding quality of this greater social contract.

The terms of that contract are as old as the Republic, and as new as the new economic order.

Every man has a right to life; and this means that he has also a right to make a comfortable living. He may by sloth or crime decline to exercise that right; but it may not be denied him. We have no actual famine or dearth; our industrial and agricultural mechanism can produce enough and to spare. Our Government formal and informal, political and economic, owes to everyone an avenue to possess himself of a portion of that plenty sufficient for his needs, through his own work.

Every man has a right to his own property; which means a right to be assured, to the fullest extent attainable, in the safety of his savings. By no other means can men carry the burdens of those parts of life which, in the nature of things, afford no chance of labor: childhood, sickness, old age. In all thought of property, this right is paramount; all other property rights must yield to it. If, in accord with this principle, we must restrict the operations of the speculator, the manipulator, even the financier, I believe we must accept the restriction as needful, not to hamper individualism but to protect it.

These two requirements must be satisfied, in the main, by the individuals who claim and hold control of the great industrial and financial combinations which dominate so large a part of our industrial life. They have undertaken to be, not business men, but princes of property. I am not prepared to say that the system which produces them is wrong. I am very clear that they must fearlessly and competently assume the responsibility which goes with the power. So many enlightened business men know this that the statement would be little more than a platitude, were it not for an added implication.

This implication is, briefly, that the responsible heads of finance and industry instead of acting each for himself, must work together to achieve the common end. They must, where necessary, sacrifice this or that private advantage; and in reciprocal self-denial must seek a general advantage. It is here that formal Government – political Government, if you choose – comes in. Whenever in the pursuit of this objective the lone wolf, the unethical competitor, the reckless promoter, the Ishmael or Insull whose hand is against every man's, declines to join in achieving an end recognized as being for the public welfare, and threatens to drag the industry back to a state of anarchy, the Government may properly be asked to apply restraint. Likewise, should the group ever use its collective power contrary to the public welfare, the Government must be swift to enter and protect the public interest.

The Government should assume the function of economic regulation only as a last resort, to be tried only when private initiative, inspired by high responsibility, with such assistance and balance as Government can give, has finally failed. As yet there has been no final failure, because there has been no attempt; and I decline to assume that this Nation is unable to meet the situation.

The final term of the high contract was for liberty and the pursuit of happiness. We have learned a great deal of both in the past century. We know that individual liberty and individual happiness mean nothing unless both are ordered in the sense that one man's meat is not another man's poison. We know that the old "rights of personal competency," the right to read, to think, to speak, to choose and live a mode of life, must be respected at all hazards. We know that liberty to do anything which deprives others of those elemental rights is outside the protection of any compact; and that Government in this regard is the maintenance of a balance, within which every individual may have a place if he will take it; in which every individual may find safety if he wishes it; in which every individual may attain such power as his ability permits, consistent with his assuming the accompanying responsibility.

All this is a long, slow talk. Nothing is more striking than the simple innocence of the men who insist, whenever an objective is present, on the prompt production of a patent scheme guaranteed to produce a result. Human endeavor is not so simple as that. Government includes the art of formulating a policy, and using the political technique to attain so much of that policy as will receive general support; persuading, leading, sacrificing, teaching always, because the greatest duty of a statesman is to educate. But in the matters of which I have spoken, we are learning rapidly, in a severe school. The lessons so learned must not be forgotten, even in the mental lethargy of a speculative upturn. We must build toward the time when a major depression cannot occur again; and if this means sacrificing the easy profits of inflationist booms, then let them go; and good riddance.

Faith in America, faith in our tradition of personal responsibility, faith in our institutions, faith in ourselves demand that we recognize the new terms of the old social contract. We shall fulfill them, as we fulfilled the obligation of the apparent Utopia which Jefferson imagined for us in 1776, and which Jefferson, Roosevelt and Wilson sought to bring to realization. We must do so, lest a rising tide of misery, engendered by our common failure, engulf us all. But failure is not an American habit; and in the strength of great hope we must all shoulder our common load.

Source: https://teachingamericanhistory.org/library/document/commonwealth-club-address/

Document Questions

Some answers may require more space than provided.

1. Is FDR's analysis more optimistic or pessimistic about the current state of the nation? How important is Turner's "frontier thesis" in FDR's analysis? What are its implications?

2. What does FDR see as the proper relationship between business and government?

3. FDR sees the Democrats as Jeffersonians and the Republicans as Hamiltonians. Is this accurate?

4. Does FDR distinguish between "property rights" and "human rights"?

5. What about the social contract?

CHAPTER EIGHTEEN

THE FINEST HOUR

World War II

Questions

Some answers may require more space than provided.

1. Besides being preoccupied with the Great Depression, why else did Americans largely ignore foreign developments during the 1930s?

2. Why is "isolationist" not the best way to describe American sentiment?

3. "It would be more accurate to say, instead, that in the interwar years, the US was reverting to a traditional policy of acting _____ and _____, with the _____ foremost in mind." (p. 317)

4. What part of the world experienced a marked improvement in relations with the United States in the interwar years? (p. 317)

5. In the meantime, what were Germany, Italy, and Japan all up to?

6. Why was the response of the Western democracies to these expanding threats weak and/or negligible?

7. What acts of aggression occurred in 1936–38?

8. What happened to the Chinese city of Nanking?

9. How did the Western democracies respond to these events?

10. How did British and French appeasement of Hitler lead to the outbreak of World War II in Europe in September 1939? (Recall that war was already going on in China.)

11. What did the Nye Committee report about why the United States entered World War I? How did this shape American reactions to foreign crises? (p. 319)

12. "A Gallup poll in March 1937 found that 94% … preferred efforts to keep America out of any foreign war over efforts to keep such wars from breaking out – a sentiment that can justly be described as _____ since it meant foreswearing any attempt by America to influence the flow of events in the world."

13. How did the neutrality acts play into the hands of the Axis aggressors?

14. What are the elements of Blitzkrieg?

15. By June 1940, all of Western Europe was _____. Britain stood alone behind its twenty-mile-wide moat, the English Channel. (p. 321)

16. What did the British save at Dunkirk?

17. As Churchill rallied the British people, what was FDR's response?

18. How close was Hitler to winning in 1940?

19. What strategy did Hitler adopt after the defeat of the Luftwaffe? (p. 322)

20. What did American ambassador Joseph Kennedy (father of president John F. Kennedy) advocate? Why? (p. 322)

21. How would you characterize the state of American public opinion about aiding Britain?

22. On what slogan did FDR run for a third term? What was the Republican position on the world war?

23. Upon reelection, FDR pledged to make the United States the "_____ _____" – providing aid to Britain, building up American power, and stimulating the economy.

24. After laying a principled foundation for war in the _____ speech, FDR asked for and Congress passed the _____, which effectively abandoned neutrality and committed the United States to aiding Britain in almost every way. (p. 324)

25. Beginning in September 1940, FDR issued "shoot on sight" orders to American ships, launching a _____ against German submarines. Isolationist

sentiment was still strong, and FDR would have been severely criticized had the public known. (p. 324)

26. Why did Japan have to expand? What did it lack and have to import?

27. Why did Roosevelt's oil embargo push the Japanese toward war with America?

28. The United States had _____ some of the Japanese _____. They knew by November 1941 that an attack was coming – but not _____. (p. 325)

29. What was the target of the Japanese carrier strike on Pearl Harbor? Why was the attack, although devastating, really a failure?

30. How did the American people respond to the Pearl Harbor attack?

31. Why was it folly for Hitler and Mussolini to declare war on the United States – a war FDR wanted (and was already secretly fighting) but that many Americans still wanted to stay out of?

32. We often forget that Stalin's Soviet Union was as much a totalitarian aggressor in 1939 as Germany. Stalin had in fact invaded Poland from the east when Hitler invaded it from the west but joined the _____ when Hitler betrayed him – they had previously sworn a pact of alliance – and invaded Russia in June 1941. (p. 327)

33. FDR changed from Dr. _____ into Dr. _____. How did American war production increase between 1942 and 1944? (pp. 327–28)

34. How many Americans served in the armed forces?

35. What prices were frozen, and what items were rationed?

36. What did Henry J. Kaiser contribute to the war effort?

37. As during World War I, many _____ and _____ entered the workforce. Many African Americans moved from the _____ to _____ to work in factories. (pp. 328–29)

38. How were Japanese Americans treated?

39. Why was the strategy to defeat Germany first?

40. How did the United States deal with the submarine threat?

41. Although the Allies drove the enemy out of Africa and then Sicily, Italy was not a _____ but rather _____.

42. Why is strategic bombing so controversial?

43. Why was Stalin desperate for his allies to invade first Italy and then France?

44. The _____ was "not only a masterwork of large-scale military and logistical planning but also a mosaic of countless individual acts of unbelievable valor and daring." (p. 332)

45. Patton's sweep across France "_____." (p. 333)

46. What did the Battle of the Bulge achieve for Germany?

47. Why did it matter who captured Berlin first?

48. What did the Big Three decide at Yalta?

49. Who made the decision to let the Russians capture Berlin? Why?

50. How did their victories in 1942 lead the Japanese to overextend themselves?

51. What happened first at the Coral Sea and then at Midway?

52. The first large-scale battle between the U.S. Marines and U.S. Army against the Japanese army was on _____. (pp. 335–36)

53. The United States launched a two-pronged offensive against Japan: General MacArthur drove across northern new Guinea toward the Philippines, while Admiral Nimitz _____ to the north. (p. 336)

54. FDR met with MacArthur and Nimitz and decided the next target should be the Philippines. An enormous air/sea battle, _____, destroyed the remaining Japanese fleet. (p. 336)

55. What new tactic did the Japanese introduce at Leyte Gulf?

56. Describe the Battle of Okinawa. What were the implications for an invasion of Japan?

57. FDR died as the war in Europe was ending. He was succeeded by _____. (p. 336)

58. What did Eisenhower do when he saw the death camp at Ohrdruf?

59. What were the alternatives to an invasion of Japan?

60. Why didn't the United States drop a demonstration bomb and demand surrender?

61. How many people died at Hiroshima?

62. Why was the war such a shock to ideas of progress and morality?

63. How did the war permanently change America?

Objective Questions

Put in order:

_____ Battle of Okinawa
_____ Hiroshima bombing
_____ Pearl Harbor attack

Put in order:

     ____ Battle of Britain
     ____ Blitz on London
     ____ Dunkirk

Put in order:

     ____ Battle of the Bulge
     ____ Fall of Berlin
     ____ Normandy invasion

Document

FRANKLIN D. ROOSEVELT, STATE OF THE UNION ADDRESS, "THE FOUR FREEDOMS," 1941

January 6, 1941

Mr. President, Mr. Speaker, Members of the Seventy-seventh Congress:

I address you, the Members of the Seventy-seventh Congress, at a moment unprecedented in the history of the Union. I use the word "unprecedented," because at no previous time has American security been as seriously threatened from without as it is today....

Even when the World War broke out in 1914, it seemed to contain only small threat of danger to our own American future. But, as time went on, the American people began to visualize what the downfall of democratic nations might mean to our own democracy.

We need not overemphasize imperfections in the Peace of Versailles. We need not harp on failure of the democracies to deal with problems of world reconstruction. We should remember that the Peace of 1919 was far less unjust than the kind of "pacification" which began even before Munich, and which is being carried on under the new order of tyranny that seeks to spread over every continent today. The American people have unalterably set their faces against that tyranny.

Every realist knows that the democratic way of life is at this moment being directly assailed in every part of the world – assailed either by arms, or by secret spreading of poisonous propaganda by those who seek to destroy unity and promote discord in nations that are still at peace.

During sixteen long months this assault has blotted out the whole pattern of democratic life in an appalling number of independent nations, great and small. The assailants are still on the march, threatening other nations, great and small.

Therefore, as your President, performing my constitutional duty to "give to the Congress information of the state of the Union," I find it, unhappily, necessary to report that the future and the safety of our country and of our democracy are overwhelmingly involved in events far beyond our borders.

Armed defense of democratic existence is now being gallantly waged in four continents. If that defense fails, all the population and all the resources of Europe, Asia, Africa and Australasia will be dominated by the conquerors. Let us remember that the total of those populations and their resources in those four continents greatly exceeds the sum total of the population and the resources of the whole of the Western Hemisphere – many times over.

In times like these it is immature – and incidentally, untrue – for anybody to brag that an unprepared America, single-handed, and with one hand tied behind its back, can hold off the whole world.

No realistic American can expect from a dictator's peace international generosity, or return of true independence, or world disarmament, or freedom of expression, or freedom of religion – or even good business....

The need of the moment is that our actions and our policy should be devoted primarily – almost exclusively – to meeting this foreign peril. For all our domestic problems are now a part of the great emergency.

Just as our national policy in internal affairs has been based upon a decent respect for the rights and the dignity of all our fellow men within our gates, so our national policy in foreign affairs has been based on a decent respect for the rights and dignity of all nations, large and small. And the justice of morality must and will win in the end. Our national policy is this:

First, by an impressive expression of the public will and without regard to partisanship, we are committed to all-inclusive national defense.

Second, by an impressive expression of the public will and without regard to partisanship, we are committed to full support of all those resolute peoples, everywhere, who are resisting aggression and are thereby keeping war away from our Hemisphere. By this support, we express our determination that the democratic cause shall prevail; and we strengthen the defense and the security of our own nation.

Third, by an impressive expression of the public will and without regard to partisanship, we are committed to the proposition that principles of morality and considerations for our own security will never permit us to acquiesce in a peace dictated by aggressors and sponsored by appeasers.

We know that enduring peace cannot be bought at the cost of other people's freedom.

In the recent national election there was no substantial difference between the two great parties in respect to that national policy. No issue was fought out on this line before the American electorate. Today it is abundantly evident that American citizens everywhere are demanding and supporting speedy and complete action in recognition of obvious danger.

Therefore, the immediate need is a swift and driving increase in our armament production....

A free nation has the right to expect full cooperation from all groups. A free nation has the right to look to the leaders of business, of labor, and of agriculture to take the lead in stimulating effort, not among other groups but within their own groups.

The best way of dealing with the few slackers or trouble makers in our midst is, first, to shame them by patriotic example, and, if that fails, to use the sovereignty of Government to save Government.

As men do not live by bread alone, they do not fight by armaments alone. Those who man our defenses, and those behind them who build our defenses, must have the stamina and the courage which come from unshakable belief in the manner of life which they are defending. The mighty action that we are calling for cannot be based on a disregard of all things worth fighting for.

The Nation takes great satisfaction and much strength from the things which have been done to make its people conscious of their individual stake in the preservation of democratic life in America. Those things have toughened the fiber of our people, have renewed their faith and strengthened their devotion to the institutions we make ready to protect.

Certainly this is no time for any of us to stop thinking about the social and economic problems which are the root cause of the social revolution which is today a supreme factor in the world.

For there is nothing mysterious about the foundations of a healthy and strong democracy. The basic things expected by our people of their political and economic systems are simple. They are:

Equality of opportunity for youth and for others.

Jobs for those who can work.

Security for those who need it.

The ending of special privilege for the few.

The preservation of civil liberties for all.

The enjoyment of the fruits of scientific progress in a wider and constantly rising standard of living.

These are the simple, basic things that must never be lost sight of in the turmoil and unbelievable complexity of our modern world. The inner and abiding strength of our economic and political systems is dependent upon the degree to which they fulfill these expectations.

Many subjects connected with our social economy call for immediate improvement. As examples:

We should bring more citizens under the coverage of old-age pensions and unemployment insurance.

We should widen the opportunities for adequate medical care.

We should plan a better system by which persons deserving or needing gainful employment may obtain it.

I have called for personal sacrifice. I am assured of the willingness of almost all Americans to respond to that call.

A part of the sacrifice means the payment of more money in taxes. In my Budget Message I shall recommend that a greater portion of this great defense program be paid for from taxation than we are paying today. No person should try, or be allowed, to get rich out of this program; and the principle of tax payments in accordance with ability to pay should be constantly before our eyes to guide our legislation.

If the Congress maintains these principles, the voters, putting patriotism ahead of pocketbooks, will give you their applause.

In the future days, which we seek to make secure, we look forward to a world founded upon four essential human freedoms.

The first is freedom of speech and expression – everywhere in the world.

The second is freedom of every person to worship God in his own way – everywhere in the world.

The third is freedom from want – which, translated into world terms, means economic understandings which will secure to every nation a healthy peacetime life for its inhabitants – everywhere in the world.

The fourth is freedom from fear – which, translated into world terms, means a world-wide reduction of armaments to such a point and in such a thorough fashion that no nation will be in a position to commit an act of physical aggression against any neighbor – anywhere in the world.

That is no vision of a distant millennium. It is a definite basis for a kind of world attainable in our own time and generation. That kind of world is the very antithesis of the so-called new order of tyranny which the dictators seek to create with the crash of a bomb.

To that new order we oppose the greater conception – the moral order. A good society is able to face schemes of world domination and foreign revolutions alike without fear.

Since the beginning of our American history, we have been engaged in change – in a perpetual peaceful revolution – a revolution which goes on steadily, quietly adjusting itself to changing conditions – without the concentration camp or the quick-lime in the ditch. The world order which we seek is the cooperation of free countries, working together in a friendly, civilized society.

This nation has placed its destiny in the hands and heads and hearts of its millions of free men and women; and its faith in freedom under the guidance of God. Freedom means the supremacy of human rights everywhere. Our support goes to those who struggle to gain those rights or keep them. Our strength is our unity of purpose. To that high concept there can be no end save victory.

Document Questions

Some answers may require more space than provided.

1. What is the situation in the world at the time of this speech (January 6, 1941?)

2. Is this a wartime speech?

3. How will the United States assist the democratic nations?

4. What is the United States' diplomatic stance toward "the dictators"?

5. What domestic programs does FDR mention – briefly?

6. This is called the "Four Freedoms" speech. Why does FDR end with those principles?

CHAPTER NINETEEN

ALL THOUGHTS AND THINGS WERE SPLIT

The Cold War

Questions

Some answers may require more space than provided.

1. The end of the war was also the end of the Depression. What was the greatest fear felt by the American public?

2. Were those fears realized?

3. The forced savings of _____ (e.g., no new automobiles, as Detroit was making military vehicles) meant lots of pent-up _____, which American business was eager to meet. (p. 342)

4. What happened to GNP between 1945 and 1970?

5. How did the automobile industry fare?

6. How did housing patterns change?

7. What did the GI Bill do for veterans?

8. Between the end of the war and 1960, the American population increased by _____, almost all from the "baby boom." (p. 344)

9. What psychological stresses did Americans, and especially returning veterans, face?

10. What is the theme of Sloan Wilson's *The Man in the Grey Flannel Suit*?

11. Why was the Cold War always especially frightening?

12. One historian called postwar America a "_____." (p. 346)

13. What was Truman's personal background and early career? How did he overcome his earlier association with the corrupt _____ machine and become respected enough to be chosen to succeed FDR? (pp. 346–47)

14. FDR "had been formed in the well-pedigreed political tradition of Jefferson and Wilson; Truman was a product of the great _____ of Jackson and Lincoln, both of them _____." (p. 348)

15. What happened in the midterm elections of 1946?

16. The Republicans overrode a Truman veto to pass in 1947 the _____, designed to pare back the power of labor unions. (p. 348)

17. Why was the wartime alliance between Stalin's Soviet Union and the Western democracies short-lived?

18. Who coined the widely accepted term or metaphor for the division between the free world and the Communist?

19. Did the Russians have legitimate grievances against the Americans and British? Did those grievances justify Soviet deceptions and broken promises?

20. Stalin tried to dominate _____, gaining control of the eastern Mediterranean and threatening the _____. (p. 350)

21. How did George Kennan help lay down the theoretical basis for the Cold War?

22. Why did "containment" of Soviet power have to include an economic as well as a political and diplomatic and military component?

23. Who would the Marshall Plan have helped? Who refused the help?

24. How much money did the Marshall Plan provide to Europe? What was the result?

25. Where is Berlin located in respect to East and West Germany? How did Stalin threaten the Western occupation of West Berlin? How did the United States respond?

26. What is NATO?

27. What role did Truman play in the creation of Israel?

28. Why was Truman's reelection in 1948 an uphill fight?

29. How did Truman win?

30. What was happening in China? How did the United States respond?

31. To what extent was the second "Red Scare" justified? Why?

32. Why did Korea become a hot battlefield in the Cold War?

33. How did Truman respond?

34. How did the war go?

35. Why did Truman fire MacArthur?

35. What did firing MacArthur cost Truman?

37. Who was right, in your opinion?

38. What was Eisenhower's background before being elected president?

39. What was Eisenhower's domestic program?

40. What was Eisenhower's Cold War strategy?

41. American goals in the Cold War were to effectively _____
_____ but also _____. These were
often incompatible. (p. 361)

42. Why did the CIA's actions in Iran produce favorable short-term success but
have far less favorable long-term consequences?

43. Why did the United States take France's side in Indochina?

44. How was Indochina divided?

45. Who did Eisenhower support in South Vietnam?

46. What happened in the Suez Crisis?

47. How did Cuba change from Batista's dictatorship to Castro's?

48. Is it just coincidence that the civil rights movement gained strength and eventually prevailed during the Cold War?

Put in order:

_____ Marshall Plan
_____ Korean War
_____ Suez Crisis

GEORGE KENNAN, THE SOURCES OF SOVIET CONDUCT, 1947

PART I

The political personality of Soviet power as we know it today is the product of ideology and circumstances: ideology inherited by the present Soviet leaders from the movement in which they had their political origin, and circumstances of the power which they now have exercised for nearly three decades in Russia. There can be few tasks of psychological analysis more difficult than to try to trace the interaction of these two forces and the relative role of each in the determination of official Soviet conduct. yet the attempt must be made if that conduct is to be understood and effectively countered.

It is difficult to summarize the set of ideological concepts with which the Soviet leaders came into power. Marxian ideology, in its Russian-Communist projection, has always been in process of subtle evolution. The materials on which it bases itself are extensive and complex. But the outstanding features of Communist thought as it existed in 1916 may perhaps be summarized as follows: (a) that the central factor in the life of man, the factor which determines the character of public life and the "physiognomy of society," is the system by which material goods are produced and exchanged; (b) that the capitalist system of production is a nefarious one which inevitably leads to the exploitation of the working class by the capital-owning class and is incapable of developing adequately the economic resources of society or of distributing fairly the material good produced by human labor; (c) that capitalism contains the seeds of its own destruction and must, in view of the inability of the capital-owning class to adjust itself to economic change, result eventually and inescapably in a revolutionary transfer of power to the working class; and (d) that imperialism, the final phase of capitalism, leads directly to war and revolution.

The rest may be outlined in Lenin's own words: "Unevenness of economic and political development is the inflexible law of capitalism. It follows from this that the victory of Socialism may come originally in a few capitalist countries or even in a single capitalist country. The victorious proletariat of that country, having expropriated the capitalists and having organized Socialist production at home, would rise against the remaining capitalist world, drawing to itself in the process the oppressed classes of other countries." It must be noted that there was no assumption that capitalism would perish without proletarian revolution. A final push was needed from a revolutionary proletariat movement in order to tip over the tottering structure. But it was regarded as inevitable that sooner or later that push be given.

For 50 years prior to the outbreak of the Revolution, this pattern of thought had exercised great fascination for the members of the Russian revolutionary movement. Frustrated, discontented, hopeless of finding self-expression – or too impatient to seek it – in the confining limits of the Tsarist political system, yet lacking wide popular support or their choice of bloody revolution as a means of social betterment, these revolutionists found in Marxist theory a highly convenient rationalization for their own instinctive desires. It afforded pseudo-scientific justification for their impatience, for their categoric denial of all value in the Tsarist system, for their yearning for power and revenge and for their inclination to cut corners in the pursuit of it. It is therefore no wonder that they had come to believe implicitly in the truth and soundness of the Marxist–Leninist teachings, so congenial to their own impulses and emotions. Their sincerity need not be impugned. This is a phenomenon as old as human nature itself. It has never been more aptly described than by Edward Gibbon, who wrote in *The Decline and Fall of the Roman Empire*: "From enthusiasm to imposture the step is perilous and slippery; the demon of Socrates affords a memorable instance of how a wise man may deceive himself, how a good man may deceive others, how the conscience may slumber in a mixed and middle state between self-illusion and voluntary fraud." And it was with this set of conceptions that the members of the Bolshevik Party entered into power.

Now it must be noted that through all the years of preparation for revolution, the attention of these men, as indeed of Marx himself, had been centered less on the future form which Socialism would take than on the necessary overthrow of rival power which, in their view, had to precede the introduction of Socialism. Their views, therefore, on the positive program to be put into effect, once power was attained, were for the most part nebulous, visionary and impractical. Beyond the nationalization of industry and the expropriation of large private capital holdings there was no agreed program. The treatment of the peasantry, which, according to the Marxist formulation was not of the proletariat, had always been a vague spot in the pattern of Communist thought: and it remained an object of controversy and vacillation for the first ten years of Communist power.

The circumstances of the immediate post-revolution period – the existence in Russia of civil war and foreign intervention, together with the obvious fact that the Communists represented only a tiny minority of the Russian people – made the establishment of dictatorial power a necessity. The experiment with war Communism and the abrupt attempt to eliminate private production and trade had unfortunate economic consequences and caused further bitterness against the new revolutionary regime. While the temporary relaxation of the effort to communize Russia, represented by the New Economic Policy, alleviated some of this economic distress and thereby served its purpose, it also made it evident that the "capitalistic sector of society" was still prepared to profit at once from any relaxation of governmental pressure, and would, if permitted to continue to exist, always constitute a powerful opposing element to the Soviet regime and a serious rival for influence in the country. Somewhat the same situation prevailed with respect to the individual peasant who, in his own small way, was also a private producer.

Lenin, had he lived, might have proved a great enough man to reconcile these conflicting forces to the ultimate benefit of Russian society, though this is questionable. But be that as it may, Stalin, and those whom he led in the struggle for succession to Lenin's position of leadership, were not the men to tolerate rival political forces in the sphere of power which they coveted. Their sense of insecurity was too great. Their particular brand of fanaticism, unmodified by any of the Anglo-Saxon traditions of compromise, was too fierce and too jealous to envisage any permanent sharing of power. From the Russian–Asiatic world out of which they had emerged they carried with them a skepticism as to the possibilities of permanent and peaceful coexistence of rival forces. Easily persuaded of their own doctrinaire "rightness," they insisted on the submission or destruction of all competing power. Outside the Communist Party, Russian society was to have no rigidity. There were to be no forms of collective human activity or association which would not be dominated by the Party. No other force in Russian society was to be permitted to achieve vitality or integrity. Only the Party was to have structure. All else was to be an amorphous mass.

And within the Party the same principle was to apply. The mass of Party members might go through the motions of election, deliberation, decision and action; but in these motions they were to be animated not by their own individual wills but by the awesome breath of the Party leadership and the over-brooding presence of "the word."

Let it be stressed again that subjectively these men probably did not seek absolutism for its own sake. They doubtless believed – and found it easy to believe – that they alone knew what was good for society and that they would accomplish that good once their power was secure and unchallengeable. But in seeking that security of their own rule they were prepared to recognize no restrictions, either of God or man, on the character of their methods. And until such time as that security might be achieved, they placed far down on their scale of operational priorities the comforts and happiness of the peoples entrusted to their care.

Now the outstanding circumstance concerning the Soviet regime is that down to the present day this process of political consolidation has never been completed and the men in the Kremlin have continued to be predominantly absorbed with the struggle to secure and make absolute the power which they seized in November 1917. They have endeavored to secure it primarily against forces at home, within Soviet society itself. But they have also endeavored to secure it against the outside world. For ideology, as we have seen, taught them that the outside world was hostile and that it was their duty eventually to over-throw the political forces beyond their borders. Then powerful hands of Russian history and tradition reached up to sustain them in this feeling. Finally, their own aggressive intransigence with respect to the outside world began to find its own reaction; and they were soon forced, to use another Gibbonesque phrase, "to chastise the contumacy" which they themselves had provoked. It is an undeniable privilege of every man to prove himself right in the thesis that the world is his enemy; for if he reiterates it frequently enough and makes it the background of his conduct he is bound eventually to be right.

Now it lies in the nature of the mental world of the Soviet leaders, as well as in the character of their ideology, that no opposition to them can be officially recognized as having any merit or justification whatsoever. Such opposition can flow, in theory, only from the hostile and incorrigible forces of dying capitalism. As long as remnants of capitalism were officially recognized as existing in Russia, it was possible to place on them, as an internal element, part of the blame for the maintenance of a dictatorial form of society. But as these remnants were liquidated, little by little, this justification fell away, and when it was indicated officially that they had been finally destroyed, it disappeared altogether. And this fact created one of the most basic of the compulsions which came to act upon the Soviet regime: since capitalism no longer existed in Russia and since it could not be admitted that there could be serious or widespread opposition to the Kremlin springing spontaneously from the liberated masses under its authority, it became necessary to justify the retention of the dictatorship by stressing the menace of capitalism abroad.

This began at an early date. In 1924 Stalin specifically defended the retention of the "organs of suppression," meaning, among others, the army and the secret police, on the ground that "as long as there is a capitalistic encirclement there will be danger of intervention with all the consequences that flow from that danger." In accordance with that theory, and from that time on, all internal opposition forces in Russia have consistently been portrayed as the agents of foreign forces of reaction antagonistic to Soviet power.

By the same token, tremendous emphasis has been placed on the original Communist thesis of a basic antagonism between the capitalist and Socialist worlds. It is clear, from many indications, that this emphasis is not founded in reality. The real facts concerning it have been confused by the existence abroad of genuine resentment provoked by Soviet philosophy and tactics and occasionally by the existence of great centers of military power, notably the Nazi regime in Germany and the Japanese Government of the late 1930s, which indeed have aggressive designs against the Soviet Union. But there is ample evidence that the stress laid in Moscow on the menace confronting Soviet society from the world outside its borders is founded not in the realities of foreign antagonism but in the necessity of explaining away the maintenance of dictatorial authority at home.

Now the maintenance of this pattern of Soviet power, namely, the pursuit of unlimited authority domestically, accompanied by the cultivation of the semi-myth of implacable foreign hostility, has gone far to shape the actual machinery of Soviet power as we know it today. Internal organs of administration which did not serve this purpose withered on the vine. Organs which did serve this purpose became vastly swollen. The security of Soviet power came to rest on the iron discipline of the Party, on the severity and ubiquity of the secret police, and on the uncompromising economic monopolism of the state. The "organs of suppression," in which the Soviet leaders had sought security from rival forces, became in large measures the masters of those whom they were designed to serve. Today the major part of the structure of Soviet power is committed to the perfection of the dictatorship and to the maintenance of the concept of Russia as in a state of siege, with the enemy lowering beyond the walls. And the millions of human beings who form that part of the structure of power must defend at all costs this concept of Russia's position, for without it they are themselves superfluous.

As things stand today, the rulers can no longer dream of parting with these organs of suppression. The quest for absolute power, pursued now for nearly three decades with a ruthlessness unparalleled (in scope at least) in modern times, has again produced internally, as it did externally, its own reaction. The excesses of the police apparatus have fanned the potential opposition to the regime into something far greater and more dangerous than it could have been before those excesses began.

But least of all can the rulers dispense with the fiction by which the maintenance of dictatorial power has been defended. For this fiction has been canonized in Soviet philosophy by the excesses already committed in its name; and it is now anchored in the Soviet structure of thought by bonds far greater than those of mere ideology.

PART II

So much for the historical background. What does it spell in terms of the political personality of Soviet power as we know it today?

Of the original ideology, nothing has been officially junked. Belief is maintained in the basic badness of capitalism, in the inevitability of its destruction, in the obligation of the proletariat to assist in that destruction and to take power into its own hands. But stress has come to be laid primarily on those concepts which relate most specifically to the Soviet regime itself: to its position as the sole truly Socialist regime in a dark and misguided world, and to the relationships of power within it.

The first of these concepts is that of the innate antagonism between capitalism and Socialism. We have seen how deeply that concept has become imbedded in foundations of Soviet power. It has profound implications for Russia's conduct as a member of international society. It means that there can never be on Moscow's side an sincere assumption of a community of aims between the Soviet Union and powers which are regarded as capitalist. It must inevitably be assumed in Moscow that the aims of the capitalist world are antagonistic to the Soviet regime, and therefore to the interests of the peoples it controls. If the Soviet government occasionally sets its signature to documents which would indicate the contrary, this is to be regarded as a tactical maneuver permissible in dealing with the enemy (who is without honor) and should be taken in the spirit of *caveat emptor*. Basically, the antagonism remains. It is postulated. And from it flow many of the phenomena which we find disturbing in the Kremlin's conduct of foreign policy: the secretiveness, the lack of frankness, the duplicity, the wary suspiciousness, and the basic unfriendliness of purpose. These phenomena are there to stay, for the foreseeable future. There can be variations of degree and of emphasis. When there is something the Russians want from us, one or the other of these features of their policy may be thrust temporarily into the background; and when that happens there will always be Americans who will leap forward with gleeful announcements that "the Russians have changed," and some who will even try to take credit for having brought about such "changes." But we should not be misled by tactical maneuvers. These characteristics of Soviet policy, like the postulate from which they flow, are basic to the internal nature of Soviet power, and will be with us, whether in the foreground or the background, until the internal nature of Soviet power is changed.

This means we are going to continue for a long time to find the Russians difficult to deal with. It does not mean that they should be considered as embarked upon a do-or-die program to overthrow our society by a given date. The theory of the inevitability of the eventual fall of capitalism has the fortunate connotation that there is no hurry about it. The forces of progress can take their time in preparing the final coup de grâce. Meanwhile, what is vital is that the "Socialist fatherland" – that oasis of power which has already been won for Socialism in the person of the Soviet Union – should be cherished and defended by all good Communists at home and abroad, its fortunes promoted, its enemies badgered and confounded. The promotion of premature, "adventuristic" revolutionary projects abroad which might embarrass Soviet power in any way would be an inexcusable, even a counter-revolutionary act. The cause of Socialism is the support and promotion of Soviet power, as defined in Moscow.

This brings us to the second of the concepts important to contemporary Soviet outlook. That is the infallibility of the Kremlin. The Soviet concept of power, which permits no focal points of organization outside the Party itself, requires that the Party leadership remain in theory the sole repository of truth. For if truth were to be found elsewhere, there would be justification for its expression in organized activity. But it is precisely that which the Kremlin cannot and will not permit.

The leadership of the Communist Party is therefore always right, and has been always right ever since in 1929 Stalin formalized his personal power by announcing that decisions of the Politburo were being taken unanimously.

On the principle of infallibility there rests the iron discipline of the Communist Party. In fact, the two concepts are mutually self-supporting. Perfect discipline requires recognition of infallibility. Infallibility requires the observance of discipline. And the two go far to determine the behaviorism of the entire Soviet apparatus of power. But their effect cannot be understood unless a third factor be taken into account: namely, the fact that the leadership is at liberty to put forward for tactical purposes any particular thesis which it finds useful to the cause at any particular moment and to require the faithful and unquestioning acceptance of that thesis by the members of the movement as a whole. This means that truth is not a constant but is actually created, for all intents and purposes, by the Soviet leaders themselves. It may vary from week to week, from month to month. It is nothing absolute and immutable – nothing which flows from objective reality. It is only the most recent manifestation of the wisdom of those in whom the ultimate wisdom is supposed to reside, because they represent the logic of history. The accumulative effect of these factors is to give to the whole subordinate apparatus of Soviet power an unshakable stubbornness and steadfastness in its orientation. This orientation can be changed at will by the Kremlin but by no other power. Once a given party line has been laid down on a given issue of current policy, the whole Soviet governmental machine, including the mechanism of diplomacy, moves inexorably along the prescribed path, like a persistent toy automobile wound up and headed in a given direction, stopping only when it meets with some unanswerable force. The individuals who are the components of this machine are unamenable to argument or reason, which comes to them from outside sources. Their whole training has taught them to mistrust and discount the glib persuasiveness of the outside world. Like the white dog before the phonograph, they hear only the "master's voice." And if they are to be called off from the purposes last dictated to them, it is the master who must call them off. Thus the foreign representative cannot hope that his words will make any impression on them. The most that he can hope is that they will be transmitted to those at the top, who are capable of changing the party line. But even those are not likely to be swayed by any normal logic in the words of the bourgeois representative. Since there can be no appeal to common purposes, there can be no appeal to common mental approaches. For this reason, facts speak louder than words to the ears of the Kremlin; and words carry the greatest weight when they have the ring of reflecting, or being backed up by, facts of unchallengeable validity.

But we have seen that the Kremlin is under no ideological compulsion to accomplish its purposes in a hurry. Like the Church, it is dealing in ideological concepts which are of long-term validity, and it can afford to be patient. It has no right to risk the existing achievements of the revolution for the sake of vain baubles of the future. The very teachings of Lenin himself require great caution and flexibility in the pursuit of Communist purposes. Again, these precepts are fortified by the lessons of Russian history: of centuries of obscure battles between nomadic forces over the stretches of a vast unfortified plain. Here caution, circumspection, flexibility and deception are the valuable qualities; and their value finds a natural appreciation in the Russian or the oriental mind. Thus the Kremlin has no compunction about retreating in the face of superior forces. And being under the compulsion of no timetable, it does not get panicky under the necessity for such retreat. Its political action is a fluid stream which moves constantly, wherever it is permitted to move, toward a given goal. Its main concern is to make sure that it has filled every nook and cranny available to it in the basin of world power. But if it finds unassailable barriers in its path, it accepts these philosophically and accommodates itself to them. The main thing is that there should always be pressure, unceasing constant pressure, toward the desired goal. There is no trace of any feeling in Soviet psychology that that goal must be reached at any given time.

These considerations make Soviet diplomacy at once easier and more difficult to deal with than the diplomacy of individual aggressive leaders like Napoleon and Hitler. On the one hand it is more sensitive to contrary force, more ready to yield on individual sectors of the diplomatic front when that force is felt to be too strong, and thus more rational in the logic and rhetoric of power. On the other hand it cannot be easily defeated or discouraged by a single victory on the part of its opponents. And the patient persistence by which it is animated means that it can be effectively countered not by sporadic acts which represent the momentary whims of democratic opinion but only by intelligent long-range policies on the part of Russia's adversaries – policies no less steady in their purpose, and no less variegated and resourceful in their application, than those of the Soviet Union itself.

In these circumstances it is clear that the main element of any United States policy toward the Soviet Union must be that of long-term, patient but firm and vigilant containment of Russian expansive tendencies. It is important to note, however, that such a policy has nothing to do with outward histrionics: with threats or blustering or superfluous gestures of outward "toughness." While the Kremlin is basically flexible in its reaction to political realities, it is by no means unamenable to considerations of prestige. Like almost any other government, it can be placed by tactless and threatening gestures in a position where it cannot afford to yield even though this might be dictated by its sense of realism. The Russian leaders are keen judges of human psychology, and as such they are highly conscious that loss of temper and of self-control is never a source of strength in political affairs. They are quick to exploit such evidences of weakness. For these reasons it is a *sine qua non* of successful dealing with Russia that the foreign government in question should remain at all times cool and collected and that its demands on Russian policy should be put forward in such a manner as to leave the way open for a compliance not too detrimental to Russian prestige.

PART III

In the light of the above, it will be clearly seen that the Soviet pressure against the free institutions of the western world is something that can be contained by the adroit and vigilant application of counter-force at a series of constantly shifting geographical and political points, corresponding to the shifts and maneuvers of

Soviet policy, but which cannot be charmed or talked out of existence. The Russians look forward to a duel of infinite duration, and they see that already they have scored great successes. It must be borne in mind that there was a time when the Communist Party represented far more of a minority in the sphere of Russian national life than Soviet power today represents in the world community.

But if the ideology convinces the rulers of Russia that truth is on their side and they can therefore afford to wait, those of us on whom that ideology has no claim are free to examine objectively the validity of that premise. The Soviet thesis not only implies complete lack of control by the west over its own economic destiny, it likewise assumes Russian unity, discipline and patience over an infinite period. Let us bring this apocalyptic vision down to earth, and suppose that the western world finds the strength and resourcefulness to contain Soviet power over a period of ten to fifteen years. What does that spell for Russia itself?

The Soviet leaders, taking advantage of the contributions of modern techniques to the arts of despotism, have solved the question of obedience within the confines of their power. Few challenge their authority; and even those who do are unable to make that challenge valid as against the organs of suppression of the state.

The Kremlin has also proved able to accomplish its purpose of building up Russia, regardless of the interests of the inhabitants, and industrial foundation of heavy metallurgy, which is, to be sure, not yet complete but which is nevertheless continuing to grow and is approaching those of the other major industrial countries. All of this, however, both the maintenance of internal political security and the building of heavy industry, has been carried out at a terrible cost in human life and in human hopes and energies. It has necessitated the use of forced labor on a scale unprecedented in modern times under conditions of peace. It has involved the neglect or abuse of other phases of Soviet economic life, particularly agriculture, consumers' goods production, housing and transportation.

To all that, the war has added its tremendous toll of destruction, death and human exhaustion. In consequence of this, we have in Russia today a population which is physically and spiritually tired. The mass of the people are disillusioned, skeptical and no longer as accessible as they once were to the magical attraction which Soviet power still radiates to its followers abroad. The avidity with which people seized upon the slight respite accorded to the Church for tactical reasons during the war was eloquent testimony to the fact that their capacity for faith and devotion found little expression in the purposes of the regime.

In these circumstances, there are limits to the physical and nervous strength of people themselves. These limits are absolute ones, and are binding even for the cruelest dictatorship, because beyond them people cannot be driven.

The forced labor camps and the other agencies of constraint provide temporary means of compelling people to work longer hours than their own volition or mere economic pressure would dictate; but if people survive them at all they become old before their time and must be considered as human casualties to the demands of dictatorship. In either case their best powers are no longer available to society and can no longer be enlisted in the service of the state.

Here only the younger generations can help. The younger generation, despite all vicissitudes and sufferings, is numerous and vigorous; and the Russians are a talented people. But it still remains to be seen what will be the effects on mature performance of the abnormal emotional strains of childhood which Soviet dictatorship created and which were enormously increased by the war. Such things as normal security and placidity of home environment have practically ceased to exist in the Soviet Union outside of the most remote farms and villages. And observers are not yet sure whether that is not going to leave its mark on the over-all capacity of the generation now coming into maturity.

In addition to this, we have the fact that Soviet economic development, while it can list certain formidable achievements, has been precariously spotty and uneven. Russian Communists who speak of the "uneven development of capitalism" should blush at the contemplation of their own national economy. Here certain branches of economic life, such as the metallurgical and machine industries, have been pushed out of all proportion to other sectors of the economy. Here is a nation striving to become in a short period one of the great industrial nations of the world while it still has no highway network worthy of the name and only a relatively primitive network of railways. Much has been done to increase efficiency of labor and to teach primitive peasants something about the operation of machines. But maintenance is still a crying deficiency of all Soviet economy. Construction is hasty and poor in quality. Depreciation must be enormous. And in vast sectors of economic life it has not yet been possible to instill into labor anything like that general culture of production and technical self-respect which characterizes the skilled worker of the west.

It is difficult to see how these deficiencies can be corrected at an early date by a tired and dispirited population working largely under the shadow of fear and compulsion. And as long as they are not overcome, Russia will remain economically as vulnerable, and in a certain sense an impotent, nation, capable of exporting its enthusiasms and of radiating the strange charm of its primitive political vitality but unable to back up those articles of export by the real evidences of material power and prosperity.

Meanwhile, a great uncertainty hangs over the political life of the Soviet Union. That is the uncertainty involved in the transfer of power from one individual or group of individuals to others.

This is, of course, outstandingly the problem of the personal position of Stalin. We must remember that his succession to Lenin's pinnacle of pre-eminence in the Communist movement was the only such transfer of individual authority which the Soviet Union has experienced. That transfer took 12 years to consolidate. It cost the lives of millions of people and shook the state to its foundations. The attendant tremors were felt all through the international revolutionary movement, to the disadvantage of the Kremlin itself.

It is always possible that another transfer of pre-eminent power may take place quietly and inconspicuously, with no repercussions anywhere. But again, it is possible that the questions involved may unleash, to use some of Lenin's words, one of those "incredibly swift transitions" from "delicate deceit" to "wild violence" which characterize Russian history, and may shake Soviet power to its foundations.

But this is not only a question of Stalin himself. There has been, since 1938, a dangerous congealment of political life in the higher circles of Soviet power. The All-Union Congress of Soviets, in theory the supreme body of the Party, is supposed to meet not less often than once in three years. It will soon be eight full years since its last meeting. During this period membership in the Party has numerically doubled. Party mortality during the war was enormous; and today well over half of the Party members are persons who have entered since the last Party congress was held. meanwhile, the same small group of men has carried on at the top through an amazing series of national vicissitudes. Surely there is some reason why the experiences of the war brought basic political changes to every one of the great governments of the west. Surely the causes of that phenomenon are basic enough to be present somewhere in the obscurity of Soviet political life, as well. And yet no recognition has been given to these causes in Russia.

It must be surmised from this that even within so highly disciplined an organization as the Communist Party there must be a growing divergence in age, outlook and interest between the great mass of Party members, only so recently recruited into the movement, and the little self-perpetuating clique of men at the top, whom most of these Party members have never met, with whom they have never conversed, and with whom they can have no political intimacy.

Who can say whether, in these circumstances, the eventual rejuvenation of the higher spheres of authority (which can only be a matter of time) can take place smoothly and peacefully, or whether rivals in the quest for higher power will not eventually reach down into these politically immature and inexperienced masses in order to find support for their respective claims? If this were ever to happen, strange consequences could flow for the Communist Party: for the membership at large has been exercised only in the practices of iron discipline and obedience and not in the arts of compromise and accommodation. And if disunity were ever to seize and paralyze the Party, the chaos and weakness of Russian society would be revealed in forms beyond description. For we have seen that Soviet power is only concealing an amorphous mass of human beings among whom no independent organizational structure is tolerated. In Russia there is not even such a thing as local government. The present generation of Russians have never known spontaneity of collective action. If, consequently, anything were ever to occur to disrupt the unity and efficacy of the Party as a political instrument, Soviet Russia might be changed overnight from one of the strongest to one of the weakest and most pitiable of national societies.

Thus the future of Soviet power may not be by any means as secure as Russian capacity for self-delusion would make it appear to the men of the Kremlin. That they can quietly and easily turn it over to others remains to be proved. Meanwhile, the hardships of their rule and the vicissitudes of international life have taken a heavy toll of the strength and hopes of the great people on whom their power rests. It is curious to note that the ideological power of Soviet authority is strongest today in areas beyond the frontiers of Russia, beyond the reach of its police power. This phenomenon brings to mind a comparison used by Thomas Mann in his great novel *Buddenbrooks*. Observing that human institutions often show the greatest outward brilliance at a moment when inner decay is in reality farthest advanced, he compared one of those stars whose light shines most brightly on this world when in reality it has long since ceased to exist. And who can say with assurance that the strong light still cast by the Kremlin on the dissatisfied peoples of the western world is not the powerful afterglow of a constellation which is in actuality on the wane? This cannot be proved. And it cannot be disproved. But the possibility remains (and in the opinion of this writer it is a strong one) that Soviet power, like the capitalist world of its conception, bears within it the seeds of its own decay, and that the sprouting of these seeds is well advanced.

PART IV

It is clear that the United States cannot expect in the foreseeable future to enjoy political intimacy with the Soviet regime. It must continue to regard the Soviet Union as a rival, not a partner, in the political arena. It must continue to expect that Soviet policies will reflect no abstract love of peace and stability, no real faith in the possibility of a permanent happy coexistence of the Socialist and capitalist worlds, but rather a cautious, persistent pressure toward the disruption and, weakening of all rival influence and rival power.

Balanced against this are the facts that Russia, as opposed to the western world in general, is still by far the weaker party, that Soviet policy is highly flexible, and that Soviet society may well contain deficiencies which will eventually weaken its own total potential. This would of itself warrant the United States entering with reasonable confidence upon a policy of firm containment, designed to confront the Russians with unalterable counter-force at every point where they show signs of encroaching upon the interests of a peaceful and stable world.

But in actuality the possibilities for American policy are by no means limited to holding the line and hoping for the best. It is entirely possible for the United States to influence by its actions the internal developments, both within Russia and throughout the international Communist movement, by which Russian policy is largely determined. This is not only a question of the modest measure of informational activity which this government can conduct in the Soviet Union and elsewhere, although that, too, is important. It is rather a question of the degree to which the United States can create among the peoples of the world generally the impression of a country which knows what it wants, which is coping successfully with the problem of its internal life and with the responsibilities of a World Power, and which has a spiritual vitality capable of holding its own among the major ideological currents of the time. To the extent that such an impression can be created and maintained, the aims of Russian Communism must appear sterile and quixotic, the hopes and enthusiasm of Moscow's supporters must wane, and added strain must be imposed on the Kremlin's foreign policies. For the palsied decrepitude of the capitalist world is the keystone of Communist philosophy. Even the failure of the United States to experience the early economic depression which the ravens of the Red Square have been predicting with such complacent confidence since hostilities ceased would have deep and important repercussions throughout the Communist world.

By the same token, exhibitions of indecision, disunity and internal disintegration within this country have an exhilarating effect on the whole Communist movement. At each evidence of these tendencies, a thrill of hope and excitement goes through the Communist world; a new jauntiness can be noted in the Moscow tread; new groups of foreign supporters climb on to what they can only view as the band wagon of international politics; and Russian pressure increases all along the line in international affairs.

It would be an exaggeration to say that American behavior unassisted and alone could exercise a power of life and death over the Communist movement and bring about the early fall of Soviet power in Russia. But the United States has it in its power to increase enormously the strains under which Soviet policy must operate, to force upon the Kremlin a far greater degree of moderation and circumspection than it has had to observe in recent years, and in this way to promote tendencies which must eventually find their outlet in either the breakup or the gradual mellowing of Soviet power. For no mystical, Messianic movement – and particularly not that of the Kremlin – can face frustration indefinitely without eventually adjusting itself in one way or another to the logic of that state of affairs.

Thus the decision will really fall in large measure in this country itself. The issue of Soviet-American relations is in essence a test of the overall worth of the United States as a nation among nations. To avoid destruction the United States need only measure up to its own best traditions and prove itself worthy of preservation as a great nation.

Surely, there was never a fairer test of national quality than this. In the light of these circumstances, the thoughtful observer of Russian–American relations will find no cause for complaint in the Kremlin's challenge to American society. He will rather experience a certain gratitude to a Providence which, by providing the American people with this implacable challenge, has made their entire security as a nation dependent on their pulling themselves together and accepting the responsibilities of moral and political leadership that history plainly intended them to bear.

Document Questions

Some answers may require more space than provided.

1. Which does Kennan think is the more important influence on Soviet conduct: ideology or circumstances?

2. Is real peace or friendship possible between the capitalist world and the Soviet Union?

3. What are the implications of this assumption of antagonism?

4. What should the U.S. policy be toward the Soviets?

5. What weaknesses may a policy of containment exacerbate within the Soviet system?

6. What does Kennan hope for the future?

CHAPTER TWENTY

OUT OF BALANCE

The Turbulent Sixties

Questions

Some answers may require more space than provided.

1. Could Eisenhower have won a third term? Why couldn't he run?

2. Of what did Eisenhower warn in his Farewell Address to the Nation?

3. Yet Eisenhower had presided over the consolidation of the "_____" state, in which the demands of expensive New Deal programs and constant military readiness dictated a sprawling federal government. (p. 367)

4. The great need was for _____, a word Eisenhower used ten times in his farewell speech. (p. 367)

5. Why was the 1960 campaign noteworthy?

6. What tone did JFK's inaugural address set?

7. Who did JFK recruit to run his administration?

8. How effective was JFK in getting his programs enacted by Congress?

9. What was the effect of slashing income tax rates?

10. Why was JFK so committed to the exploration of space?

11. How effective was JFK's Cuban policy?

12. What happened when JFK met Soviet leader Khrushchev two months later?

13. Who won the Cuban Missile Crisis?

14. What other foreign policy headache did JFK inherit?

15. What was the effect of Kennedy's assassination?

16. What progress did the civil rights movement make after World War II?

17. LBJ was described as _____ – yet he had a heart for the underprivileged. This led to his _____ programs, which went far beyond what the New Deal had created. (pp. 376–77)

18. How did the Republican Party split in 1964?

19. What were the two consoling features of Goldwater's loss for conservatives?

20. What were the main elements of Johnson's Great Society?

21. How successful was the Great Society?

22. How did the emerging Black Power movement coexist with King's emphasis on nonviolence?

23. What was the Gulf of Tonkin Resolution?

24. To what extent was the U.S. involvement in Vietnam a product of the doctrine of containment? What were the difficulties of this?

25. Why did popular support for the war drop?

26. "Although often speaking a _____ language, members of the counterculture tended to behave as _____." (p. 382)

27. When and what was the Fourth Great Awakening?

28. Why did LBJ not run again?

29. Why did America seem to be falling apart in 1968?

30. Who was the third candidate in 1968? How did the election come out?

31. What did Nixon's victory (and Wallace's showing) indicate?

Objective Questions

Put in order:

    _____ Cuban Missile Crisis
    _____ George Wallace gets forty-two electoral votes
    _____ Gulf of Tonkin Resolution

Put in order:

    _____ assassinations of MLK and Robert Kennedy
    _____ Great Society
    _____ Peace Corps established

Document

REV. MARTIN LUTHER KING JR., "I HAVE A DREAM," AUGUST 28, 1963

I am happy to join with you today in what will go down in history as the greatest demonstration for freedom in the history of our nation.

Five score years ago, a great American, in whose symbolic shadow we stand today, signed the Emancipation Proclamation. This momentous decree came as a great beacon light of hope to millions of Negro slaves who had been seared in the flames of withering injustice. It came as a joyous daybreak to end the long night of their captivity.

But one hundred years later, the Negro still is not free. One hundred years later, the life of the Negro is still sadly crippled by the manacles of segregation and the chains of discrimination. One hundred years later, the Negro lives on a lonely island of poverty in the midst of a vast ocean of material prosperity. One hundred years later, the Negro is still languished in the corners of American society and finds himself an exile in his own land. And so we've come here today to dramatize a shameful condition.

In a sense we've come to our nation's capital to cash a check. When the architects of our republic wrote the magnificent words of the Constitution and the Declaration of Independence, they were signing a promissory note to which every American was to fall heir. This note was a promise that all men, yes, black men as well as white men, would be guaranteed the "unalienable Rights" of "Life, Liberty and the pursuit of Happiness." It is obvious today that America has defaulted on this promissory note, insofar as her citizens of color are concerned. Instead of honoring this sacred obligation, America has given the Negro people a bad check, a check which has come back marked "insufficient funds."

But we refuse to believe that the bank of justice is bankrupt. We refuse to believe that there are insufficient funds in the great vaults of opportunity of this nation. And so, we've come to cash this check, a check that will give us upon demand the riches of freedom and the security of justice.

We have also come to this hallowed spot to remind America of the fierce urgency of Now. This is no time to engage in the luxury of cooling off or to take the tranquilizing drug of gradualism. Now is the time to make real the promises of democracy. Now is the time to rise from the dark and desolate valley of segregation to the sunlit path of racial justice. Now is the time to lift our nation from the quicksands of racial injustice to the solid rock of brotherhood. Now is the time to make justice a reality for all of God's children.

It would be fatal for the nation to overlook the urgency of the moment. This sweltering summer of the Negro's legitimate discontent will not pass until there is an invigorating autumn of freedom and equality. Nineteen sixty-three is not an end, but a beginning. And those who hope that the Negro needed to blow off steam and will now be content will have a rude awakening if the nation returns to business as usual. And there will be neither rest nor tranquility in America until the Negro is granted his citizenship rights. The whirlwinds of revolt will continue to shake the foundations of our nation until the bright day of justice emerges.

But there is something that I must say to my people, who stand on the warm threshold which leads into the palace of justice: In the process of gaining our rightful place, we must not be guilty of wrongful deeds. Let us not seek to satisfy our thirst for freedom by drinking from the cup of bitterness and hatred. We must forever conduct our struggle on the high plane of dignity and discipline. We must not allow our creative protest to degenerate into physical violence. Again and again, we must rise to the majestic heights of meeting physical force with soul force.

The marvelous new militancy which has engulfed the Negro community must not lead us to a distrust of all white people, for many of our white brothers, as evidenced by their presence here today, have come to realize that their destiny is tied up with our destiny. And they have come to realize that their freedom is inextricably bound to our freedom.

We cannot walk alone.

And as we walk, we must make the pledge that we shall always march ahead.

We cannot turn back.

There are those who are asking the devotees of civil rights, "When will you be satisfied?" We can never be satisfied as long as the Negro is the victim of the unspeakable horrors of police brutality. We can never be satisfied as long as our bodies, heavy with the fatigue of travel, cannot gain lodging in the motels of the highways and the hotels of the cities. We cannot be satisfied as long as the Negro's basic mobility is from a smaller ghetto to a larger one. We can never be satisfied as long as our children are stripped of their self-hood and robbed of their dignity by signs stating: "For Whites Only." We cannot be satisfied as long as a Negro in Mississippi cannot vote and a Negro in New York believes he has nothing for which to vote. No, no, we are not satisfied, and we will not be satisfied until "justice rolls down like waters, and righteousness like a mighty stream."

I am not unmindful that some of you have come here out of great trials and tribulations. Some of you have come fresh from narrow jail cells. And some of you have come from areas where your quest – quest for freedom left you battered by the storms of persecution and staggered by the winds of police brutality. You have been the veterans of creative suffering. Continue to work with the faith that unearned suffering is redemptive. Go back to Mississippi, go back to Alabama, go back to South Carolina, go back to Georgia, go back to Louisiana, go back to the slums and ghettos of our northern cities, knowing that somehow this situation can and will be changed.

Let us not wallow in the valley of despair, I say to you today, my friends.

And so even though we face the difficulties of today and tomorrow, I still have a dream. It is a dream deeply rooted in the American dream.

I have a dream that one day this nation will rise up and live out the true meaning of its creed: "We hold these truths to be self-evident, that all men are created equal."

I have a dream that one day on the red hills of Georgia, the sons of former slaves and the sons of former slave owners will be able to sit down together at the table of brotherhood.

I have a dream that one day even the state of Mississippi, a state sweltering with the heat of injustice, sweltering with the heat of oppression, will be transformed into an oasis of freedom and justice.

I have a dream that my four little children will one day live in a nation where they will not be judged by the color of their skin but by the content of their character.

I have a *dream* today!

I have a dream that one day, down in Alabama, with its vicious racists, with its governor having his lips dripping with the words of "interposition" and "nullification" – one day right there in Alabama little black boys and black girls will be able to join hands with little white boys and white girls as sisters and brothers.

I have a *dream* today!

I have a dream that one day every valley shall be exalted, and every hill and mountain shall be made low, the rough places will be made plain, and the crooked places will be made straight; "and the glory of the Lord shall be revealed and all flesh shall see it together."

This is our hope, and this is the faith that I go back to the South with.

With this faith, we will be able to hew out of the mountain of despair a stone of hope. With this faith, we will be able to transform the jangling discords of our nation into a beautiful symphony of brotherhood. With this faith, we will be able to work together, to pray together, to struggle together, to go to jail together, to stand up for freedom together, knowing that we will be free one day.

And this will be the day – this will be the day when all of God's children will be able to sing with new meaning:

My country 'tis of thee, sweet land of liberty, of thee I sing. Land where my fathers died, land of the Pilgrim's pride, From every mountainside, let freedom ring!

And if America is to be a great nation, this must become true.

And so let freedom ring from the prodigious hilltops of New Hampshire.

Let freedom ring from the mighty mountains of New York.

Let freedom ring from the heightening Alleghenies of Pennsylvania.

Let freedom ring from the snow-capped Rockies of Colorado.

Let freedom ring from the curvaceous slopes of California.

But not only that:

Let freedom ring from Stone Mountain of Georgia.

Let freedom ring from Lookout Mountain of Tennessee.

Let freedom ring from every hill and molehill of Mississippi.

From every mountainside, let freedom ring.

And when this happens, and when we allow freedom ring, when we let it ring from every village and every hamlet, from every state and every city, we will be able to speed up that day when *all* of God's children, black men and white men, Jews and Gentiles, Protestants and Catholics, will be able to join hands and sing in the words of the old Negro spiritual:

> *Free at last! Free at last!*
> *Thank God Almighty, we are free at last!*

Document Questions

Some answers may require more space than provided.

1. Why do you think King begins his speech with an invocation of Abraham Lincoln and the Emancipation Proclamation?

2. What is the importance of his use of the image of "cashing a check"?

3. What does King mean by "the fierce urgency of Now"?

4. What does King mean in saying "we cannot walk alone"?

5. How strong a role does King's religious faith play in this speech? Where does one see it emerge?

CHAPTER TWENTY-ONE

FALL AND RESTORATION

From Nixon to Reagan

Questions

Some answers may require more space than provided.

1. How was Nixon like Truman?

2. Nixon is a good example of why "it becomes more and more difficult to write about history with _____ and _____ the more closely one's subject matter approaches _____." (p. 386)

3. Nixon was a _____ politician but also had a talent for _____ and _____ building. (p. 389)

4. "Balancing an assertive and consistently _____ policy with largely _____, Nixon was always able to put together effective electoral combinations and eventually brought his formerly embattled party within hailing distance of majority status." (pp. 387–88)

5. What was Nixon's biggest piece of unfinished business upon coming into the White House? How did he deal with it?

6. How did Nixon revise China policy?

7. Why could only Nixon have opened diplomacy with China?

8. Nixon's domestic policy was far less successful. Why?

9. What is *stagflation*?

10. What was Nixon's New Federalism?

11. Nixon was reelected easily. But why was George McGovern in a sense the Democrats' Goldwater?

12. What was "Watergate"? (pp. 392–93)

13. What was Schlesinger's argument in *The Imperial Presidency*?

14. Who were the main victims of Nixon's downfall?

15. What event was most noteworthy of a generally very successful Bicentennial celebration?

16. How did the election of 1976 turn out?

17. How did Carter signal his rejection of the "imperial presidency"?

18. Why was Carter ineffective in dealing with energy policy and inflation?

19. What was Carter's great foreign policy triumph?

20. What was Carter's great foreign policy disaster?

21. How did Carter respond to the Soviet invasion of Afghanistan?

22. What are "transactional" and "transformative" leaders?

23. What were the groups composing the rising conservative movement that chose Reagan as its standard-bearer? What were the basics of conservative ideology?

24. How did Reagan's early life and career shape him?

25. Reagan was thoroughly conservative and skilled at coalition building, joining the _____ in the so-called Religious Right with _____, and both sets of social conservatives with _____. (pp. 401–2)

26. What was the outcome of the 1980 election?

27. What was Reagan's tax policy? What was the result?

28. What was Reagan's chief regret and failure?

29. What was Reagan's strategy for the Cold War?

30. How did Reagan win?

31. How did Reagan handle the "Euromissile crisis"?

32. Was Reagan or Gorbachev more responsible for the collapse of the Soviet Union? Did Soviet Communism fall? Or was it pushed?

Objective Questions

Put in order:

_____ Camp David Accords
_____ "evil empire" speech
_____ opening of diplomatic relations with China

Put in order:

_____ Ford presidency
_____ New Federalism
_____ Watergate

RONALD REAGAN, REMARKS AT THE BRANDENBURG GATE, WEST BERLIN, JUNE 12, 1987

Chancellor Kohl, Governing Mayor Diepgen, ladies and gentlemen: Twenty-four years ago, President John F. Kennedy visited Berlin, and speaking to the people of this city and the world at the city hall. Well since then two other presidents have come, each in his turn to Berlin. And today, I, myself, make my second visit to your city.

We come to Berlin, we American Presidents, because it's our duty to speak in this place of freedom. But I must confess, we're drawn here by other things as well; by the feeling of history in this city – more than 500 years older than our own nation; by the beauty of the Grunewald and the Tiergarten; most of all, by your courage and determination. Perhaps the composer, Paul Linke, understood something about American Presidents. You see, like so many Presidents before me, I come here today because wherever I go, whatever I do: *Ich hab noch einen Koffer in Berlin* [I still have a suitcase in Berlin].

Our gathering today is being broadcast throughout Western Europe and North America. I understand that it is being seen and heard as well in the East. To those listening throughout Eastern Europe, I extend my warmest greetings and the good will of the American people. To those listening in East Berlin, a special word: Although I cannot be with you, I address my remarks to you just as surely as to those standing here before me. For I join you, as I join your fellow countrymen in the West, in this firm, this unalterable belief: *Es gibt nur ein Berlin* [There is only one Berlin].

Behind me stands a wall that encircles the free sectors of this city, part of a vast system of barriers that divides the entire continent of Europe. From the Baltic South, those barriers cut across Germany in a gash of barbed wire, concrete, dog runs, and guard towers. Farther south, there may be no visible, no obvious wall. But there remain armed guards and checkpoints all the same – still a restriction on the right to travel, still an instrument to impose upon ordinary men and women the will of a totalitarian state.

Yet, it is here in Berlin where the wall emerges most clearly; here, cutting across your city, where the news photo and the television screen have imprinted this brutal division of a continent upon the mind of the world.

Standing before the Brandenburg Gate, every man is a German separated from his fellow men.

Every man is a Berliner, forced to look upon a scar.

President Von Weizsäcker has said, "The German question is open as long as the Brandenburg Gate is closed." Well today – today I say: As long as this gate is closed, as long as this scar of a wall is permitted to stand, it is not the German question alone that remains open, but the question of freedom for all mankind.

Yet, I do not come here to lament. For I find in Berlin a message of hope, even in the shadow of this wall, a message of triumph.

In this season of spring in 1945, the people of Berlin emerged from their air-raid shelters to find devastation. Thousands of miles away, the people of the United States reached out to help. And in 1947 Secretary of State – as you've been told – George Marshall announced the creation of what would become known as the Marshall Plan. Speaking precisely 40 years ago this month, he said: "Our policy is directed not against any country or doctrine, but against hunger, poverty, desperation, and chaos."

In the Reichstag a few moments ago, I saw a display commemorating this 40th anniversary of the Marshall Plan. I was struck by a sign – the sign on a burnt-out, gutted structure that was being rebuilt. I understand that Berliners of my own generation can remember seeing signs like it dotted throughout the western sectors of the city. The sign read simply: "The Marshall Plan is helping here to strengthen the free world." A strong, free world in the West – that dream became real. Japan rose from ruin to become an economic giant. Italy, France, Belgium – virtually every nation in Western Europe saw political and economic rebirth; the European Community was founded.

In West Germany and here in Berlin, there took place an economic miracle, the *Wirtschaftswunder* [Miracle on the Rhine]. Adenauer, Erhard, Reuter, and other leaders understood the practical importance of liberty – that just as truth can flourish only when the journalist is given freedom of speech, so prosperity can come about only when the farmer and businessman enjoy economic freedom. The German leaders – the German leaders reduced tariffs, expanded free trade, lowered taxes. From 1950 to 1960 alone, the standard of living in West Germany and Berlin doubled.

Where four decades ago there was rubble, today in West Berlin there is the greatest industrial output of any city in Germany: busy office blocks, fine homes and apartments, proud avenues, and the spreading lawns of parkland. Where a city's culture seemed to have been destroyed, today there are two great universities, orchestras and an opera, countless theaters, and museums. Where there was want, today there's abundance – food, clothing, automobiles – the wonderful goods of the Kudamm. From devastation, from utter ruin, you Berliners have, in freedom, rebuilt a city that once again ranks as one of the greatest on earth. Now the Soviets may have had other plans. But my friends, there were a few things the Soviets didn't count on: *Berliner Herz, Berliner Humor, ja, und Berliner Schnauze* [Berliner heart, Berliner humor, yes, and a Berliner Schnauze].

In the 1950s – In the 1950s Khrushchev predicted: "We will bury you."

But in the West today, we see a free world that has achieved a level of prosperity and well-being unprecedented in all human history. In the Communist world, we see failure, technological backwardness, declining standards of health, even want of the most basic kind – too little food. Even today, the Soviet Union still cannot feed itself. After these four decades, then, there stands before the entire world one great and inescapable conclusion: Freedom leads to prosperity. Freedom replaces the ancient hatreds among nations with comity and peace. Freedom is the victor.

And now – Now the Soviets themselves may, in a limited way, be coming to understand the importance of freedom. We hear much from Moscow about a new policy of reform and openness. Some political prisoners have been released. Certain foreign news broadcasts are no longer being jammed. Some economic enterprises have been permitted to operate with greater freedom from state control.

Are these the beginnings of profound changes in the Soviet state? Or are they token gestures intended to raise false hopes in the West, or to strengthen the Soviet system without changing it? We welcome change and openness; for we believe that freedom and security go together, that the advance of human liberty – the advance of human liberty can only strengthen the cause of world peace.

There is one sign the Soviets can make that would be unmistakable, that would advance dramatically the cause of freedom and peace.

General Secretary Gorbachev, if you seek peace, if you seek prosperity for the Soviet Union and Eastern Europe, if you seek liberalization: Come here to this gate.

Mr. Gorbachev, open this gate.

Mr. Gorbachev – Mr. Gorbachev, tear down this wall!

I understand the fear of war and the pain of division that afflict this continent, and I pledge to you my country's efforts to help overcome these burdens. To be sure, we in the West must resist Soviet expansion. So, we must maintain defenses of unassailable strength. Yet we seek peace; so we must strive to reduce arms on both sides.

Beginning 10 years ago, the Soviets challenged the Western alliance with a grave new threat, hundreds of new and more deadly SS-20 nuclear missiles capable of striking every capital in Europe. The Western alliance responded by committing itself to a counter-deployment (unless the Soviets agreed to negotiate a better solution) – namely, the elimination of such weapons on both sides. For many months, the Soviets refused to bargain in earnestness. As the alliance, in turn, prepared to go forward with its counter-deployment, there were difficult days, days of protests like those during my 1982 visit to this city; and the Soviets later walked away from the table.

But through it all, the alliance held firm. And I invite those who protested then – I invite those who protest today – to mark this fact: Because we remained strong, the Soviets came back to the table. Because we remained strong, today we have within reach the possibility, not merely of limiting the growth of arms, but of eliminating, for the first time, an entire class of nuclear weapons from the face of the earth.

As I speak, NATO ministers are meeting in Iceland to review the progress of our proposals for eliminating these weapons. At the talks in Geneva, we have also proposed deep cuts in strategic offensive weapons. And the Western allies have likewise made far-reaching proposals to reduce the danger of conventional war and to place a total ban on chemical weapons.

While we pursue these arms reductions, I pledge to you that we will maintain the capacity to deter Soviet aggression at any level at which it might occur. And in cooperation with many of our allies, the United States is pursuing the Strategic Defense Initiative – research to base deterrence not on the threat of offensive retaliation, but on defenses that truly defend; on systems, in short, that will not target populations, but shield them. By these means we seek to increase the safety of Europe and all the world. But we must remember a crucial fact: East and West do not mistrust each other because we are armed; we are armed because we mistrust each other. And our differences are not about weapons but about liberty. When President Kennedy spoke at the City Hall those 24 years ago, freedom was encircled; Berlin was under siege. And today, despite all the pressures upon this city, Berlin stands secure in its liberty. And freedom itself is transforming the globe.

In the Philippines, in South and Central America, democracy has been given a rebirth. Throughout the Pacific, free markets are working miracle after miracle of economic growth. In the industrialized nations, a technological revolution is taking place, a revolution marked by rapid, dramatic advances in computers and telecommunications.

In Europe, only one nation and those it controls refuse to join the community of freedom. Yet in this age of redoubled economic growth, of information and innovation, the Soviet Union faces a choice: It must make fundamental changes, or it will become obsolete.

Today, thus, represents a moment of hope. We in the West stand ready to cooperate with the East to promote true openness, to break down barriers that separate people, to create a safer, freer world. And surely there is no better place than Berlin, the meeting place of East and West, to make a start.

Free people of Berlin: Today, as in the past, the United States stands for the strict observance and full implementation of all parts of the Four Power Agreement of 1971. Let us use this occasion, the 750th anniversary of this city, to usher in a new era, to seek a still fuller, richer life for the Berlin of the future. Together, let us maintain and develop the ties between the Federal Republic and the Western sectors of Berlin, which is permitted by the 1971 agreement.

And I invite Mr. Gorbachev: Let us work to bring the Eastern and Western parts of the city closer together, so that all the inhabitants of all Berlin can enjoy the benefits that come with life in one of the great cities of the world.

To open Berlin still further to all Europe, East and West, let us expand the vital air access to this city, finding ways of making commercial air service to Berlin more convenient, more comfortable, and more economical. We look to the day when West Berlin can become one of the chief aviation hubs in all central Europe.

With – With our French – With our French and British partners, the United States is prepared to help bring international meetings to Berlin. It would be only fitting for Berlin to serve as the site of United Nations meetings, or world conferences on human rights and arms control, or other issues that call for international cooperation.

There is no better way to establish hope for the future than to enlighten young minds, and we would be honored to sponsor summer youth exchanges, cultural events, and other programs for young Berliners from the East. Our French and British friends, I'm certain, will do the same. And it's my hope that an authority can be found in East Berlin to sponsor visits from young people of the Western sectors.

One final proposal, one close to my heart: Sport represents a source of enjoyment and ennoblement, and you may have noted that the Republic of Korea – South Korea – has offered to permit certain events of the 1988 Olympics to take place in the North. International sports competitions of all kinds could take place in both parts of this city. And what better way to demonstrate to the world the openness of this city than to offer in some future year to hold the Olympic games here in Berlin, East and West.

In these four decades, as I have said, you Berliners have built a great city. You've done so in spite of threats – the Soviet attempts to impose the East-mark, the blockade. Today the city thrives in spite of the challenges implicit in the very presence of this wall. What keeps you here? Certainly there's a great deal to be said for your fortitude, for your defiant courage.

But I believe there's something deeper, something that involves Berlin's whole look and feel and way of life – not mere sentiment. No one could live long in Berlin without being completely disabused of illusions. Something, instead, that has seen the difficulties of life in Berlin but chose to accept them, that continues to build this good and proud city in contrast to a surrounding totalitarian presence, that refuses to release human energies or aspirations, something that speaks with a powerful voice of affirmation, that says "yes" to this city, yes to the future, yes to freedom. In a word, I would submit that what keeps you in Berlin – is "love."

Love both profound and abiding.

Perhaps this gets to the root of the matter, to the most fundamental distinction of all between East and West. The totalitarian world produces backwardness because it does such violence to the spirit, thwarting the human impulse to create, to enjoy, to worship. The totalitarian world finds even symbols of love and of worship an affront.

Years ago, before the East Germans began rebuilding their churches, they erected a secular structure: the television tower at Alexander Platz. Virtually ever since, the authorities have been working to correct what they view as the tower's one major flaw: treating the glass sphere at the top with paints and chemicals of every kind. Yet even today when the sun strikes that sphere, that sphere that towers over all Berlin, the light makes the sign of the cross. There in Berlin, like the city itself, symbols of love, symbols of worship, cannot be suppressed.

As I looked out a moment ago from the Reichstag, that embodiment of German unity, I noticed words crudely spray-painted upon the wall, perhaps by a young Berliner (quote):

"This wall will fall. Beliefs become reality."

Yes, across Europe, this wall will fall, for it cannot withstand faith; it cannot withstand truth. The wall cannot withstand freedom.

And I would like, before I close, to say one word. I have read, and I have been questioned since I've been here about certain demonstrations against my coming. And I would like to say just one thing, and to those who demonstrate so. I wonder if they have ever asked themselves that if they should have the kind of government they apparently seek, no one would ever be able to do what they're doing again.

Thank you and God bless you all. Thank you.

Document Questions

Some answers may require more space than provided.

1. Why does Reagan call Berlin "this place of freedom"?

2. The most famous lines of the speech are directed at Soviet general secretary Mikhail Gorbachev. What are they?

3. What are some of the places in which Reagan is seeing a new birth of freedom?

4. What is Reagan's advice for the Soviet Union?

5. What was the crisis over the SS-20s, and why was it so important?

6. How does Reagan turn the tables against the protesters against his visit?

CHAPTER TWENTY-TWO

THE WORLD SINCE THE COLD WAR

Questions

Some answers may require more space than provided.

1. "Part of the discipline of thinking historically is developing the ability to be _____ of what we think we see plainly before our eyes and of what ' _____ ' in the present moment." (p. 408)

2. "If history teaches us anything, it is that we only rarely have the power to grasp the _____ as they are occurring. Live long enough, and you will find out how true that is." (p. 408)

3. Most of the rest of this chapter comprises summaries, in turn, of the presidencies of George H. W. Bush, Bill Clinton, George W. Bush, Barak Obama, and Donald Trump. How aware does each seem to have been of the new range of "characteristic problems and issues that have emerged" since the end of the Cold War, and how effective does each seem to have been in dealing with them? What are those problems and issues?

4. George H. W. Bush presided over the collapse of the Soviet Union but did so with sober and cautious restraint. He "could sense that with the end of the Cold War, there were profound changes coming, many of which would be hard to predict." Was Bush's presidency a success? Why or why not?

5. The Cold War had provided "_____ to American foreign policy and much of American domestic life, even the nation's _____, for half a century." (p. 411)

6. What do you believe is most likely to take the place of the Cold War as an ordering principle for the United States' disposition toward the rest of the world? In answering, lay out the possibilities in broad strokes (unilateral, bilateral, muiltilateral, etc.).

7. How did Desert Storm reflect a world picture that corresponded to the writing of Francis Fukuyama? What did he mean that we had reached "the end of history"?

8. What was Samuel Huntington's theory in *The Clash of Civilizations* about the new world "order"? (p. 413)

9. Historian Daniel T. Rodgers says we are living in an "_____" in which all shared narratives are called into question. (p. 414)

10. Was Bill Clinton's presidency a success? Why or why not?)

11. The nation rallied behind George W. Bush after the 9/11 attacks, but this harmony did not last long. Are the occasions for national unity fewer and farther between? And shorter lived? And are any other events besides an attack from outside likely to produce such unity? Think back over your study of American history to see if you can think of examples.

12. What were the political effects of the Great Recession of 2007–8?

13. Barack Obama's election itself was epochal, but the record of his presidency less so. Would you judge that he was a success? Why or why not?

14. "It is far too early at this juncture to make any judgments or predictions about Donald Trump's success or failure. But two things can be said with relative confidence. First, while Trump seems unlikely to be the architect of a fresh national consensus, he has brought to the fore certain ideas, notably the emphasis on _____, that appear to be on the rise in much of the world, as in Great Britain and Italy.... And second, his election itself and the brutal, nonstop political combat that has ensued since it are symptomatic of the _____ _____felt by a significant portion of the American public." (p. 419)

15. What is the great unresolved and bipartisan problem illustrating the dysfunction of our political system?

16. Review the opening passage from John Dos Passos. It is just when old institutions are caving in and being replaced by new ones that we most need to look _____. (p. 422)

Objective Question

Put in order:

_____ 9/11 attacks
_____ Desert Storm
_____ execution of Saddam Hussein

Document

GEORGE W. BUSH, REMARKS AT THE NATIONAL DAY OF PRAYER AND REMEMBRANCE SERVICE, WASHINGTON NATIONAL CATHEDRAL, SEPTEMBER 14, 2001

We are here in the middle hour of our grief. So many have suffered so great a loss, and today we express our nation's sorrow. We come before God to pray for the missing and the dead, and for those who loved them. On Tuesday, our country was attacked with deliberate and massive cruelty. We have seen the images of fire and ashes and bent steel.

Now come the names, the list of casualties we are only beginning to read:

They are the names of men and women who began their day at a desk or in an airport, busy with life.

They are the names of people who faced death and in their last moments called home to say, be brave and I love you.

They are the names of passengers who defied their murderers and prevented the murder of others on the ground.

They are the names of men and women who wore the uniform of the United States and died at their posts.

They are the names of rescuers – the ones whom death found running up the stairs and into the fires to help others.

We will read all these names. We will linger over them and learn their stories, and many Americans will weep.

To the children and parents and spouses and families and friends of the lost, we offer the deepest sympathy of the nation. And I assure you, you are not alone. Just three days removed from these events, Americans do not yet have the distance of history, but our responsibility to history is already clear: to answer these attacks and rid the world of evil.

War has been waged against us by stealth and deceit and murder. This nation is peaceful, but fierce when stirred to anger. This conflict was begun on the timing and terms of others; it will end in a way and at an hour of our choosing. Our purpose as a nation is firm, yet our wounds as a people are recent and unhealed and lead us to pray. In many of our prayers this week, there's a searching and an honesty. At St. Patrick's Cathedral in New York, on Tuesday, a woman said, "I pray to God to give us a sign that He's still here."

Others have prayed for the same, searching hospital to hospital, carrying pictures of those still missing. God's signs are not always the ones we look for. We learn in tragedy that His purposes are not always our own, yet the prayers of private suffering, whether in our homes or in this great cathedral are known and heard and understood. There are prayers that help us last through the day or endure the night. There are prayers of friends and strangers that give us strength for the journey, and there are prayers that yield our will to a Will greater than our own.

This world He created is of moral design. Grief and tragedy and hatred are only for a time. Goodness, remembrance and love have no end, and the Lord of life holds all who die and all who mourn.

It is said that adversity introduces us to ourselves. This is true of a nation as well. In this trial, we have been reminded and the world has seen that our fellow Americans are generous and kind, resourceful and brave.

We see our national character in rescuers working past exhaustion, in long lines of blood donors, in thousands of citizens who have asked to work and serve in any way possible.

And we have seen our national character in eloquent acts of sacrifice:

Inside the World Trade Center, one man who could have saved himself stayed until the end and at the side of his quadriplegic friend.

A beloved priest died giving the last rites to a firefighter.

Two office workers, finding a disabled stranger, carried her down 68 floors to safety.

A group of men drove through the night from Dallas to Washington to bring skin grafts for burned victims.

In these acts and many others, Americans showed a deep commitment to one another and an abiding love for our country.

Today, we feel what Franklin Roosevelt called "the warm courage of national unity." This is a unity of every faith and every background. It has joined together political parties and both houses of Congress. It is evident in services of prayer and candlelight vigils and American flags, which are displayed in pride and waved in defiance. Our unity is a kinship of grief and a steadfast resolve to prevail against our enemies. And this unity against terror is now extending across the world.

America is a nation full of good fortune, with so much to be grateful for, but we are not spared from suffering. In every generation, the world has produced enemies of human freedom. They have attacked America because we are freedom's home and defender, and the commitment of our Fathers is now the calling of our time.

On this national day of prayer and remembrance, we ask Almighty God to watch over our nation and grant us patience and resolve in all that is to come.

We pray that He will comfort and console those who now walk in sorrow. We thank Him for each life we now must mourn, and the promise of a life to come.

As we've been assured, neither death nor life nor angels nor principalities, nor powers nor things present nor things to come nor height nor depth can separate us from God's love. May He bless the souls of the departed. May He comfort our own. And may He always guide our country.

God bless America.

Document Questions

Some answers may require more space than provided.

1. Bush's speech came three days after the 9/11 attacks on New York, Washington, D.C., and Pennsylvania by Islamist terrorists and was delivered at the National Cathedral in Washington. How does the speech reflect those things?

2. "Our responsibility to history is already clear: to answer these attacks and rid the world of evil." Was this an appropriate response?

3. How does Bush answer those who fear that God might not "still be here"?

4. What positive signs does Bush see coming out of these horrible events?

5. How does Bush present the motives of the attackers?

THE SHAPE OF AMERICAN PATRIOTISM

Questions

Some answers may require more space than provided.

1. What is the difference between being objective and being neutral?

2. "The two things, _____, are not necessarily enemies. _____ is the foundation of the wisest criticism, and criticism is the essential partner of an honest and enduring _____." (p. 423)

3. "We live in a country, let us hope, in which our flaws can always be openly discussed, and where criticism and dissent can be regarded not as _____ _____ but as essential ingredients in the flourishing of our polity and our common life." Yet we must not take this for granted; it is far from universal and does not perpetuate itself. (pp. 423–24)

4. Why is patriotism often treated as a dangerous sentiment, when it is such a natural thing?

5. Why is refining and elevating American patriotism not an easy task?

6. What was the debate over the word *homeland* after 9/11?

7. What is the fundamental clash of perceptions about American national identity?

8. As a nation of immigrants, Americans are made "_____ as by a process of _____ that make America what it is." (p. 425)

9. Hamilton contended in *Federalist* 1 that America was to be a _____ for all humankind, deciding whether it is possible for good governments to be constructed by "_____" rather than relying on "_____." (p. 425)

10. What is the other element, besides a strong sense of universalism, in American national self-consciousness and patriotism, if it is not "blood and soil"?

11. One finds this second element of national consciousness less in _____ and more in _____. (p. 427)

12. "So there is a vital _____ in the makeup of American patriotism, a _____ between its universalizing ideals and its particularizing sentiments, with their emphasis upon memory, history, tradition, culture, and the land.... It would be a mistake to insist on one while excluding the other." (pp. 427–28)

13. Lincoln appealed to both in turn, with "the mystic chords of _____, stretching from every battle-field, and patriot grave, to every living heart and hearthstone," but also America as "the last best hope of earth." (p. 428)

14. How does each of the following quotations illustrate different aspects of American patriotism? Can you think of others?

> A. Walt Whitman, "I Hear American Singing," from *Leaves of Grass* (1867 edition)
>
> I hear America singing, the varied carols I hear,
> Those of mechanics, each one singing his as it should be blithe
>   and strong,
> The carpenter singing his as he measures his plank or beam,
> The mason singing his as he makes ready for work, or leaves off work,
> The boatman singing what belongs to him in his boat, the deckhand
>   singing on the steamboat deck,

The shoemaker singing as he sits on his bench, the hatter singing
      as he stands,
The wood-cutter's song, the ploughboy's on his way in the morning,
      or at noon intermission or at sundown,

The delicious singing of the mother, or of the young wife at work,
      or of the girl sewing or washing,
Each singing what belongs to him or her and to none else,
The day what belongs to the day – at night the party of young fellows,
      robust, friendly,
Singing with open mouths their strong melodious songs

Source: https://poets.org/poem/i-hear-america-singing

B. Katharine Lee Bates, "America the Beautiful" (1911 version)

O beautiful for spacious skies,
For amber waves of grain,
For purple mountain majesties
Above the fruited plain!
America! America!
God shed His grace on thee
And crown thy good with brotherhood
From sea to shining sea!

O beautiful for pilgrim feet,
Whose stern, impassioned stress
A thoroughfare for freedom beat
Across the wilderness!
America! America!
God mend thine every flaw,
Confirm thy soul in self-control,
Thy liberty in law!

O beautiful for heroes proved
In liberating strife,
Who more than self their country loved
And mercy more than life!
America! America!
May God thy gold refine,

Till all success be nobleness,
And every gain divine!

O beautiful for patriot dream
That sees beyond the years
Thine alabaster cities gleam
Undimmed by human tears!
America! America!
God shed His grace on thee
And crown thy good with brotherhood
From sea to shining sea!

Source: https://openlibrary.org/works/OL3462961W/America_
the_beautiful

C. Lee Greenwood, "God Bless the USA" (1983)

If tomorrow all my things were gone,
I'd worked for all my life.
And I had to start again,
With just my children and my wife.

I'd thank my lucky stars,
To be livin' here today.
'Cause the flag still stands for freedom,
And they can't take that away.

And I'm proud to be an American,
Where at least I know I'm free.
And I won't forget the men who died,
Who gave that right to me.
And I gladly stand up,
Next to you and defend her still today.
'Cause there ain't no doubt I love this land,
God bless the USA.
From the lakes of Minnesota,
To the hills of Tennessee.
Across the plains of Texas,
From sea to shining sea.

From Detroit down to Houston,
And New York to L.A.
Well there's pride in every American heart,
And its time we stand and say

That I'm proud to be an American,
Where at least I know I'm free.
And I won't forget the men who died,
Who gave that right to me.
And I gladly stand up,
Next to you and defend her still today.
'Cause there ain't no doubt I love this land,
God bless the USA.

Source: https://www.azlyrics.com/lyrics/leegreenwood/proudtobean
american.html

D. Langston Hughes, "Let America Be America Again" (1936)

Let America be America again.
Let it be the dream it used to be.
Let it be the pioneer on the plain
Seeking a home where he himself is free.

(America never was America to me.)

Let America be the dream the dreamers dreamed –
Let it be that great strong land of love
Where never kings connive nor tyrants scheme
That any man be crushed by one above.

(It never was America to me.)

O, let my land be a land where Liberty
Is crowned with no false patriotic wreath,
But opportunity is real, and life is free,
Equality is in the air we breathe.

(There's never been equality for me,
Nor freedom in this "homeland of the free.")

Say, who are you that mumbles in the dark?
And who are you that draws your veil across the stars?

I am the poor white, fooled and pushed apart,
I am the Negro bearing slavery's scars.
I am the red man driven from the land,
I am the immigrant clutching the hope I seek –
And finding only the same old stupid plan
Of dog eat dog, of mighty crush the weak.

I am the young man, full of strength and hope,
Tangled in that ancient endless chain
Of profit, power, gain, of grab the land!
Of grab the gold! Of grab the ways of satisfying need!
Of work the men! Of take the pay!
Of owning everything for one's own greed!

I am the farmer, bondsman to the soil.
I am the worker sold to the machine.
I am the Negro, servant to you all.
I am the people, humble, hungry, mean –
Hungry yet today despite the dream.
Beaten yet today – O, Pioneers!
I am the man who never got ahead,
The poorest worker bartered through the years.

Yet I'm the one who dreamt our basic dream
In the Old World while still a serf of kings,
Who dreamt a dream so strong, so brave, so true,
That even yet its mighty daring sings
In every brick and stone, in every furrow turned
That's made America the land it has become.
O, I'm the man who sailed those early seas
In search of what I meant to be my home –
For I'm the one who left dark Ireland's shore,
And Poland's plain, and England's grassy lea,
And torn from Black Africa's strand I came
To build a "homeland of the free."

The free?

Who said the free? Not me?
Surely not me? The millions on relief today?
The millions shot down when we strike?
The millions who have nothing for our pay?
For all the dreams we've dreamed
And all the songs we've sung
And all the hopes we've held
And all the flags we've hung,
The millions who have nothing for our pay –
Except the dream that's almost dead today.

O, let America be America again –
The land that never has been yet –
And yet must be – the land where every man is free.
The land that's mine – the poor man's, Indian's, Negro's, ME –
Who made America,
Whose sweat and blood, whose faith and pain,
Whose hand at the foundry, whose plow in the rain,
Must bring back our mighty dream again.

Sure, call me any ugly name you choose –
The steel of freedom does not stain.
From those who live like leeches on the people's lives,
We must take back our land again,
America!

O, yes,
I say it plain,
America never was America to me,
And yet I swear this oath –
America will be!

Out of the rack and ruin of our gangster death,
The rape and rot of graft, and stealth, and lies,
We, the people, must redeem
The land, the mines, the plants, the rivers.
The mountains and the endless plain –
All, all the stretch of these great green states –
And make America again!

E. Wendell Berry, from *Jayber Crow* (2000)

It was a community always disappointed in itself, disappointing its members, always trying to contain its divisions and gentle its meanness, always failing and yet always preserving a sort of goodwill. I knew that, in the midst of all the ignorance and error, this was a membership; it was the membership of Port William; it was of no other place on earth. My vision gathered the community as it never has been and never will be gathered in this world of time, for the community must always be marred by members who are indifferent to it or against it, who are nonetheless its members and nonetheless essential to it. And yet I saw them all as somehow perfected, beyond time, by one another's love, compassion, and forgiveness, as it is said we may be perfected by grace. (p. 205)

F. Abraham Lincoln, Eulogy on Henry Clay, July 6, 1852

Mr. Clay's predominant sentiment, from first to last, was a deep devotion to the cause of human liberty – a strong sympathy with the oppressed everywhere, and an ardent wish for their elevation. With him, this was a primary and all controlling passion. Subsidiary to this was the conduct of his whole life. He loved his country partly because it was his own country, but mostly because it was a free country; and he burned with a zeal for its advancement, prosperity and glory, because he saw in such, the advancement, prosperity and glory, of human liberty, human right and human nature. He desired the prosperity of his countrymen partly because they were his countrymen, but chiefly to show to the world that freemen could be prosperous.

MAP EXERCISES

Exercise 1 · Statehood

Write the initials of each state in the circles, and within the state, write the date it joined the union and its number (out of fifty) in reaching statehood. (For the smaller states along the East Coast, the circles and two lines are out in the ocean or in Canada.) (**Students will find this information with map exercise 2.** Yes, it is important enough to do twice. Be able to name the states without help.)

The original thirteen should be numbered and dated twice: first, use the order in which they voted in the Continental and Confederation Congresses (North to South), with the year for each being 1776; second, use the order in which they ratified the U.S. Constitution (Delaware was first, Rhode Island thirteenth), with the dates being from 1787 through 1790.

The original thirteen might have used two possible models in managing and developing the western territories. They could have played "mother country" under the mercantilist doctrine of the French, British, and Spanish empires, exploiting the West while limiting its political power. Alternately, they could have followed the example of the Roman republic, in which conquered Italian cities were granted Roman citizenship and were represented in the Senate. (Rome abandoned this inspired approach when it conquered aliens outside of Italy, and the republic turned into an oppressive empire.) The Confederation Congress wisely rejected the mercantilist approach and adopted (in the northwest land ordinances of 1784 and 1787) the Roman model; the West would be organized into territories with limited self-government, and when population growth reached a certain level, each territory would write a state constitution and apply to join the union as a new state on a level of full equality with the original thirteen.

Modern Americans tend to think in terms of North versus South as the main sectional conflict, but in fact, the seventeenth and eighteenth centuries were characterized much more by East versus West: Bacon's Rebellion, the Paxton Boys, the Regulator movement, Shays' Rebellion, and the Whiskey Rebellion are examples. Had the Congress not set up the system for adding new states, it is likely this pattern of conflict between East and West would have continued, and even intensified. The Confederation is generally accounted a weak government, but in this vital matter of western land policy, the Congress produced legislation as far-reaching and beneficial as anything any Congress ever did.

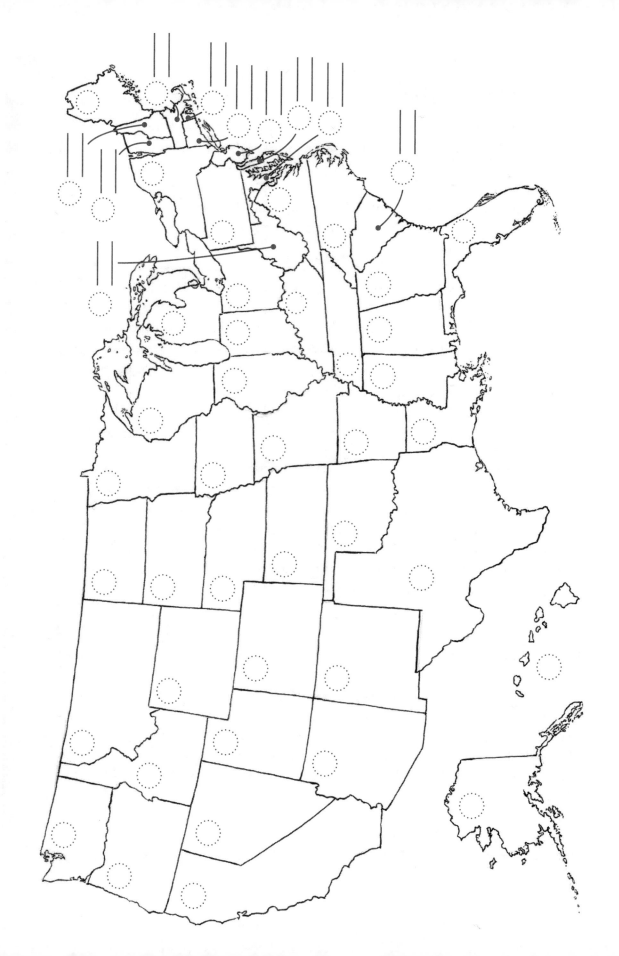

Exercise 2 · Regions

Use a heavy line to group the states into regions. The U.S. State Department lists six: **New England, the Mid-Atlantic, the South, the Midwest, the Southwest, and the West.** Note that which region a state goes in is sometimes debatable. For example, is Texas part of the South or of the Southwest? Texas is very large. Its eastern area is piney woods and cotton, definitely part of the South. Its western areas, however, range from Great Plains to craggy mountains and arid desert. Those parts definitely belong to the Southwest.

The concept of "region" used to be much more influential than it is today, when we have a national culture knit together by systems of rapid communication and transportation. In the nineteenth century, though, the various regions were not only geographically different but also tended to be culturally distinct and largely self-contained, each having its own religious practices, its own customs, and even its own ways of speaking. The most extreme contrast was between New England and the South, which were divergent in almost every way and not merely in their views about slavery. Despite the current dominance of our national culture, many of these regional differences persist even today and often are proudly celebrated (see Texas above). It's good to be aware of them.

Note the prevalence of straight-line boundaries for many western states. This reflects the fact that decisions about territorial sizes (and also names) were made in the East, by a Congress largely ignorant of western geography and primarily concerned with packaging and selling the western lands, which might begin to be settled even before they were fully explored.

Within each state and next to the dot representing its capital, write the number and the abbreviation from the following list. Watch the country grow!

1. Delaware (DE), 1787	Dover	
2. Pennsylvania (PA), 1787	Harrisburg	
3. New Jersey (NJ), 1787	Trenton	
4. Georgia (GA), 1788	Atlanta	
5. Connecticut (CT), 1788	Hartford	
6. Massachusetts (MA), 1788	Boston	
7. Maryland (MD), 1788	Annapolis	
8. South Carolina (SC), 1788	Columbia	
9. New Hampshire (NH), 1788	Concord	
10. Virginia (VA), 1788	Richmond	
11. New York (NY), 1788	Albany	
12. North Carolina (NC), 1789	Raleigh	

13. Rhode Island (RI), 1790	Providence	
14. Vermont (VT), 1791	Montpelier	
15. Kentucky (KY), 1792	Frankfort	
16. Tennessee (TN), 1796	Nashville	
17. Ohio (OH), 1803	Columbus	
18. Louisiana (LA), 1812	Baton Rouge	
19. Indiana (IN), 1816	Indianapolis	
20. Mississippi (MS), 1817	Jackson	
21. Illinois (IL), 1818	Springfield	
22. Alabama (AL), 1819	Montgomery	
23. Maine (ME), 1820	Augusta	
24. Missouri (MO), 1821	Jefferson City	

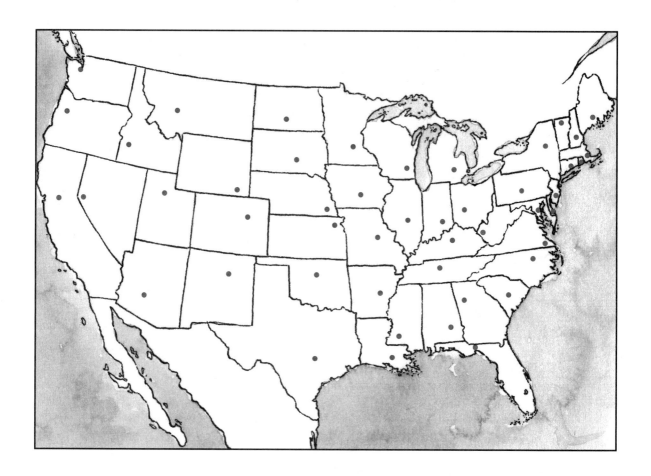

25. Arkansas (AR), 1836	Little Rock	39. North Dakota (ND), 1889	Bismarck
26. Michigan (MI), 1837	Lansing	40. South Dakota (SD), 1889	Pierre
27. Florida (FL), 1845	Tallahassee	41. Montana (MT), 1889	Helena
28. Texas (TX), 1845	Austin	42. Washington (WA), 1889	Olympia
29. Iowa (IA), 1846	Des Moines	43. Idaho (ID), 1890	Boise
30. Wisconsin (WI), 1848	Madison	44. Wyoming (WY), 1890	Cheyenne
31. California (CA), 1850	Sacramento	45. Utah (UT), 1896	Salt Lake City
32. Minnesota (MN), 1858	St. Paul	46. Oklahoma (OK), 1907	Oklahoma City
33. Oregon (OR), 1859	Salem	47. New Mexico (NM), 1912	Santa Fe
34. Kansas (KS), 1861	Topeka	48. Arizona (AZ), 1912	Phoenix
35. West Virginia (WV), 1863	Charleston		
36. Nevada (NV), 1864	Carson City	(Alaska and Hawai'i are not shown on this map.)	
37. Nebraska (NE), 187	Lincoln	49. Alaska (AK), 1958	Juneau
38. Colorado (CO), 1876	Denver	50. Hawai'i (HI), 1959	Honolulu

Exercise 3 · Landforms

Color differently each of the following geographic features and identify it with the appropriate number:

1. **Mississippi River:** Aka "Old Man River" or "the Big Muddy"; "There is on the globe one single spot, the possessor of which is our natural and habitual enemy. It is New Orleans, through which the produce of three eighths of our territory must pass to market." – President Thomas Jefferson to Robert Livingston, his ambassador to France, early in 1802, just before the Louisiana Purchase

2. **Missouri River:** As the song "Shenandoah" says, "I'm bound away, across the wide Missouri"

3. **Ohio River:** Mark Twain commented on the contrast between the thriving free territory on its north bank and the less prosperous slave territory on its south bank

4. **Colorado River:** Flows through the Grand Canyon and out to the Pacific via the Gulf of California

5. **Columbia River:** The great river of the northwest, the boundary between the states of Oregon and Washington

6. **Appalachian Mountain** chain: Aka "the Blue Ridge"; first great barrier to English settlement

7. **Rocky Mountain** range: "The Rockies" are relatively wide and less steep; the "Great Divide" ("where the rivers change direction, across the Great Divide") runs along their peak; beaver were trapped for fur

8. The **Sierra Nevada** mountains: The "High Sierra"; a "great granite fortress" paralleling the Pacific coast

9. The **Great Plains:** For a long time called "the Great American Desert," as trees do not grow there, but the soil is fertile once steel plows and windmills come into use; vast herds of bison roamed

10. The **Great Basin:** Discovered by John C. Fremont and containing Death Valley, it covers much of the land between the Sierra Nevada and the Rockies and does not drain into an ocean

11. The **Great Lakes:** Put the appropriate letter in each – A. Erie; B. Huron; C. Ontario; D. Michigan; E. Superior

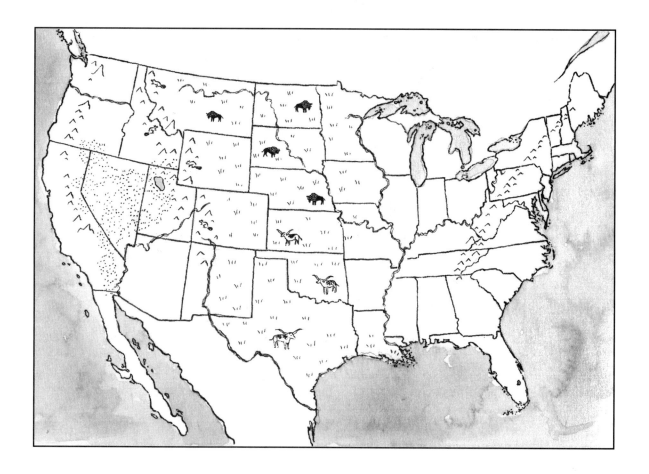

12. The **Rio Grande**: Disputed border between Mexico and Texas; herds of long-horn cattle were driven up from Texas to market at the railhead in Abilene, Kansas

The continental United States is divided into three watersheds: the eastern one flows into the Atlantic; the central one (between the Appalachians and the Rockies) flows into the Gulf of Mexico at New Orleans, and the western one (west of the Great Divide) flows into the Pacific directly or via the Colorado or Columbia river. Before the development of paved turnpikes and railroads in the early 1800s, the rivers and lakes were the only effective lines of transportation and retained their importance with the steamboat.

Exercise 4 · Eastern Waterways

Identify each town, city, or fort on the map (the dots) with the appropriate number from the following list. Identify each river by writing its name on the line extending out into the ocean, where the river reaches the sea, or along the river itself. Name the Great Lakes.

1, 2, 3, 4, 5. Montgomery, AL; Columbus, GA; Macon, GA; Augusta, GA; Columbia, SC

6, 7, 8, 9, 10, 11, 12. Raleigh, NC; Durham, NC; Richmond, VA; Washington, DC; Baltimore, MD; Wilmington, DE; Philadelphia, PA

13, 14. New York City and Long Island

15, 16. Boston, MA, and Cape Cod

17. Albany, NY – where the Mohawk River meets the Hudson River

18. Pittsburgh, PA – originally the French Fort Duquesne, renamed Fort Pitt when the British captured it

19. Detroit, MI – the main British fort in the Northwest, developed into a major manufacturing city

20. Fort Ticonderoga dominates the passage between Lake Champlain and Lake George

21, 22. Montreal and Quebec, the main French settlements along the Saint Lawrence River

Rivers are generally navigable from the ocean to the first waterfall. The "fall line" connects the first waterfall on each river and is the boundary between the tidewater and the piedmont. Southern towns (the South had few big cities) tended to be located along the fall line, as shown on the map.

Southern rivers tend to have gentle slopes, making them excellent for navigation. Northern rivers, especially in New England, tend to fall more steeply, with more waterfalls: poor for navigation, but excellent as power sources for mills and, eventually, factories.

The following rivers are drawn on the map: Alabama, Apalachicola, Satilla, Altamaha, Ogeechee, Savannah (state line between Georgia and South Carolina), Edisto, Ashley and Cooper (flow into Charleston Harbor), Santee, Pee Dee, Roanoke,

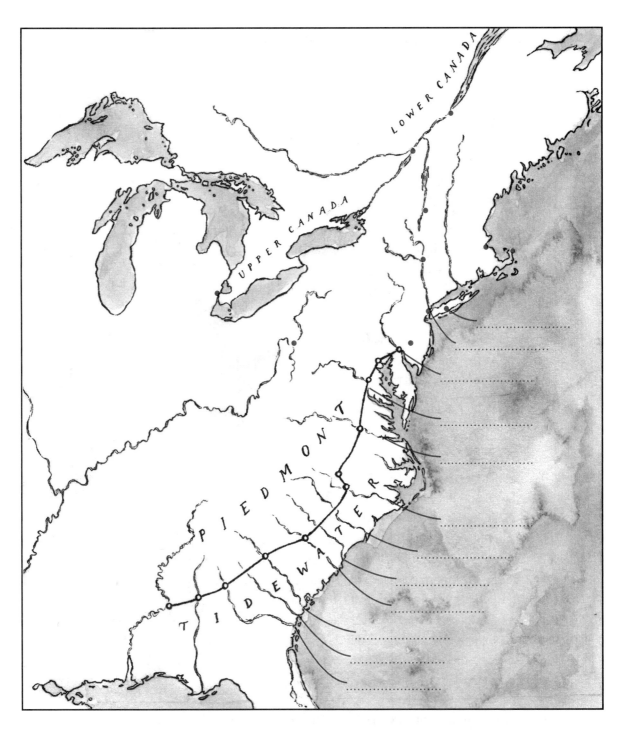

James (Richmond), Potomac, Delaware, Hudson, Monongahela, Allegheny, Ohio ("three rivers" at Pittsburgh), Mohawk, Connecticut, Richelieu (with Lakes Champlain and George), Ottawa (boundary between Lower and Upper Canada), St. Lawrence.

Exercise 5 · The Missouri Compromise

Identify and outline in blue each free state or territory; how many free states are there?

Identify and outline in red each slave state or territory; how many slave states are there?

Use a green marker to trace the line 36°30′. Use another color to trace the Mason–Dixon line.

Note the "unorganized territory" north of Arkansas and Missouri; it was closed to slavery, but no one knew how many states it would become.

Note that Texas is at this time a Spanish possession, about to be Mexican, when it wins its independence in 1821.

The Mason–Dixon line was surveyed in the 1760s and marked the boundary between the free state of Pennsylvania and the slave states of Maryland and Virginia; it also separated Delaware from Maryland. The phrase "below the Mason–Dixon line" came to mean the slaveholding South.

The 36°30′ line similarly divided the western territories into slave and free, but only for the nation as it existed in 1820 (the Louisiana Purchase being the western limit). Would its effect extend to California after the United States acquired Texas and the Mexican Cession? That was by no means settled.

The great political issue was not slavery where it already existed; the question was whether the West (all of that land out there, representing growth and the future) would be part of the North, and open to free labor, or part of the South, with slavery as the main labor system and basis of society.

Because northern population growth had far outstripped the South's (even counting the slaves as three-fifths), the free states dominated the House of Representatives. The slave states could use the Senate to protect themselves against any federal action or policy, as long as the slave and free states remained equal in number. This is why the admission of Maine (formerly part of Massachusetts) as a free state had to be balanced by the admission of Missouri.

The Missouri Compromise "worked": slavery was not a major issue for the next quarter-century. But the rapid and immense growth of the nation between 1845 and 1850 as a result of the annexation of Texas and the Mexican Cession reopened the question of the expansion of slavery into the West. Compromise would be far more difficult, and ultimately impossible, next time around, in 1850 and after.

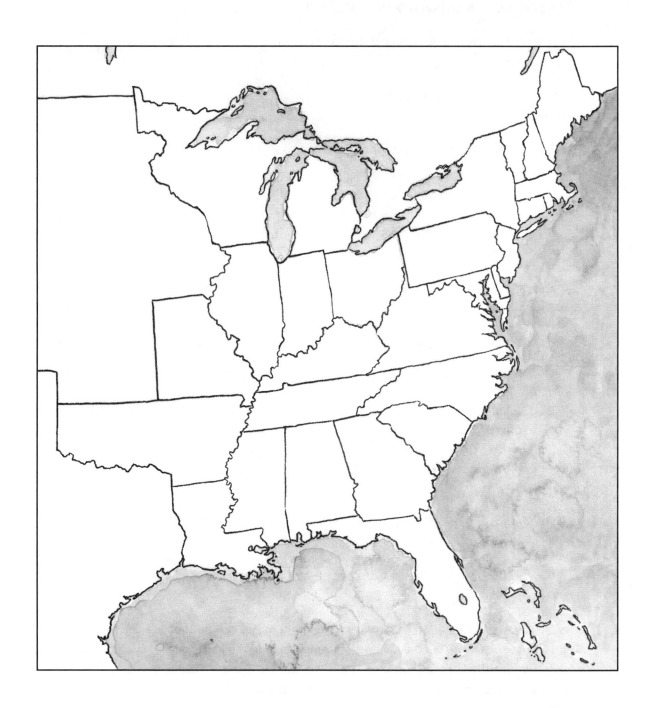

Exercise 6 · Westward Expansion

Note that this map is similar to the one on p. 158 of the text, to which students should refer.

Color each area differently, and write the appropriate number from the following list:

1. the original thirteen states that declared independence in 1776

2. ceded to the United States by Britain in 1783, due in part to the victories of George Rogers Clark

3. the Louisiana Purchase from France, 1803; note that it is far more than today's state of Louisiana

4. adjustments to the U.S.–Canadian border, negotiated with Britain, 1818 and 1842 (Webster–Ashburton Treaty)

5. Florida, ceded by Spain in 1819 (after Jackson had conquered it without permission!)

6. Texas, which won independence from Mexico in 1837 and was an independent republic until 1845, when it became a state

7. the Oregon Territory, as negotiated by treaty with Britain in 1846, splitting the original area north and south; the northern half became British Columbia, a Canadian province

8. the Mexican Cession, the fruits of the American victory in the War with Mexico, 1848

9. the Gadsden Purchase from Mexico, the best route for a southern transcontinental railroad, 1853

As the nation grew, it had to be explored. **Highlight in red the path of the Lewis and Clark expedition, 1803–6,** the first of many expeditions into the unknown land. (Jefferson instructed Lewis and Clark to be on the lookout for mammoths; their skeletons proved that they had existed in Virginia, and they were not known to be extinct.)

Note that the western coast was settled and entered the Union as states (California and Oregon) long before the center of the continent (which became the

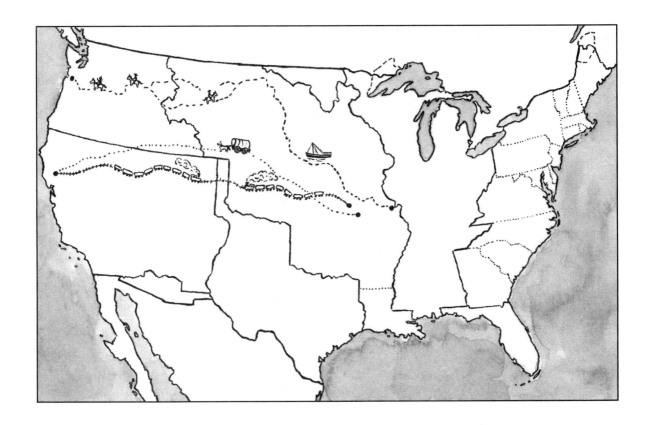

"middle border"). **Highlight in green the path of the 49ers,** who had to cross the Great Plains and the Rockies to get to where the gold was.

There were eventually three major transcontinental railroads, which opened up the Great Plains to settlement as well as "tying east to west with a ribbon of steel." **Highlight in yellow the path of the first one,** the Union Pacific, meeting the Central Pacific at Promontory, Utah, 1869.

Exercise 7 · The Civil War

Identify and outline in red the eleven Confederate states; identify and outline in green the four border states (slave states that did not secede); identify and outline in blue each Union state. What was the status of Oklahoma? How did West Virginia become a state?

Locate each place on the map by writing its number beside the correct dot:

1. **Appomattox:** Lee surrendered to Grant, April 15, 1865

2. **Atlanta:** its fall in July 1864 ensured Lincoln's reelection

3. **Charleston:** "cradle of secession," where the war began at Fort Sumter, April 1861

4. **Chickamauga:** bloody Confederate victory in 1863 led to the siege of Chattanooga until lifted by Grant

5. **Gettysburg:** Union victory that turned back Lee's invasion, July 1–3, 1863

6. **Mobile:** Alabama seaport captured by Farragut's fleet, August 1864

7. **New Orleans:** "Bayou City"; captured by Farragut, 1862

8. **Richmond:** capital of the Confederacy; defended by Lee's army

9. **St. Louis:** pro-Union city in a border state; rural areas were pro-Confederate

10. **Savannah:** Georgia seaport closed by blockade

11. **Shiloh:** first large battle in the West; Grant won on the second day after almost being driven into the river

12. **Vicksburg:** Confederate fortress blocking the Mississippi River; surrendered to Grant, July 4, 1863

13. **Washington, DC:** U.S. capital; surrounded by slave states and vulnerable to Confederate attack

There were four main "theaters" of war: Virginia ("the east"); Tennessee and the Gulf States ("the west"); the Trans-Mississippi west (Louisiana, Arkansas, and Texas); and the blockade of the southern coast. The Confederates were able to defend Virginia until 1865, but the blockade strangled the southern economy (the "Anaconda Plan"), and the opening of the Mississippi River in 1863 split the Confederacy into two.

Sherman's 1864 march "from Atlanta to the sea" (Savannah) split it again and devastated the countryside.

Exercise 8 · Reconstruction

Outline in heavy black the five military districts during congressional ("Radical") Reconstruction. Which former Confederate state was not included? Why?

Within each state, write its name, its date (year) of readmission to the Union, and the year when its Reconstruction state government was replaced by a white-majority (former Confederate, "Redeemer") state government. (The dates for each state are given; write them on the map.)

Using two differently colored highlighters, show which southern states gave their electoral votes to Republican Hayes and which to Democrat Tilden in the disputed election of 1876.

Alabama: 1868, 1874

Arkansas: 1868, 1874

Florida: 1868, 1877

Georgia: 1870, 1872

Louisiana: 1868, 1877

Mississippi: 1870, 1876

North Carolina: 1868, 1870

South Carolina: 1868, 1876

Tennessee: 1866, 1869; home of President Johnson and heavily Unionist in its eastern area

Texas: 1870, 1873

Virginia: 1870, 1869; its post-Reconstruction constitution was relatively moderate; trading continued black suffrage for restoration of ex-Confederate suffrage

Overall Reconstruction was at best disjointed and fragmented. The victorious North had many other pressing concerns (the new immigration, railroad construction, etc.) and grew less and less interested in reconstructing the South, and particularly in protecting the freedmen. The former Confederates, on the other hand, were focused on regaining control of their states. The names they gave to groups reflect this southern bias: "Carpetbaggers" and "Scalawags," "Radical" or "Black Reconstruction," "Redeemers" or "Bourbons."

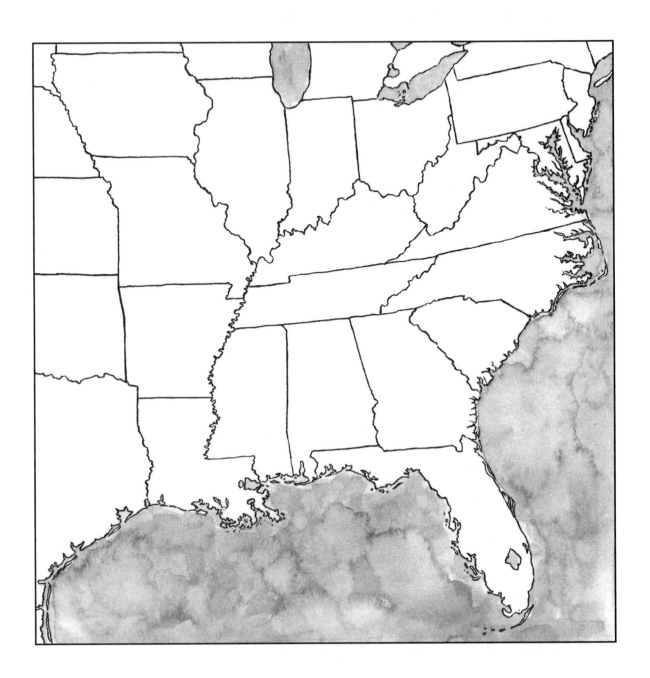

Exercise 9 · U.S. Overseas Expansion

Locate the following on the map and write the appropriate number beside the dot (the dots for the Philippines and Guam, and for the Caribbean, are found on the inset maps, for clarity; some of these places are tiny):

1. **Alaska:** purchased from Russia in 1867; "Seward's folly," which proved immensely valuable

2. **Aleutians:** volcanic islands extending from Alaska almost to Russia; part of the Alaskan Purchase

3. **Cuba:** freed from Spanish rule in 1898 and given independence; U.S. retains Guantánamo Naval Base

4. **Guam:** captured from Spain in 1898; the westernmost U.S. possession; a small island but an important base between Hawai'i and the Philippines

5. **Hawai'i:** a kingdom and then a republic heavily influenced by American merchants and missionaries during the 1800s; annexed by the United States in 1898; Pearl Harbor is the main U.S. naval base in the Pacific

6. **Panama:** seceded from Columbia with U.S. backing in 1903 so that the canal could be built; vital to both the world economy and U.S. defense by allowing warships to pass freely from ocean to ocean

7. **Philippines:** islands captured from Spain in 1898; fought a war for independence against the United States, which freed them by treaty in 1945; Manila is the site of the main U.S. naval base in the eastern Pacific

8. **Puerto Rico:** freed from Spanish rule in 1898; an unincorporated U.S. possession whose residents are U.S. citizens but regularly reject statehood and accompanying taxes

9. **Virgin Islands:** some belong to Britain, the rest to the United States, either taken from Spain in 1898 or purchased from Denmark in 1917

Most of these were conquered in the Spanish-American War of 1898. Inspired by American naval officer **Alfred T. Mahan's** books on sea power, they provide a chain of naval bases enabling the U.S. Navy to operate across the Pacific.

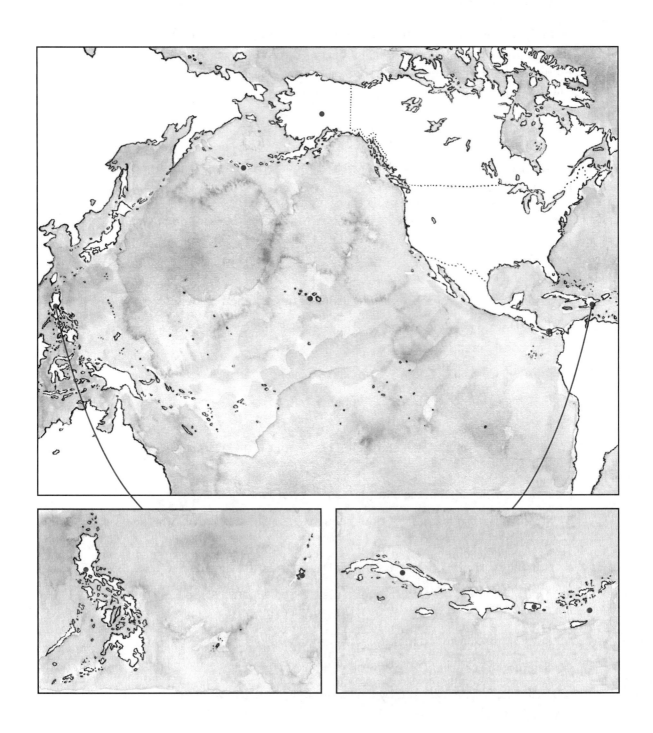

Exercise 10 · Europe in World War II

Write its name in each country. Use three differently colored highlighters to show which countries were originally part of the Axis, which were conquered by the Axis and then liberated by the Allies, and which were neutral throughout the war. Two countries will not be in any of these three categories.

Which country opposed Hitler throughout and was never conquered? (Hint: It was because the German army could not walk on water.) Which country began the war as a German ally until being invaded and half-conquered by Hitler? (Hint: It invaded Poland at the same time Germany did.)

Put each number in the following list beside the appropriate dot on the map:

1. **Ardennes:** forested area that was the site of the Battle of the Bulge, December 1944

2. **Berlin:** conquered by the Red Army in one of the bloodiest battles of the war

3. **Casablanca:** site of the conference between FDR and Churchill that demanded unconditional surrender

4. **Dresden:** German city destroyed by American and British fire-bombing

5. **El Alamein:** British field marshal Montgomery turns back Rommel's drive toward Egypt

6. **Leningrad:** formerly St. Petersburg; besieged by the Germans but never conquered

7. **London:** main target of the Blitz (the German word for "lightning")

8. **Moscow:** German patrols got close enough to see the Kremlin, but it was never conquered

9. **Normandy:** French peninsula; site of D-Day invasion

10. **Paris:** Patton was ordered to bypass the city so De Gaulle's Free French could liberate it

11. **Rome:** Mussolini hoped to restore it to its former glory

12. **Salerno:** site of Italian D-Day invasion

13. **Sicily:** the ball being kicked by the Italian boot; invaded by the Americans and the British in 1943

14. **Stalingrad:** turning point in the war; saw the surrender of the German Sixth Army

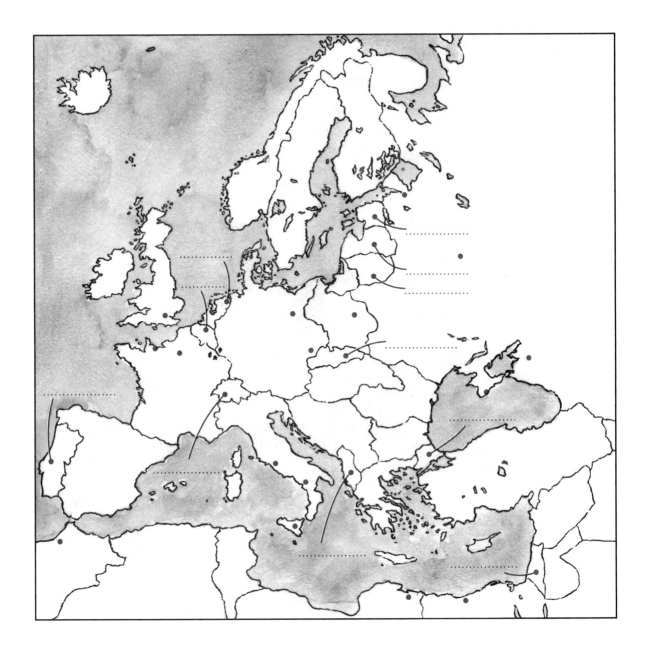

15. **Tobruk:** Libyan port defended by the Australians against Rommel's Afrika Korps

16. **Warsaw:** liberated by the Polish underground army, which was then crushed by the Germans while the Red Army paused its advance until the Germans eliminated the Polish resistance

17. **Yalta:** city in southern Russia; site of the last conference of FDR, Churchill, and Stalin

Exercise 11 · World War II in the South Pacific

It is hard to comprehend the sheer immensity of the war in the Pacific. From the Aleutians down to Australia and from the coast of California to the Philippines is about a quarter of the earth's surface. Strategy revolved around distances; tiny islands became important because they provided bases for long-range aircraft. The "fold" shown on the map represents about four hundred miles of water.

Locate the following on the map, and write the appropriate number beside the dot:

1. **Australia:** British Commonwealth nation the Japanese never quite reached

2. **Guadalcanal:** first U.S. counteroffensive; U.S. Marines on land and "iron bottom sound" offshore

3. **Hiroshima:** first Japanese city destroyed by the atomic bomb

4. **Hong Kong:** Chinese city and British possession easily captured by the Japanese

5. **Iwo Jima:** tiny island captured by U.S. Marines in a bloody assault, early 1945

6. **Korea:** peninsula between China and Japan; conquered by Japan

7. **Leyte Gulf:** giant air–naval battle near the Philippines, 1944; saw destruction of the Japanese fleet

8. **Manchuria:** industrialized northern part of China conquered by the Japanese

9. **Manila:** capital of the Philippines; captured by the Japanese and then liberated by MacArthur

10. **Midway:** air–naval battle in which the Japanese lost four aircraft carriers; turning point in the war

11. **Nagasaki:** second Japanese city destroyed by the atomic bomb

12. **Nanking:** Chinese city sacked by the Japanese army, with many atrocities

13. **New Guinea:** long lizard-island; heavy jungle; saw bitter fighting

14. **Okinawa:** site of last major battle and one of the bloodiest; the Japanese army fought almost to the last man

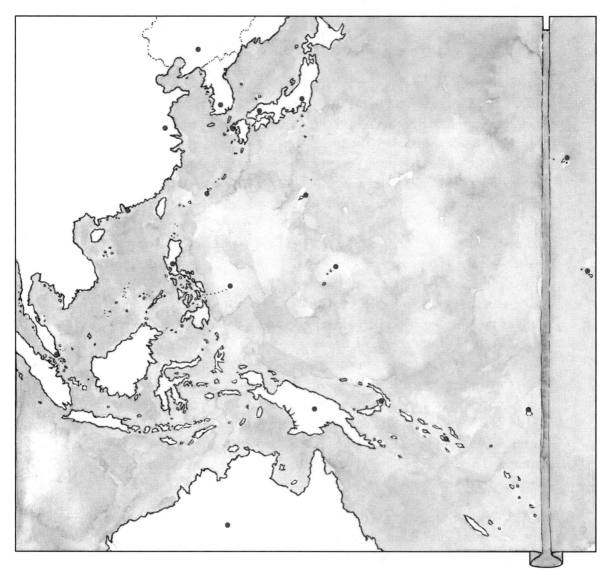

15. **Pearl Harbor:** near Honolulu, HI; main U.S. naval base in the Pacific

16. **Rabaul:** north of New Guinea and Australia; Japan's main naval–air base in the South Pacific

17. **Saipan:** one of the Mariana Islands; captured by the United States in June–July 1944; many civilian casualties

18. **Singapore:** British city in Indonesia; invulnerable from sea attack but captured from the land side

19. **Tarawa:** first U.S. Marine invasion of a Japanese-held island, November 1943

20. **Tokyo:** Japanese capital; subjected to heavy fire-bombing

Exercise 12 · Europe During the Cold War

Locate the "Iron Curtain" (Churchill's phrase) separating East and West Germany and the NATO nations from the Warsaw Pact. West Germany was the combined American, British, and French zones; the Russian zone became East Germany. **Locate the city of Berlin,** captured by the Red Army with horrendous casualties, after Eisenhower forbade Patton from taking the city. (Great prestige attaches to whoever captures the enemy capital, and it is possible that the loss of life would have been far less, as many Germans were eager to surrender to the Americans or British and terrified of the Russians.) Berlin was then divided into four zones just as Germany had been, and the American, British, and French zones became West Berlin. The free city was about a hundred miles inside East Germany and "behind the Iron Curtain." Until the Soviets built the **Berlin Wall (mark it** – it is also part of the "Iron Curtain") separating East Berlin from West, many Germans fled the Communist-controlled area into the west. Berlin was both strategically and symbolically the focal point of the Cold War, which ended when the Wall came down. ("Mr. Gorbachev, tear down this wall!") "And the wall came a tumbling down."

On the larger map of Europe, write the number from the following list in the appropriate country. Use three differently colored highlighters to show whether each country is part of NATO (North Atlantic Treaty Organization), part of the Warsaw Pact (WP), or neutral. Note that the most powerful NATO nation, and its organizer, is the United States, not on the map. (Canada is also a member of NATO.)

1. **West Germany:** the combined American, British, and French zones, deliberately kept nonnuclear but encouraged to build a powerful army; a large U.S. Army force was also stationed here, as a "trip wire"

2. **East Germany:** also heavily militarized by the Soviets; had war broken out between NATO and the Warsaw Pact, Germans would have been fighting Germans, which may be one reason why war never came

3, 4, 5, 6, 7, 8, 9, 10. **France, Italy, Belgium, Netherlands, Denmark, Norway, Iceland, Portugal:** members of NATO; individually vulnerable to Communist political or military attack but united to resist it

11. **Great Britain:** key NATO member and still a major nuclear power

12, 13. **Greece** and **Turkey:** NATO allies yet bitter rivals and often enemies

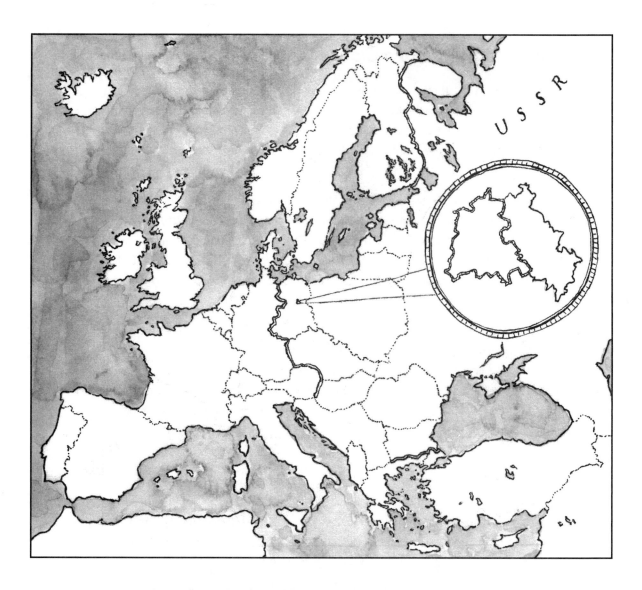

14. Poland: invaded from both sides; subject to massacres; betrayed and enslaved—but a Polish pope and a Polish labor movement were key in bringing down the Soviet Union

15, 16, 17, 18, 19. Albania, Bulgaria, Czechoslovakia, Hungary, Romania, the other Warsaw Pact nations

20, 21, 22, 23, 24, 25, 26. Sweden, Switzerland, Austria, Yugoslavia, Spain, Finland, Ireland: neutrals

The USSR is marked and extends all the way to the Pacific. It absorbed several previously independent nations, such as Estonia, Latvia, Ukraine, and Georgia (not the U.S. state!), among others.

The United States at a Glance

We've provided an otherwise blank map of the United States with state boundaries, and another with physical features added. **These can be copied and used for further study or for practice at naming the states.** The following list gives suggestions of other topics – and there are many more – that may be investigated with one of these maps.

1. Presidential elections are decided in the Electoral College. The electoral votes (EVs) of each state may change as a result of the ten-year census. Students may recreate an election by putting its number of EVs in each state and indicating with different colors which candidate (and party) got them. The most important elections are generally considered 1800, 1824, 1840, 1860, 1876, 1896, 1912, 1932, 1960, 1980, and 2000, but any are worth looking at.

2. Western states typically contain large tracts of land still owned and controlled by the U.S. government. Texas is an exception, because the republic retained ownership of its public lands by treaty when it joined the Union. (This is one reason why Texas has developed rapidly.) Students might research and indicate within each state what percentage of its land is controlled by the government in Washington, D.C. (Checking the internet for stories about the "Sagebrush Rebellion" might be a place to start.)

3 There have been many more expeditions and treks across the country than those shown on map 4. Possibilities for further study include Spanish and French explorers, such as Coronado and LaSalle; Americans like John C. Fremont; and groups such as the Mormons. Most of these are best studied by drawing their route onto the second map, as the "lay of the land" would largely determine where they went.

4. The Native American cultures are a fertile field for investigation. Possibilities include the various language groups, the level of culture (hunter-gatherers, villagers, or civilizations) of each nation or tribe, and the various wars and migrations both before and after contact with Europeans. Students might trace the paths of, for example, the flight of the Nez Pierce under Chief Joseph, the great Comanche Linnville raid of 1840, the campaigns of Geronimo, the Trail of Tears, and many others.

5. Transportation lines are immensely important – first the navigable rivers, then the railroads, and now the interstate highway system. These may best be done on the second map because geography restricts what can go where.

There are as many possible uses for these maps as there is interest or imagination!

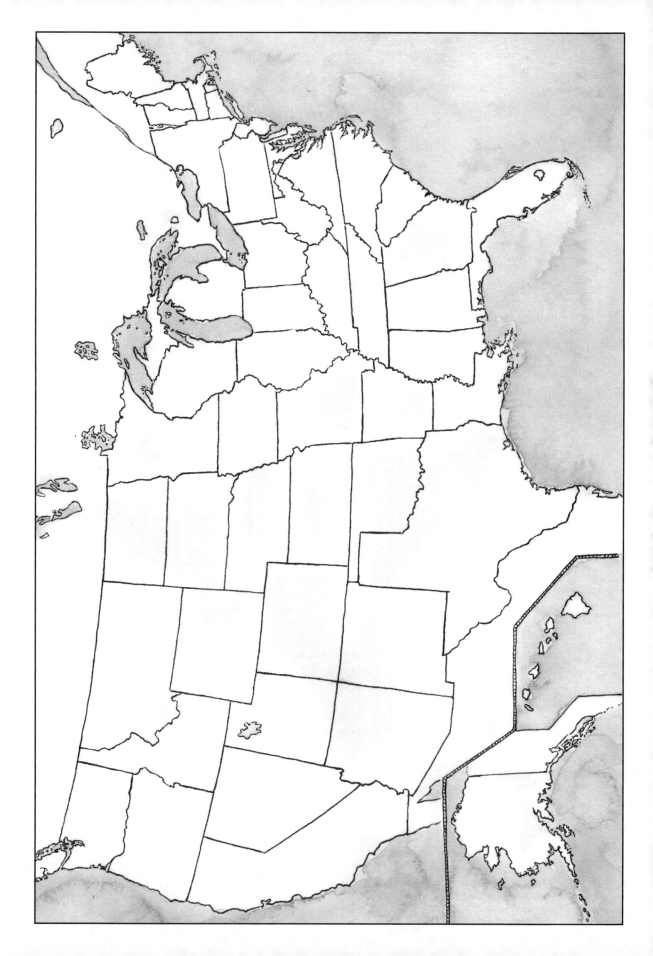

This map shows key rivers, mountain ranges, and rainfall. Rainfall is denoted with dots – the more dense the dots, the more rain in the region.

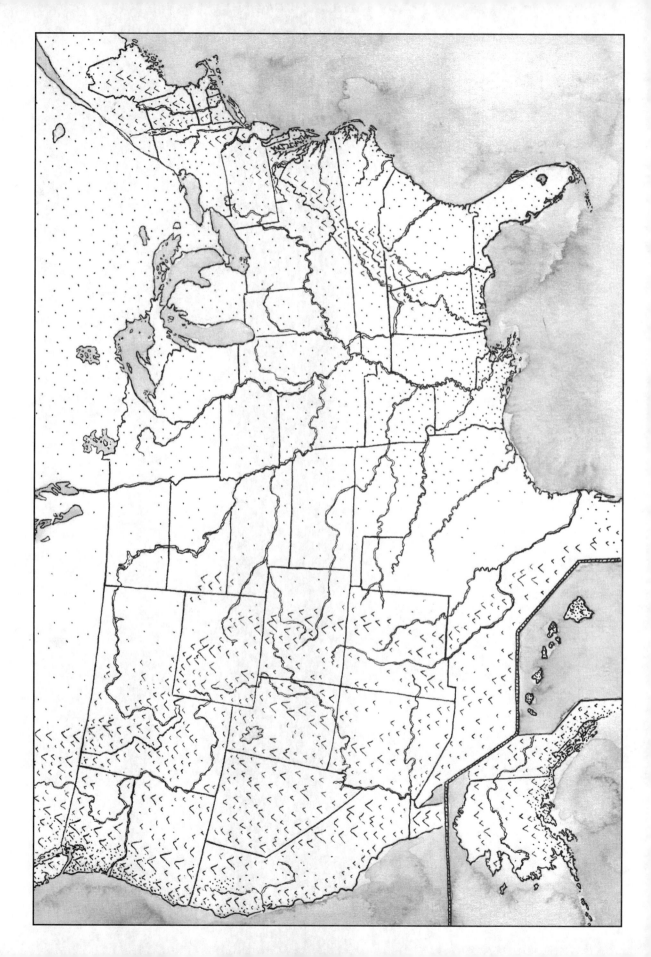

SUPPLEMENTAL MATERIALS

A QUICK AND EASY GUIDE TO THE ENGLISH AND BRITISH MONARCHY

From Colonization to the American Revolution

TUDOR DYNASTY (five rulers in three generations)

> Henry VII (r. 1485–1509): took the throne by force

> Henry VIII (r. 1509–47): six wives; broke England away from Roman Catholic Church; succeeded by three children

> Edward VI (r. 1547–53): Henry VIII's sickly son; Church of England became more Protestant during his reign

> Mary I (r. 1553–58): "Bloody Mary"; Henry VIII's eldest daughter; tried to restore the Catholic Church; died after a brief reign

> Elizabeth I (r. 1558–1603): "Virgin Queen" under whom expansion to Ireland and America began; stable on the throne once it was established that she would not marry; the Stuart king of Scotland would succeed her

> Tudor dynastic instability and weakness prevented English expansion overseas until Elizabeth, but began the establishment of English sea power (defeat of the Spanish Armada in 1588), the English conquest of Ireland, and its attempted colonization of Virginia and set the stage for the English Civil Wars of the mid-1600s.

STUART DYNASTY (six rulers in four generations)

Twelve of the thirteen colonies were settled under Stuart rule. Circumstances in England led directly to various groups wanting or needing to go to America.

> James VI of Scotland/James I of England (r. England 1603–25): king of Scotland who took the English throne by prearrangement when Elizabeth died; this is the "James" of Jamestown and the King James Bible; refused to give the Puritans what they demanded, stating "no bishops, no king," and persecuted them so that many left for New England

> Charles I (r. 1625–49): drove many Puritans to Massachusetts Colony; tried to rule without Parliament; executed after losing Civil Wars

Interregnum (1649–60): England ruled by Puritan military dictator Oliver Cromwell; some royalists ("Cavaliers") fled to Virginia

Restoration (1660): King and Parliament restored after Cromwell's death in 1659

Charles II (r. 1660–84): the "merry monarch" under whom was much colonization; New York, New Jersey, Pennsylvania, and the Carolinas ("Restoration colonies") established; was careful not to challenge Parliament's authority

James II (r. 1684–88): brother of Charles II; former naval commander and Duke of York; overthrown by Parliament in Glorious Revolution of 1688 because he was Catholic

Mary II and husband, William of Orange (r. 1689–1702): Mary was the daughter of James II; Protestant rulers of the Netherlands invited by Parliament to succeed James II – note that Parliament is hiring and firing kings

Anne (r. 1702–14): sister of Mary; also Protestant; ruled until she died childless; succeeded by the Hanover Dynasty

HANOVER DYNASTY

Protestant kings of Hanover in Germany; became rulers of England beginning in 1714 until the present day. George I spoke no English, George II only poor English; George III (king in 1776) was the first fully English monarch from the family, which changed its name from Hanover to Windsor during World War I (because Hanover was part of Germany and on the other side). The Colony of Georgia established in 1732 under George II (last of thirteen, and only one established after 1700)

THE DECLARATION OF INDEPENDENCE

Note: The following text is a transcription of the Stone Engraving of the parchment Declaration of Independence (the document on display in the Rotunda at the National Archives Museum). The spelling and punctuation reflect the original.

In Congress, July 4, 1776

The unanimous Declaration of the thirteen united States of America, When in the Course of human events, it becomes necessary for one people to dissolve the political bands which have connected them with another, and to assume among the powers of the earth, the separate and equal station to which the Laws of Nature and of Nature's God entitle them, a decent respect to the opinions of mankind requires that they should declare the causes which impel them to the separation.

We hold these truths to be self-evident, that all men are created equal, that they are endowed by their Creator with certain unalienable Rights, that among these are Life, Liberty and the pursuit of Happiness. – That to secure these rights, Governments are instituted among Men, deriving their just powers from the consent of the governed, – That whenever any Form of Government becomes destructive of these ends, it is the Right of the People to alter or to abolish it, and to institute new Government, laying its foundation on such principles and organizing its powers in such form, as to them shall seem most likely to effect their Safety and Happiness. Prudence, indeed, will dictate that Governments long established should not be changed for light and transient causes; and accordingly all experience hath shewn, that mankind are more disposed to suffer, while evils are sufferable, than to right themselves by abolishing the forms to which they are accustomed. But when a long train of abuses and usurpations, pursuing invariably the same Object evinces a design to reduce them under absolute Despotism, it is their right, it is their duty, to throw off such Government, and to provide new Guards for their future security. – Such has been the patient sufferance of these Colonies; and such is now the necessity which constrains them to alter their former Systems of Government. The history of the present King of Great Britain is a history of repeated injuries and usurpations, all having in direct object the establishment of an absolute Tyranny over these States. To prove this, let Facts be submitted to a candid world.

He has refused his Assent to Laws, the most wholesome and necessary for the public good.

He has forbidden his Governors to pass Laws of immediate and pressing importance, unless suspended in their operation till his Assent should be obtained; and when so suspended, he has utterly neglected to attend to them.

He has refused to pass other Laws for the accommodation of large districts of people, unless those people would relinquish the right of Representation in the Legislature, a right inestimable to them and formidable to tyrants only.

He has called together legislative bodies at places unusual, uncomfortable, and distant from the depository of their public Records, for the sole purpose of fatiguing them into compliance with his measures.

He has dissolved Representative Houses repeatedly, for opposing with manly firmness his invasions on the rights of the people.

He has refused for a long time, after such dissolutions, to cause others to be elected; whereby the Legislative powers, incapable of Annihilation, have returned to the People at large for their exercise; the State remaining in the mean time exposed to all the dangers of invasion from without, and convulsions within.

He has endeavoured to prevent the population of these States; for that purpose obstructing the Laws for Naturalization of Foreigners; refusing to pass others to encourage their migrations hither, and raising the conditions of new Appropriations of Lands.

He has obstructed the Administration of Justice, by refusing his Assent to Laws for establishing Judiciary powers.

He has made Judges dependent on his Will alone, for the tenure of their offices, and the amount and payment of their salaries.

He has erected a multitude of New Offices, and sent hither swarms of Officers to harrass our people, and eat out their substance.

He has kept among us, in times of peace, Standing Armies without the Consent of our legislatures.

He has affected to render the Military independent of and superior to the Civil power.

He has combined with others to subject us to a jurisdiction foreign to our constitution, and unacknowledged by our laws; giving his Assent to their Acts of pretended Legislation:

For Quartering large bodies of armed troops among us:

For protecting them, by a mock Trial, from punishment for any Murders which they should commit on the Inhabitants of these States:

For cutting off our Trade with all parts of the world:

For imposing Taxes on us without our Consent:

For depriving us in many cases, of the benefits of Trial by Jury:

For transporting us beyond Seas to be tried for pretended offences

For abolishing the free System of English Laws in a neighbouring Province, establishing therein an Arbitrary government, and enlarging its Boundaries so as to render it at once an example and fit instrument for introducing the same absolute rule into these Colonies:

For taking away our Charters, abolishing our most valuable Laws, and altering fundamentally the Forms of our Governments:

For suspending our own Legislatures, and declaring themselves invested with power to legislate for us in all cases whatsoever.

He has abdicated Government here, by declaring us out of his Protection and waging War against us.

He has plundered our seas, ravaged our Coasts, burnt our towns, and destroyed the lives of our people.

He is at this time transporting large Armies of foreign Mercenaries to compleat the works of death, desolation and tyranny, already begun with circumstances of Cruelty & perfidy scarcely paralleled in the most barbarous ages, and totally unworthy the Head of a civilized nation.

He has constrained our fellow Citizens taken Captive on the high Seas to bear Arms against their Country, to become the executioners of their friends and Brethren, or to fall themselves by their Hands.

He has excited domestic insurrections amongst us, and has endeavoured to bring on the inhabitants of our frontiers, the merciless Indian Savages, whose known rule of warfare, is an undistinguished destruction of all ages, sexes and conditions.

In every stage of these Oppressions We have Petitioned for Redress in the most humble terms: Our repeated Petitions have been answered only by repeated injury. A Prince whose character is thus marked by every act which may define a Tyrant, is unfit to be the ruler of a free people.

Nor have We been wanting in attentions to our Brittish brethren. We have warned them from time to time of attempts by their legislature to extend an unwarrantable jurisdiction over us. We have reminded them of the circumstances of our emigration and settlement here. We have appealed to their native justice and magnanimity, and we have conjured them by the ties of our common kindred to disavow these usurpations, which, would inevitably interrupt our connections and correspondence. They too have been deaf to the voice of justice and of consanguinity. We must, therefore, acquiesce in the necessity, which denounces our Separation, and hold them, as we hold the rest of mankind, Enemies in War, in Peace Friends.

We, therefore, the Representatives of the united States of America, in General Congress, Assembled, appealing to the Supreme Judge of the world for the rectitude of our intentions, do, in the Name, and by Authority of the good People of these Colonies, solemnly publish and declare, That these United Colonies are, and of Right ought to be Free and Independent States; that they are Absolved from all Allegiance to the British Crown, and that all political connection between them and the State of Great Britain, is and ought to be totally dissolved; and that as Free and Independent States, they have full Power to levy War, conclude Peace, contract Alliances, establish Commerce, and to do all other Acts and Things which Independent States may of right do. And for the support of this Declaration, with a firm reliance on the protection of divine Providence, we mutually pledge to each other our Lives, our Fortunes and our sacred Honor.

Source: https://www.archives.gov/founding-docs/declaration-transcript

THE U.S. CONSTITUTION

(Including the Bill of Rights and All Other Amendments)

We the People of the United States, in Order to form a more perfect Union, establish Justice, insure domestic Tranquility, provide for the common defence, promote the general Welfare, and secure the Blessings of Liberty to ourselves and our Posterity, do ordain and establish this Constitution for the United States of America.

ARTICLE I

Section 1: Congress

All legislative Powers herein granted shall be vested in a Congress of the United States, which shall consist of a Senate and House of Representatives.

Section 2: The House of Representatives

The House of Representatives shall be composed of Members chosen every second Year by the People of the several States, and the Electors in each State shall have the Qualifications requisite for Electors of the most numerous Branch of the State Legislature.

No Person shall be a Representative who shall not have attained to the Age of twenty five Years, and been seven Years a Citizen of the United States, and who shall not, when elected, be an Inhabitant of that State in which he shall be chosen.

Representatives and direct Taxes shall be apportioned among the several States which may be included within this Union, according to their respective Numbers, which shall be determined by adding to the whole Number of free Persons, including those bound to Service for a Term of Years, and excluding Indians not taxed, three fifths of all other Persons. The actual Enumeration shall be made within three Years after the first Meeting of the Congress of the United States, and within every subsequent Term of ten Years, in such Manner as they shall by Law direct. The number of Representatives shall not exceed one for every thirty Thousand, but each State shall have at Least one Representative; and until such enumeration shall be made, the State of New Hampshire shall be entitled to chuse three, Massachusetts eight, Rhode-Island and Providence Plantations one, Connecticut five, New-York six, New Jersey four, Pennsylvania eight, Delaware one, Maryland six, Virginia ten, North Carolina five, South Carolina five, and Georgia three.

When vacancies happen in the Representation from any State, the Executive Authority thereof shall issue Writs of Election to fill such Vacancies.

The House of Representatives shall chuse their Speaker and other Officers; and shall have the sole Power of Impeachment.

Section 3: The Senate

The Senate of the United States shall be composed of two Senators from each State, chosen by the Legislature thereof, for six Years; and each Senator shall have one Vote.

Immediately after they shall be assembled in Consequence of the first Election, they shall be divided as equally as may be into three Classes. The Seats of the Senators of the first Class shall be vacated at the Expiration of the second Year, of the second Class at the Expiration of the fourth Year, and of the third Class at the Expiration of the sixth Year, so that one third may be chosen every second Year; and if Vacancies happen by Resignation, or otherwise, during the Recess of the Legislature of any State, the Executive thereof may make temporary Appointments until the next Meeting of the Legislature, which shall then fill such Vacancies.

No Person shall be a Senator who shall not have attained to the Age of thirty Years, and been nine Years a Citizen of the United States, and who shall not, when elected, be an Inhabitant of that State for which he shall be chosen.

The Vice President of the United States shall be President of the Senate, but shall have no Vote, unless they be equally divided.

The Senate shall chuse their other Officers, and also a President pro tempore, in the Absence of the Vice President, or when he shall exercise the Office of President of the United States.

The Senate shall have the sole Power to try all Impeachments. When sitting for that Purpose, they shall be on Oath or Affirmation. When the President of the United States is tried, the Chief Justice shall preside: And no Person shall be convicted without the Concurrence of two thirds of the Members present.

Judgment in Cases of Impeachment shall not extend further than to removal from Office, and disqualification to hold and enjoy any Office of honor, Trust or Profit under the United States: but the Party convicted shall nevertheless be liable and subject to Indictment, Trial, Judgment and Punishment, according to Law.

Section 4: Elections

The Times, Places and Manner of holding Elections for Senators and Representatives, shall be prescribed in each State by the Legislature thereof; but the Congress may at any time by Law make or alter such Regulations, except as to the Places of chusing Senators.

The Congress shall assemble at least once in every Year, and such Meeting shall be on the first Monday in December, unless they shall by Law appoint a different Day.

Section 5: Powers and Duties of Congress

Each House shall be the Judge of the Elections, Returns and Qualifications of its own Members, and a Majority of each shall constitute a Quorum to do Business; but a smaller Number may adjourn from day to day, and may be authorized to compel the Attendance of absent Members, in such Manner, and under such Penalties as each House may provide.

Each House may determine the Rules of its Proceedings, punish its Members for disorderly Behaviour, and, with the Concurrence of two thirds, expel a Member.

Each House shall keep a Journal of its Proceedings, and from time to time publish the same, excepting such Parts as may in their Judgment require Secrecy; and the Yeas and Nays of the Members of either House on any question shall, at the Desire of one fifth of those Present, be entered on the Journal.

Neither House, during the Session of Congress, shall, without the Consent of the other, adjourn for more than three days, nor to any other Place than that in which the two Houses shall be sitting.

Section 6: Rights and Disabilities of Members

The Senators and Representatives shall receive a Compensation for their Services, to be ascertained by Law, and paid out of the Treasury of the United States. They shall in all Cases, except Treason, Felony and Breach of the Peace, be privileged from Arrest during their Attendance at the Session of their respective Houses, and in going to and returning from the same; and for any Speech or Debate in either House, they shall not be questioned in any other Place.

No Senator or Representative shall, during the Time for which he was elected, be appointed to any civil Office under the Authority of the United States, which shall have been created, or the Emoluments whereof shall have been encreased during such time; and no Person holding any Office under the

United States, shall be a Member of either House during his Continuance in Office.

Section 7: Legislative Process

All Bills for raising Revenue shall originate in the House of Representatives; but the Senate may propose or concur with Amendments as on other Bills.

Every Bill which shall have passed the House of Representatives and the Senate, shall, before it become a Law, be presented to the President of the United States; If he approve he shall sign it, but if not he shall return it, with his Objections to that House in which it shall have originated, who shall enter the Objections at large on their Journal, and proceed to reconsider it. If after such Reconsideration two thirds of that House shall agree to pass the Bill, it shall be sent, together with the Objections, to the other House, by which it shall likewise be reconsidered, and if approved by two thirds of that House, it shall become a Law. But in all such Cases the Votes of both Houses shall be determined by Yeas and Nays, and the Names of the Persons voting for and against the Bill shall be entered on the Journal of each House respectively. If any Bill shall not be returned by the President within ten Days (Sundays excepted) after it shall have been presented to him, the Same shall be a Law, in like Manner as if he had signed it, unless the Congress by their Adjournment prevent its Return, in which Case it shall not be a Law.

Every Order, Resolution, or Vote to which the Concurrence of the Senate and House of Representatives may be necessary (except on a question of Adjournment) shall be presented to the President of the United States; and before the Same shall take Effect, shall be approved by him, or being disapproved by him, shall be repassed by two thirds of the Senate and House of Representatives, according to the Rules and Limitations prescribed in the Case of a Bill.

Section 8: Powers of Congress

The Congress shall have Power To lay and collect Taxes, Duties, Imposts and Excises, to pay the Debts and provide for the common Defence and general Welfare of the United States; but all Duties, Imposts and Excises shall be uniform throughout the United States;

To borrow Money on the credit of the United States;

To regulate Commerce with foreign Nations, and among the several States, and with the Indian Tribes;

To establish a uniform Rule of Naturalization, and uniform Laws on the subject of Bankruptcies throughout the United States;

To coin Money, regulate the Value thereof, and of foreign Coin, and fix the Standard of Weights and Measures;

To provide for the Punishment of counterfeiting the Securities and current Coin of the United States;

To establish Post Offices and post Roads;

To promote the Progress of Science and useful Arts, by securing for limited Times to Authors and Inventors the exclusive Right to their respective Writings and Discoveries;

To constitute Tribunals inferior to the supreme Court;

To define and punish Piracies and Felonies committed on the high Seas, and Offenses against the Law of Nations;

To declare War, grant Letters of Marque and Reprisal, and make Rules concerning Captures on Land and Water;

To raise and support Armies, but no Appropriation of Money to that Use shall be for a longer Term than two Years;

To provide and maintain a Navy;

To make Rules for the Government and Regulation of the land and naval Forces;

To provide for calling forth the Militia to execute the Laws of the Union, suppress Insurrections and repel Invasions;

To provide for organizing, arming, and disciplining, the Militia, and for governing such Part of them as may be employed in the Service of the United States, reserving to the States respectively, the Appointment of the Officers, and the Authority of training the Militia according to the discipline prescribed by Congress;

To exercise exclusive Legislation in all Cases whatsoever, over such District (not exceeding ten Miles square) as may, by Cession of particular States, and the Acceptance of Congress, become the Seat of the Government of the United States, and to exercise like Authority over all Places purchased by the Consent of the Legislature of the State in which the Same shall be, for the Erection of Forts, Magazines, Arsenals, dock-Yards and other needful Buildings; And

To make all Laws which shall be necessary and proper for carrying into Execution the foregoing Powers, and all other Powers vested by this Constitution in the Government of the United States, or in any Department or Officer thereof.

Section 9: Powers Denied Congress

The Migration or Importation of such Persons as any of the States now existing shall think proper to admit, shall not be prohibited by the Congress prior to the Year one thousand eight hundred and eight, but a Tax or duty may be imposed on such Importation, not exceeding ten dollars for each Person.

The Privilege of the Writ of Habeas Corpus shall not be suspended, unless when in Cases of Rebellion or Invasion the public Safety may require it.

No Bill of Attainder or ex post facto Law shall be passed.

No Capitation, or other direct, Tax shall be laid, unless in Proportion to the Census or Enumeration herein before directed to be taken.

No Tax or Duty shall be laid on Articles exported from any State.

No Preference shall be given by any Regulation of Commerce or Revenue to the Ports of one State over those of another: nor shall Vessels bound to, or from, one State, be obliged to enter, clear, or pay Duties in another.

No Money shall be drawn from the Treasury, but in Consequence of Appropriations made by Law; and a regular Statement and Account of the Receipts and Expenditures of all public Money shall be published from time to time.

No Title of Nobility shall be granted by the United States: And no Person holding any Office of Profit or Trust under them, shall, without the Consent of the Congress, accept of any present, Emolument, Office, or Title, of any kind whatever, from any King, Prince, or foreign State.

Section 10: Powers Denied to the States

No State shall enter into any Treaty, Alliance, or Confederation; grant Letters of Marque and Reprisal; coin Money; emit Bills of Credit; make any Thing but gold and silver Coin a Tender in Payment of Debts; pass any Bill of Attainder, ex post facto Law, or Law impairing the Obligation of Contracts, or grant any Title of Nobility.

No State shall, without the Consent of the Congress, lay any Imposts or Duties on Imports or Exports, except what may be absolutely necessary for executing it's inspection Laws: and the net Produce of all Duties and Imposts, laid by any State on Imports or Exports, shall be for the Use of the Treasury of the United States; and all such Laws shall be subject to the Revision and Controul of the Congress.

No State shall, without the Consent of Congress, lay any Duty of Tonnage, keep Troops, or Ships of War in time of Peace, enter into any Agreement or Compact with another State, or with a foreign Power, or engage in War, unless actually invaded, or in such imminent Danger as will not admit of delay.

ARTICLE II

Section I

The executive Power shall be vested in a President of the United States of America.

He shall hold his Office during the Term of four Years, and, together with the Vice President, chosen for the same Term, be elected, as follows:

Each State shall appoint, in such Manner as the Legislature thereof may direct, a Number of Electors, equal to the whole Number of Senators and Representatives to which the State may be entitled in the Congress: but no Senator or Representative, or Person holding an Office of Trust or Profit under the United States, shall be appointed an Elector.

The Electors shall meet in their respective States, and vote by Ballot for two Persons, of whom one at least shall not be an Inhabitant of the same State with themselves. And they shall make a List of all the Persons voted for, and of the Number of Votes for each; which List they shall sign and certify, and transmit sealed to the Seat of the Government of the United States, directed to the President of the Senate. The President of the Senate shall, in the Presence of the Senate and House of Representatives, open all the Certificates, and the Votes shall then be counted. The Person having the greatest Number of Votes shall be the President, if such Number be a Majority of the whole Number of Electors appointed; and if there be more than one who have such Majority, and have an equal Number of Votes, then the House of Representatives shall immediately chuse by Ballot one of them for President; and if no Person have a Majority, then from the five highest on the List the said House shall in like Manner chuse the President. But in chusing the President, the Votes shall be taken by States, the Representation from each State having one Vote; A quorum for this Purpose shall consist of a Member or Members from two thirds of the States, and a Majority of all the States shall be necessary to a Choice. In every Case, after the Choice of the President, the Person having the greatest Number of Votes of the Electors shall be the Vice President. But if there should remain two or more who have equal Votes, the Senate shall chuse from them by Ballot the Vice President.

The Congress may determine the Time of chusing the Electors, and the Day on which they shall give their Votes; which Day shall be the same throughout the United States.

No Person except a natural born Citizen, or a Citizen of the United States, at the time of the Adoption of this Constitution, shall be eligible to the Office of President; neither shall any person be eligible to that Office who shall not have attained to the Age of thirty five Years, and been fourteen Years a Resident within the United States.

In Case of the Removal of the President from Office, or of his Death, Resignation, or Inability to discharge the Powers and Duties of the said Office, the Same shall devolve on the Vice President, and the Congress may by Law provide for the Case of Removal, Death, Resignation or Inability, both of the President and Vice President, declaring what Officer shall then act as President, and such Officer shall act accordingly, until the Disability be removed, or a President shall be elected.

The President shall, at stated Times, receive for his Services, a Compensation, which shall neither be increased nor diminished during the Period for which he shall have been elected, and he shall not receive within that Period any other Emolument from the United States, or any of them.

Before he enter on the Execution of his Office, he shall take the following Oath or Affirmation: – "I do solemnly swear (or affirm) that I will faithfully execute the Office of President of the United States, and will to the best of my Ability, preserve, protect and defend the Constitution of the United States."

Section 2

The President shall be Commander in Chief of the Army and Navy of the United States, and of the Militia of the several States, when called into the actual Service of the United States; he may require the Opinion, in writing, of the principal Officer in each of the executive Departments, upon any Subject relating to the Duties of their respective Offices, and he shall have Power to grant Reprieves and Pardons for Offenses against the United States, except in Cases of Impeachment.

He shall have Power, by and with the Advice and Consent of the Senate, to make Treaties, provided two thirds of the Senators present concur; and he shall nominate, and by and with the Advice and Consent of the Senate, shall appoint Ambassadors, other public Ministers and Consuls, Judges of the supreme Court, and all other Officers of the United States, whose Appointments are not herein otherwise provided for, and which shall be established by Law: but the Congress may by Law vest the Appointment of such inferior Officers, as they think proper, in the President alone, in the Courts of Law, or in the Heads of Departments.

The President shall have Power to fill up all Vacancies that may happen during the Recess of the Senate, by granting Commissions which shall expire at the End of their next Session.

Section 3

He shall from time to time give to the Congress Information of the State of the Union, and recommend to their Consideration such Measures as he shall judge necessary and expedient; he may, on extraordinary Occasions, convene both Houses, or either of them, and in Case of Disagreement between them, with Respect to the Time of Adjournment, he may adjourn them to such Time as he shall think proper; he shall receive Ambassadors and other public Ministers; he shall take Care that the Laws be faithfully executed, and shall Commission all the Officers of the United States.

Section 4

The President, Vice President and all civil Officers of the United States, shall be removed from Office on Impeachment for, and Conviction of, Treason, Bribery, or other high Crimes and Misdemeanors.

ARTICLE III

Section 1

The judicial Power of the United States, shall be vested in one supreme Court, and in such inferior Courts as the Congress may from time to time ordain and establish. The Judges, both of the supreme and inferior Courts, shall hold their Offices during good Behaviour, and shall, at stated Times, receive for their Services, a Compensation, which shall not be diminished during their Continuance in Office.

Section 2

The judicial Power shall extend to all Cases, in Law and Equity, arising under this Constitution, the Laws of the United States, and Treaties made, or which shall be made, under their Authority; – to all Cases affecting Ambassadors, other public Ministers and Consuls; – to all Cases of admiralty and maritime Jurisdiction; – to Controversies to which the United States shall be a Party; – to Controversies between two or more States; – between a State and Citizens of another State; – between Citizens of different States; – between Citizens of the same State claiming Lands under Grants of different States, and between a State, or the Citizens thereof, and foreign States, Citizens or Subjects.

In all Cases affecting Ambassadors, other public Ministers and Consuls, and those in which a State shall be Party, the supreme Court shall have original Jurisdiction. In all the other Cases before mentioned, the supreme Court shall have appellate Jurisdiction, both as to Law and Fact, with such Exceptions, and under such Regulations as the Congress shall make.

The Trial of all Crimes, except in Cases of Impeachment; shall be by Jury; and such Trial shall be held in the State where the said Crimes shall have been committed; but when not committed within any State, the Trial shall be at such Place or Places as the Congress may by Law have directed.

Section 3

Treason against the United States, shall consist only in levying War against them, or in adhering to their Enemies, giving them Aid and Comfort. No Person shall be convicted of Treason unless on the Testimony of two Witnesses to the same overt Act, or on Confession in open Court.

The Congress shall have Power to declare the Punishment of Treason, but no Attainder of Treason shall work Corruption of Blood, or Forfeiture except during the Life of the Person attainted.

ARTICLE IV

Section 1

Full Faith and Credit shall be given in each State to the public Acts, Records, and judicial Proceedings of every other State. And the Congress may by general Laws prescribe the Manner in which such Acts, Records and Proceedings shall be proved, and the Effect thereof.

Section 2

The Citizens of each State shall be entitled to all Privileges and Immunities of Citizens in the several States.

A Person charged in any State with Treason, Felony, or other Crime, who shall flee from Justice, and be found in another State, shall on Demand of the executive Authority of the State from which he fled, be delivered up, to be removed to the State having Jurisdiction of the Crime.

No Person held to Service or Labour in one State, under the Laws thereof, escaping into another, shall, in Consequence of any Law or Regulation therein, be discharged from such Service or Labour, but shall be delivered up on Claim of the Party to whom such Service or Labour may be due.

Section 3

New States may be admitted by the Congress into this Union; but no new State shall be formed or erected within the Jurisdiction of any other State; nor any State be formed by the Junction of two or more States, or Parts of States, without the Consent of the Legislatures of the States concerned as well as of the Congress.

The Congress shall have Power to dispose of and make all needful Rules and Regulations respecting the Territory or other Property belonging to the United States; and nothing in this Constitution shall be so construed as to Prejudice any Claims of the United States, or of any particular State.

Section 4

The United States shall guarantee to every State in this Union a Republican Form of Government, and shall protect each of them against Invasion; and on Application of the Legislature, or of the Executive (when the Legislature cannot be convened) against domestic Violence.

ARTICLE V

The Congress, whenever two thirds of both Houses shall deem it necessary, shall propose Amendments to this Constitution, or, on the Application of the Legislatures of two thirds of the several States, shall call a Convention for proposing Amendments, which, in either Case, shall be valid to all Intents and Purposes, as Part of this Constitution, when ratified by the Legislatures of three fourths of the several States, or by Conventions in three fourths thereof, as the one or the other Mode of Ratification may be proposed by the Congress; Provided that no Amendment which may be made prior to the Year One thousand eight hundred and eight shall in any Manner affect the first and fourth Clauses in the Ninth Section of the first Article; and that no State, without its Consent, shall be deprived of its equal Suffrage in the Senate.

ARTICLE VI

All Debts contracted and Engagements entered into, before the Adoption of this Constitution, shall be as valid against the United States under this Constitution, as under the Confederation.

This Constitution, and the Laws of the United States which shall be made in Pursuance thereof; and all Treaties made, or which shall be made, under the

Authority of the United States, shall be the supreme Law of the Land; and the Judges in every State shall be bound thereby, any Thing in the Constitution or Laws of any State to the Contrary notwithstanding.

The Senators and Representatives before mentioned, and the Members of the several State Legislatures, and all executive and judicial Officers, both of the United States and of the several States, shall be bound by Oath or Affirmation, to support this Constitution; but no religious Test shall ever be required as a Qualification to any Office or public Trust under the United States.

ARTICLE VII

The Ratification of the Conventions of nine States, shall be sufficient for the Establishment of this Constitution between the States so ratifying the Same.

First Amendment

Congress shall make no law respecting an establishment of religion, or prohibiting the free exercise thereof; or abridging the freedom of speech, or of the press; or the right of the people peaceably to assemble, and to petition the Government for a redress of grievances.

Second Amendment

A well regulated Militia, being necessary to the security of a free State, the right of the people to keep and bear Arms, shall not be infringed.

Third Amendment

No Soldier shall, in time of peace be quartered in any house, without the consent of the Owner, nor in time of war, but in a manner to be prescribed by law.

Fourth Amendment

The right of the people to be secure in their persons, houses, papers, and effects, against unreasonable searches and seizures, shall not be violated, and no Warrants shall issue, but upon probable cause, supported by Oath or affirmation, and particularly describing the place to be searched, and the persons or things to be seized.

Fifth Amendment

No person shall be held to answer for a capital, or otherwise infamous crime, unless on a presentment or indictment of a Grand Jury, except in cases arising in the land or naval forces, or in the Militia, when in actual service in time of War or public danger; nor shall any person be subject for the same offence to be twice put in jeopardy of life or limb; nor shall be compelled in any criminal case to be a witness against himself, nor be deprived of life, liberty, or property, without due process of law; nor shall private property be taken for public use, without just compensation.

Sixth Amendment

In all criminal prosecutions, the accused shall enjoy the right to a speedy and public trial, by an impartial jury of the State and district wherein the crime shall have been committed, which district shall have been previously ascertained by law, and to be informed of the nature and cause of the accusation; to be confronted with the witnesses against him; to have compulsory process for obtaining witnesses in his favor, and to have the Assistance of Counsel for his defence.

Seventh Amendment

In Suits at common law, where the value in controversy shall exceed twenty dollars, the right of trial by jury shall be preserved, and no fact tried by a jury, shall be otherwise reexamined in any Court of the United States, than according to the rules of the common law.

Eighth Amendment

Excessive bail shall not be required, nor excessive fines imposed, nor cruel and unusual punishments inflicted.

Ninth Amendment

The enumeration in the Constitution, of certain rights, shall not be construed to deny or disparage others retained by the people.

Tenth Amendment

The powers not delegated to the United States by the Constitution, nor prohibited by it to the States, are reserved to the States respectively, or to the people.

Eleventh Amendment

The Judicial power of the United States shall not be construed to extend to any suit in law or equity, commenced or prosecuted against one of the United States by Citizens of another State, or by Citizens or Subjects of any Foreign State.

Twelfth Amendment

The Electors shall meet in their respective states and vote by ballot for President and Vice-President, one of whom, at least, shall not be an inhabitant of the same state with themselves; they shall name in their ballots the person voted for as President, and in distinct ballots the person voted for as Vice-President, and they shall make distinct lists of all persons voted for as President, and of all persons voted for as Vice-President, and of the number of votes for each, which lists they shall sign and certify, and transmit sealed to the seat of the government of the United States, directed to the President of the Senate; – The President of the Senate shall, in the presence of the Senate and House of Representatives, open all the certificates and the votes shall then be counted; – The person having the greatest number of votes for President, shall be the President, if such number be a majority of the whole number of Electors appointed; and if no person have such majority, then from the persons having the highest numbers not exceeding three on the list of those voted for as President, the House of Representatives shall choose immediately, by ballot, the President. But in choosing the President, the votes shall be taken by states, the representation from each state having one vote; a quorum for this purpose shall consist of a member or members from two-thirds of the states, and a majority of all the states shall be necessary to a choice. And if the House of Representatives shall not choose a President whenever the right of choice shall devolve upon them, before the fourth day of March next following, then the Vice-President shall act as President, as in case of the death or other constitutional disability of the President. – The person having the greatest number of votes as Vice-President, shall be the Vice-President, if such number be a majority of the whole number of Electors appointed, and if no person have a majority, then from the two highest numbers on the list, the Senate shall choose the Vice-President; a quorum for the purpose shall consist of two-thirds of the whole number of Senators, and a majority of the whole number shall be necessary to a choice. But no person constitutionally ineligible to the office of President shall be eligible to that of Vice-President of the United States.

Thirteenth Amendment

Section 1

Neither slavery nor involuntary servitude, except as a punishment for crime whereof the party shall have been duly convicted, shall exist within the United States, or any place subject to their jurisdiction.

Section 2

Congress shall have power to enforce this article by appropriate legislation.

Fourteenth Amendment

Section 1

All persons born or naturalized in the United States, and subject to the jurisdiction thereof, are citizens of the United States and of the State wherein they reside. No State shall make or enforce any law which shall abridge the privileges or immunities of citizens of the United States; nor shall any State deprive any person of life, liberty, or property, without due process of law; nor deny to any person within its jurisdiction the equal protection of the laws.

Section 2

Representatives shall be apportioned among the several States according to their respective numbers, counting the whole number of persons in each State, excluding Indians not taxed. But when the right to vote at any election for the choice of electors for President and Vice-President of the United States, Representatives in Congress, the Executive and Judicial officers of a State, or the members of the Legislature thereof, is denied to any of the male inhabitants of such State, being twenty-one years of age, and citizens of the United States, or in any way abridged, except for participation in rebellion, or other crime, the basis of representation therein shall be reduced in the proportion which the number of such male citizens shall bear to the whole number of male citizens twenty-one years of age in such State.

Section 3

No person shall be a Senator or Representative in Congress, or elector of President and Vice-President, or hold any office, civil or military, under the United States, or under any State, who, having previously taken an oath, as a member of Congress, or as an officer of the United States, or as a member of any State legislature, or as an executive or judicial officer of any State, to support the Constitution of the United States, shall have engaged in insurrection or rebellion against the same, or given aid or comfort to the enemies thereof. But Congress may by a vote of two-thirds of each House, remove such disability.

Section 4

The validity of the public debt of the United States, authorized by law, including debts incurred for payment of pensions and bounties for services in suppressing insurrection or rebellion, shall not be questioned. But neither the United States nor any State shall assume or pay any debt or obligation incurred in aid of insurrection or rebellion against the United States, or any claim for the loss or emancipation of any slave; but all such debts, obligations and claims shall be held illegal and void.

Section 5

The Congress shall have the power to enforce, by appropriate legislation, the provisions of this article.

Fifteenth Amendment

Section 1

The right of citizens of the United States to vote shall not be denied or abridged by the United States or by any State on account of race, color, or previous condition of servitude.

Section 2

The Congress shall have the power to enforce this article by appropriate legislation.

Sixteenth Amendment

The Congress shall have power to lay and collect taxes on incomes, from whatever source derived, without apportionment among the several States, and without regard to any census or enumeration.

Seventeenth Amendment

The Senate of the United States shall be composed of two Senators from each State, elected by the people thereof, for six years; and each Senator shall have one vote. The electors in each State shall have the qualifications requisite for electors of the most numerous branch of the State legislatures.

When vacancies happen in the representation of any State in the Senate, the executive authority of such State shall issue writs of election to fill such vacancies: Provided, That the legislature of any State may empower the executive thereof to make temporary appointments until the people fill the vacancies by election as the legislature may direct.

This amendment shall not be so construed as to affect the election or term of any Senator chosen before it becomes valid as part of the Constitution.

Eighteenth Amendment

Section 1

After one year from the ratification of this article the manufacture, sale, or transportation of intoxicating liquors within, the importation thereof into, or the exportation thereof from the United States and all territory subject to the jurisdiction thereof for beverage purposes is hereby prohibited.

Section 2

The Congress and the several States shall have concurrent power to enforce this article by appropriate legislation.

Section 3

This article shall be inoperative unless it shall have been ratified as an amendment to the Constitution by the legislatures of the several States, as provided in the Constitution, within seven years from the date of the submission hereof to the States by the Congress.

Nineteenth Amendment

The right of citizens of the United States to vote shall not be denied or abridged by the United States or by any State on account of sex. Congress shall have power to enforce this article by appropriate legislation.

Twentieth Amendment

Section 1

The terms of the President and the Vice President shall end at noon on the 20th day of January, and the terms of Senators and Representatives at noon on the 3d day of January, of the years in which such terms would have ended if this article had not been ratified; and the terms of their successors shall then begin.

Section 2

The Congress shall assemble at least once in every year, and such meeting shall begin at noon on the 3d day of January, unless they shall by law appoint a different day.

Section 3

If, at the time fixed for the beginning of the term of the President, the President elect shall have died, the Vice President elect shall become President. If a President shall not have been chosen before the time fixed for the beginning of his term, or if the President elect shall have failed to qualify, then the Vice President elect shall act as President until a President shall have qualified; and the Congress may by law provide for the case wherein neither a President elect nor a Vice President shall have qualified, declaring who shall then act as President, or the manner in which one who is to act shall be selected, and such person shall act accordingly until a President or Vice President shall have qualified.

Section 4

The Congress may by law provide for the case of the death of any of the persons from whom the House of Representatives may choose a President whenever the right of choice shall have devolved upon them, and for the case of the death of any of the persons from whom the Senate may choose a Vice President whenever the right of choice shall have devolved upon them.

Section 5

Sections 1 and 2 shall take effect on the 15th day of October following the ratification of this article.

Section 6

This article shall be inoperative unless it shall have been ratified as an amendment to the Constitution by the legislatures of three-fourths of the several States within seven years from the date of its submission.

Twenty-First Amendment

Section 1

The eighteenth article of amendment to the Constitution of the United States is hereby repealed.

Section 2

The transportation or importation into any State, Territory, or Possession of the United States for delivery or use therein of intoxicating liquors, in violation of the laws thereof, is hereby prohibited.

Section 3

This article shall be inoperative unless it shall have been ratified as an amendment to the Constitution by conventions in the several States, as provided in the Constitution, within seven years from the date of the submission hereof to the States by the Congress.

Twenty-Second Amendment

Section 1

No person shall be elected to the office of the President more than twice, and no person who has held the office of President, or acted as President, for more than two years of a term to which some other person was elected President shall be elected to the office of President more than once. But this Article shall not apply to any person holding the office of President when this Article was proposed by Congress, and shall not prevent any person who may be holding the office of President, or acting as President, during the term within which this Article becomes operative from holding the office of President or acting as President during the remainder of such term.

Section 2

This article shall be inoperative unless it shall have been ratified as an amendment to the Constitution by the legislatures of three-fourths of the several States within seven years from the date of its submission to the States by the Congress.

Twenty-Third Amendment

Section 1

The District constituting the seat of Government of the United States shall appoint in such manner as Congress may direct: A number of electors of President and Vice President equal to the whole number of Senators and Representatives in Congress to which the District would be entitled if it were a State, but in no event more than the least populous State; they shall be in addition to those appointed by the States, but they shall be considered, for the purposes of the election of President and Vice President, to be electors appointed by a State; and they shall meet in the District and perform such duties as provided by the twelfth article of amendment.

Section 2

The Congress shall have power to enforce this article by appropriate legislation.

Twenty-Fourth Amendment

Section 1

The right of citizens of the United States to vote in any primary or other election for President or Vice President, for electors for President or Vice President, or for Senator or Representative in Congress, shall not be denied or abridged by the United States or any State by reason of failure to pay poll tax or other tax.

Section 2

The Congress shall have power to enforce this article by appropriate legislation.

Twnety-Fifth Amendment

Section 1

In case of the removal of the President from office or of his death or resignation, the Vice President shall become President.

Section 2

Whenever there is a vacancy in the office of the Vice President, the President shall nominate a Vice President who shall take office upon confirmation by a majority vote of both Houses of Congress.

Section 3

Whenever the President transmits to the President pro tempore of the Senate and the Speaker of the House of Representatives his written declaration that he is unable to discharge the powers and duties of his office, and until he transmits to them a written declaration to the contrary, such powers and duties shall be discharged by the Vice President as Acting President.

Section 4

Whenever the Vice President and a majority of either the principal officers of the executive departments or of such other body as Congress may by law provide, transmit to the President pro tempore of the Senate and the Speaker of the House of Representatives their written declaration that the President is unable to discharge the powers and duties of his office, the Vice President shall immediately assume the powers and duties of the office as Acting President.

Thereafter, when the President transmits to the President pro tempore of the Senate and the Speaker of the House of Representatives his written declaration that no inability exists, he shall resume the powers and duties of his office unless the Vice President and a majority of either the principal officers of the executive department or of such other body as Congress may by law provide, transmit within four days to the President pro tempore of the Senate and the Speaker of the House of Representatives their written declaration that the

President is unable to discharge the powers and duties of his office. Thereupon Congress shall decide the issue, assembling within forty-eight hours for that purpose if not in session. If the Congress, within twenty-one days after receipt of the latter written declaration, or, if Congress is not in session, within twenty-one days after Congress is required to assemble, determines by two-thirds vote of both Houses that the President is unable to discharge the powers and duties of his office, the Vice President shall continue to discharge the same as Acting President; otherwise, the President shall resume the powers and duties of his office.

Twenty-Sixth Amendment

Section 1

The right of citizens of the United States, who are eighteen years of age or older, to vote shall not be denied or abridged by the United States or by any State on account of age.

Section 2

The Congress shall have power to enforce this article by appropriate legislation.

27th Amendment

No law, varying the compensation for the services of the Senators and Representatives, shall take effect, until an election of representatives shall have intervened.

Source: https://constitutioncenter.org/interactive-constitution/full-text

TABLE OF U.S. PRESIDENTIAL ELECTIONS

DATE	CANDIDATES	PARTY	PERCENTAGE OF POPULAR VOTE	ELECTORAL VOTE
1789	GEORGE WASHINGTON	No Party Designations	–	69
	John Adams			34
	Other Candidates			35
1792	GEORGE WASHINGTON	No Party Designations	–	132
	John Adams			77
	George Clinton			50
	Other Candidates			5
1796	JOHN ADAMS	Federalist	–	71
	Thomas Jefferson	Democratic-Republican		68
	Thomas Pinckney	Federalist		59
	Aaron Burr	Democratic-Republican		30
	Other Candidates	–		48
1800	THOMAS JEFFERSON	Democratic-Republican	–	73
	Aaron Burr	Democratic-Republican		73
	John Adams	Federalist		65
	Charles C. Pinckney	Federalist		64
	John Jay	Federalist		1
1804	THOMAS JEFFERSON	Democratic-Republican	–	162
	Charles C. Pinckney	Federalist		14
1808	JAMES MADISON	Democratic-Republican	–	122
	Charles C. Pinckney	Federalist		47
	George Clinton	Democratic-Republican		6
1812	JAMES MADISON	Democratic-Republican	–	128
	DeWitt Clinton	Federalist		89
1816	JAMES MONROE	Democratic-Republican	–	183
	Rufus King	Federalist		34
1820	JAMES MONROE	Democratic-Republican	–	231
	John Quincy Adams	Independent		1
1824	JOHN QUINCY ADAMS	Democratic-Republican	30.5	84
	Andrew Jackson	Democratic-Republican	43.1	99
	Henry Clay	Democratic-Republican	13.2	37
	William H. Crawford	Democratic-Republican	13.1	41

DATE	CANDIDATES	PARTY	PERCENTAGE OF POPULAR VOTE	ELECTORAL VOTE
1828	ANDREW JACKSON	Democratic	56.0	178
	John Quincy Adams	National-Republican	44.0	83
1832	ANDREW JACKSON	Democratic	54.5	219
	Henry Clay	National-Republican	37.5	49
	William Wirt	Anti-Masonic	8.0*	7
	John Floyd	Democratic		11
1836	MARTIN VAN BUREN	Democratic	50.9	170
	William H. Harrison	Whig*	49.1*	73
	Hugh L. White	Whig*		26
	Daniel Webster	Whig*		14
	W. P. Mangum	Whig*		11
1840	WILLIAM H. HARRISON	Whig	53.1	234
	Martin Van Buren	Democratic	46.9	60
1844	JAMES K. POLK	Democratic	49.6	170
	Henry Clay	Whig	48.1	105
	James G. Birney	Liberty	2.3	–
1848	ZACHARY TAYLOR	Whig	47.4	163
	Lewis Cass	Democratic	42.5	127
	Martin Van Buren	Free Soil	10.1	–
1852	FRANKLIN PIERCE	Democratic	50.9	254
	Winfield Scott	Whig	44.1	42
	John P. Hale	Free Soil	5.0	–
1856	JAMES BUCHANAN	Democratic	45.3	174
	John C. Fremont	Republican	33.1	114
	Millard Fillmore	American	21.6	8
1860	ABRAHAM LINCOLN	Republican	39.8	180
	Stephen A. Douglas	Democratic	29.5	12
	John C. Breckinridge	Democratic	18.1	72
	John Bell	Constitutional Union	12.6	39
1864	ABRAHAM LINCOLN	Republican	55.0	212
	George B. McClellan	Democratic	45.0	21
1868	ULYSSES S. GRANT	Republican	52.7	214
	Horatio Seymour	Democratic	47.3	80
1872	ULYSSES S. GRANT	Republican	55.6	286
	Horace Greeley	Democratic	43.9	66
1876	RUTHERFORD B. HAYES	Republican	48.0	185
	Samuel J. Tilden	Democratic	51.0	184

DATE	CANDIDATES	PARTY	PERCENTAGE OF POPULAR VOTE	ELECTORAL VOTE
1880	JAMES A. GARFIELD	Republican	48.5	214
	Winfield S. Hancock	Democratic	48.1	155
	James B. Weaver	Greenback-Labor	3.4	–
1884	GROVER CLEVELAND	Democratic	48.5	219
	James G. Blaine	Republican	48.2	182
	Benjamin F. Butler	Greenback-Labor	1.8	–
	John P. St. John	Prohibition	1.5	–
1888	BENJAMIN HARRISON	Republican	47.9	233
	Grover Cleveland	Democratic	48.6	168
	Clinton B. Fisk	Prohibition	2.2	–
	Anson J. Streeter	Union Labor	1.3	–
1892	GROVER CLEVELAND	Democratic	46.1	277
	Benjamin Harrison	Republican	43.0	145
	James B. Weaver	People's	8.5	22
	John Bidwell	Prohibition	2.2	–
1896	WILLIAM MCKINLEY	Republican	51.1	271
	William J. Bryan	Democratic	47.7	176
1900	WILLIAM MCKINLEY	Republican	51.7	292
	William J. Bryan	Democratic; Populist	45.5	155
	John C. Wooley	Prohibition	1.5	–
1904	THEODORE ROOSEVELT	Republican	57.4	336
	Alton B. Parker	Democratic	37.6	140
	Eugene V. Debs	Socialist	3.0	–
	Silas C. Swallow	Prohibition	1.9	–
1908	WILLIAM H. TAFT	Republican	51.6	321
	William J. Bryan	Democratic	43.1	162
	Eugene V. Debs	Socialist	2.8	–
	Eugene W. Chafin	Prohibition	1.7	–
1912	WOODROW WILSON	Democratic	41.9	435
	Theodore Roosevelt	Progressive	27.4	88
	William H. Taft	Republican	23.2	8
	Eugene V. Debs	Socialist	6.0	–
	Eugene W. Chafin	Prohibition	1.4	–
1916	WOODROW WILSON	Democratic	49.4	277
	Charles E. Hughes	Republican	46.2	254
	A. L. Benson	Socialist	3.2	–
	J. Frank Hanly	Prohibition	1.2	–

DATE	CANDIDATES	PARTY	PERCENTAGE OF POPULAR VOTE	ELECTORAL VOTE
1920	WARREN G. HARDING	Republican	60.4	404
	James M. Cox	Democratic	34.2	127
	Eugene V. Debs	Socialist	3.4	–
	P. P. Christensen	Farmer-Labor	1.0	–
1924	CALVIN COOLIDGE	Republican	54.0	382
	John W. Davis	Democratic	28.8	136
	Robert M. La Follette	Progressive	16.6	13
1928	HERBERT HOOVER	Republican	58.2	444
	Alfred E. Smith	Democratic	40.9	87
1932	FRANKLIN D. ROOSEVELT	Democratic	57.4	472
	Herbert C. Hoover	Republican	39.7	59
	Norman Thomas	Socialist	2.2	–
1936	FRANKLIN D. ROOSEVELT	Democratic	60.8	523
	Alfred M. Landon	Republican	36.5	8
	William Lemke	Union	1.9	–
1940	FRANKLIN D. ROOSEVELT	Democratic	54.8	449
	Wendell L. Willkie	Republican	44.8	82
1944	FRANKLIN D. ROOSEVELT	Democratic	53.5	432
	Thomas E. Dewey	Republican	46.0	99
1948	HARRY S. TRUMAN	Democratic	49.6	303
	Thomas E. Dewey	Republican	45.1	189
	J. Strom Thurmond	States' Rights	2.4	39
	Henry A. Wallace	Progressive	2.4	–
1952	DWIGHT D. EISENHOWER	Republican	55.1	442
	Adlai E. Stevenson	Democratic	44.4	89
1956	DWIGHT D. EISENHOWER	Republican	57.6	457
	Adlai E. Stevenson	Democratic	42.1	73
1960	JOHN F. KENNEDY	Democratic	49.7	303
	Richard M. Nixon	Republican	49.5	219
1964	LYNDON B. JOHNSON	Democratic	61.1	486
	Barry M. Goldwater	Republican	38.5	52
1968	RICHARD M. NIXON	Republican	43.4	301
	Hubert H. Humphrey	Democratic	42.7	191
	George C. Wallace	American Independent	13.5	46

DATE	CANDIDATES	PARTY	PERCENTAGE OF POPULAR VOTE	ELECTORAL VOTE
1972	RICHARD M. NIXON	Republican	60.7	520
	George S. McGovern	Democratic	37.5	17
	John G. Schmitz	American	1.4	–
1976	JIMMY CARTER	Democratic	50.1	297
	Gerald R. Ford	Republican	48.0	240
1980	RONALD REAGAN	Republican	50.7	489
	Jimmy Carter	Democratic	41.0	49
	John B. Anderson	Independent	6.6	–
	Ed Clark	Libertarian	1.1	–
1984	RONALD REAGAN	Republican	58.8	525
	Walter F. Mondale	Democratic	40.6	13
1988	GEORGE H. W. BUSH	Republican	53.4	426
	Michael Dukakis	Democratic	45.6	111
1992	BILL CLINTON	Democratic	43.0	370
	George H. W. Bush	Republican	37.4	168
	H. Ross Perot	Independent	18.9	–
1996	BILL CLINTON	Democratic	49.0	379
	Bob Dole	Republican	41.0	159
	H. Ross Perot	Independent	8.0	–
2000	GEORGE W. BUSH	Republican	47.9	271
	Al Gore	Democratic	48.4	266
	Ralph Nader	Green	2.7	–
2004	GEORGE W. BUSH	Republican	50.7	286
	John F. Kerry	Democratic	48.3	251
2008	BARACK H. OBAMA	Democratic	52.9	365
	John McCain	Republican	45.7	173
2012	BARACK H. OBAMA	Democratic	51.1	332
	Mitt Romney	Republican	47.2	206
2016	DONALD J. TRUMP	Republican	46.1	304
	Hillary Clinton	Democratic	48.2	227
	Gary Johnson	Libertarian	3.3	–
	Jill Stein	Green	1.1	–

SUGGESTED TOPICS FOR ADDITIONAL RESEARCH

1. England was interested in overseas expansion as early as 1496, when John Cabot explored North America for Henry VII. But the first English colonies were not attempted for almost another century, and the first permanent settlement was Jamestown in 1607, by which time the Spanish and Portuguese had more than a century's head start. What caused the English delay?

2. Contrast the French "style" of government and politics with that of England, considering both the monarchies and the respective revolutions of the two. How might American history have been different if the French way of doing things had prevailed, rather than the English?

3. The English mostly ignored their colonies throughout the seventeenth century, later justifying it as "salutary neglect." Why did England embrace such loose "control" over its colonies? And why did England abandon this policy during the eighteenth century? How would you judge the policy, on balance? Was it a good thing, a failure, or what?

4. The Revolutionary War began in April 1775, yet independence was not declared until July 1776, more than a year later. Why did it take so long? And why was the Declaration of Independence finally adopted?

5. Generally, we think of a revolution as including a destructive phase, in which the existing system is overthrown, followed by a constructive phase, in which a new system is created. But in reality, it's usually not that simple. The two phases often overlap, and one may interfere with the other. Things can get blurry. Take the American Revolution. How and when did the colonists succeed in destroying the British system, and to what extent did they actually replace it? And to what extent did they ever *want* to destroy it? Where would your considered opinion fall on the question of whether the Revolution was about home rule or about who ruled at home?

6. To what extent were the differences between Hamilton and Jefferson the product of events of their time, and to what extent did they reflect fundamentally

different and permanent visions of how government should operate and of what America should become? How durable and pervasive have those different visions turned out to be in subsequent American history? Can you see them active in later debates and conflicts? Do you see them today? Explain.

7. Explore the meaning of the term *Jacksonian democracy*. How much was the phenomenon it described a reflection of Jackson the man, and how much was it a product of larger social forces?

8. When can it be said that the United States took control of its own destiny, as opposed to being dominated by European events and ideas? When was it finally possible to speak of America, and American developments, without constant reference to events across the Atlantic? Which changes produced this result, and why?

9. What was the origin of the states-rights/nullification/secession theory of the nature of the federal union? Which regions and which parties appealed to it, at what times, and in what circumstances? Has that theory been entirely vanquished, or does it still have a role to play? Explain.

10. The Civil War was a political and diplomatic as well as a military struggle. Considering all three aspects, and beginning with Lincoln's election in 1860, was there any way the Confederacy might have won? Explain, and offer plausible scenarios for your explanation.

11. The Civil War Amendments put an end to slavery, but they did not succeed in establishing full civic equality and liberty for African Americans. Why not? What would you identify as the most important turning points in the years since that time, in which many of these barriers have been overcome?

12. How would you respond to *Land of Hope*'s suggestion that the ugly history of Indian removal and Native displacement represented, in part, a failure of imagination on the part of American leaders?

13. The United States tried twice to conquer Canada, first in 1776 and again in the War of 1812. Why were these attempts unsuccessful? Why have they not left a legacy of distrust between Americans and Canadians, who today enjoy excellent relations and share the world's longest undefended border? Give an explanation, as well as any lessons we can learn from this story.

14. There have often been fierce debates over what name to use to label the military events of 1861–65. Why does it matter so much whether we call it a Civil War, a War between the States, a War of Southern Independence, a War of Northern Aggression, a War of Rebellion, the Second American Revolution, or any number of other names that have been employed over the years? Why do you think have there been so many names?

15. What is the significance of immigration in the American imagination and self-understanding?

16. The term *grand strategy* refers to the larger and longer-scale planning that takes place at the highest levels of government, in pursuit of the national interest as leaders understand that interest. Who in the American system is responsible for that? Outline the elements of grand strategy employed by Lincoln, Wilson, Franklin Roosevelt, and Reagan in their respective wars.

17. Why did John Brown act as he did in Kansas and at Harpers Ferry? Was he morally justified in his actions? The case of John Brown raises in a vivid way the more general question of whether and when violence is justified in a good cause. If the cause (in Brown's case, the freeing of some slaves and, ultimately, the abolition of slavery) is just, under what circumstances does this also justify deadly violence in pursuing it?

18. Which of the following do you think had the *most* to do with causing the Civil War: Eli Whitney, William Lloyd Garrison, Nat Turner, Harriet Beecher Stowe, John Brown, or Stephen A. Douglas? Justify your choice, and explain why you did not choose the others.

19. Reconstruction is often termed a tragedy. Was that so because of what happened or what did not happen? How might it have been better? How might it have been worse? Who is to blame for its failures?

20. Mahan's concept of sea power included four elements – battle fleets, merchant ships, colonies, naval bases – and was as much economic as military. How did Mahan's writing influence American foreign policy between 1890 and 1914?

21. "The Soviet Union didn't just fall; it was pushed." Is this a valid statement? Whom would you be inclined to credit more for the final outcome, Reagan or Gorbachev? (And what about George H. W. Bush?)

22. "America has been better at winning wars than at establishing a good peace afterwards." Evaluate this generalization, citing at least three specific cases.

23. What is history? Is it an art or a craft? Is it a science or a branch of literature? Is it chiefly a matter of facts or is it also a work of the imagination? Is it a source of knowledge, and if so, what kind of knowledge? How can we judge the difference between good history and bad history? What are the criteria for making that judgment?

24. How and why has the idea of a frontier been so important to Americans? Was Frederick Jackson Turner right to emphasize it? What about John F. Kennedy? Do we need to discover a new frontier for the health of our democracy? If so, why? What is a plausible candidate for that role? And how does the need for a frontier relate to our character as a Land of Hope?

25. In thinking about the requirements of American patriotism – a patriotism appropriate to a free and independent people – how do we balance the powerful need to respect and revere our institutions against the equally important right to be free to subject them to criticism? How do we weigh the claims of loyalty against the claims of dissent?

26. Do great presidents require the influence of great challenges to achieve their greatness? Is there something about human nature that *requires* the stimulus of events and circumstances to prod us to achieve feats that might otherwise be beyond us? Or are the truly great leaders the ones who come to the task having already developed the qualities of leadership, and who know how to fasten on to the possibilities of their time and make something of them? Discuss, citing specific presidencies to support your argument.

27. The doctrine of "just war" was developed by Christian thinkers in the Middle Ages to help make sound judgments about when the use of organized violence against an enemy is morally justifiable. The doctrine establishes a series of criteria all of which must be met for a war to be considered "just." After doing some outside research and studying the criteria for a just war, pick an example of an event from American history – it can be anything from the Revolutionary War to World War II to the invasion of Iraq – and evaluate it in terms of just-war theory.

28. No word is more important in American political discourse than *liberty*. Trace the evolution of Americans' conceptions of liberty, and the shifting tension between liberty and equality in American political ideas and sentiments, from the Revolution

to the present day. Has the general movement of American history been toward greater liberty or greater equality – or both? Or neither?

29. The theme of "chosenness" has long been part of American history, deriving mainly from the nation's religious heritage. The New England Puritans believed that they were creating a New Zion in the wilderness, acting on a commission from God. To what extent has that theme persisted even beyond the seventeenth-century Puritans?

30. It can be argued, as the economic historian Robert Higgs has done in his book *Crisis and Leviathan*, that emergencies, and particularly wars, have always served to strengthen the role of the central government in American history. Would you agree with this contention? Flesh out your answer by using evidence from three or four wars in different eras of American history.

31. How did the Electoral College fit into the original design of the Constitution? Why do so many students of the Constitution insist upon its importance and warn against its removal? What is their reasoning? Do you agree? Explain.

32. In a politically oriented history like *Land of Hope*, there is a tendency to downplay America's record of technological innovation as an independent driver of social and cultural change, entirely apart from politics. But that may be a mistake. Let's try to correct for that bias with the following question. In what ways, and with what results, has technological change been far more important than any other form of change in modern America? Give examples.

33. "The issues at stake in the conflict between the Federalists and Antifederalists did not go away. They have remained of central importance in American history, from the time of the debates over the Constitution through the time of the Whigs and then the Progressives, all the way up to the present conflicts between the Washington political establishment and the new populism that is challenging it." Do you agree? Please explain.

34. What has been the role of religion in American society over the course of American history? Has that role changed in recent years? If so, why? Do you think it may change again?

35. The imaginative and creative might try the following exercise. Write an extended dialogue about the meaning of America or some similarly large topic, a dialogue that could be a script for a seminar-style discussion featuring a group of important

individuals from all sorts of times and places in the American past. For example, imagine a dialogue between George Washington, Brigham Young (the great Mormon leader), Robert La Follette (the Progressive politician from Wisconsin), Catharine Beecher (the student of domestic economy and the proper role of women), and Eugene Debs (the socialist labor leader). Better yet, assemble your own list! But whatever you do, try to present each of the individuals "in character," that is, in line with what we know about him or her from history.

To get a better idea of what the results of this exercise might be, have a look at an American television show of the 1970s and 1980s called *Meeting of Minds*, created and hosted by television personality Steve Allen. The show featured actors portraying individuals from throughout human history and engaging in discussions with one another. A description of the show can be found at http://www.steveallen online.com/television_pioneer/meeting_of_minds.htm, and some of the shows themselves can be seen on YouTube and other internet sites (e.g., at https://www .youtube.com/watch?v=hKRxZSOqAYw).

A NOTE ON THE TYPE

The STUDENT WORKBOOK FOR LAND OF HOPE has been set in Le Monde Livre. Designed in 1997 by Jean-François Porchez, Le Monde Livre adapts for book typography the award-winning 1994 type family Porchez created for France's Le Monde newspaper, types now called Le Monde Journal. While the Journal types were specifically intended to be used at small sizes, the Livre family is suitable for larger, less dense settings planned for longer reading. The family was subsequently expanded with a more decorative variation (Le Monde Classic) and a sans-serif (Le Monde Sans). Graced with both style and readability, all of the Le Monde types display Porchez's considerable skill as a designer of typefaces and his deep knowledge of typographic history, particularly the rich heritage of French types from the sixteenth through nineteenth centuries. ¶ The display type is Hypatia Sans designed by Thomas W. Phinney for the Adobe Originals collection of types.

DESIGN & COMPOSITION BY CARL W. SCARBROUGH